Grant Writing

FOR

DUMMIES®

3RD EDITION

by Dr. Beverly A. Browning, MPA, DBA

WILEY

Wiley Publishing, Inc.

Grant Writing For Dummies,® 3rd Edition

Published by
Wiley Publishing, Inc.
111 River St.
Hoboken, NJ 07030-5774
www.wiley.com

Copyright © 2009 by Wiley Publishing, Inc., Indianapolis, Indiana

Published by Wiley Publishing, Inc., Indianapolis, Indiana

Published simultaneously in Canada

WILEY

About the Author

Dr. Beverly A. Browning has been consulting in the areas of grant writing, contract bid responses, and organizational development for 25 years. Her clients have included faith-based organizations, units of local and county municipal governments, state and federal government agencies, school districts and colleges, social and human service agencies, hospitals, fire departments, service associations, and Fortune 500 corporations. Dr. Browning has assisted clients and workshop participants throughout the United States in receiving awards of more than $200 million.

She is the author of more than two dozen grant-related publications, including three editions of *Grant Writing For Dummies* (2001, 2005, and 2009, Wiley), *Grant Writing for Educators* (2004, Solution-Tree), *How to Become a Grant Writing Consultant* (2001 and 2005, BBA, Inc.), *Faith-Based Grants: Aligning Your Church to Receive Abundance* (2005, BBA, Inc.), and *Perfect Phrases for Writing Grant Proposals* (2007, McGraw-Hill).

Dr. Browning holds degrees in Organizational Development, Public Administration, and Business Administration. She is a grant writing course developer and online facilitator for Education To Go, a faculty member at the U.S. Chamber of Commerce Institute for Organization Management and Rio Salado College Online, and a member of the Advisory Board for the University of Central Arkansas Community Development Institute. In 2007, she founded the Grant Writing Training Foundation (GWTF), the purpose of which is to provide affordable and relevant training in grant seeking and writing. The GWTF is a private operating foundation supported by BBA, Inc. dba Bev Browning & Associates. Dr. Browning is also the host of *Get a Grant!* on the VoiceAmerica.com Internet Radio Talk Show venue. Link to it from www. bevbrowning.com.

Dedication

In the past, I've dedicated books to fans, friends, and even some family members. In this third edition of *Grant Writing For Dummies,* I'd like to thank everyone (and there are literally thousands upon thousands of you worldwide) who has made my *For Dummies* book a best-selling reference book. You are my sunshine, my inspiration to keep writing, and the reason that I constantly reinvent myself to keep up with the times and needs of readers and clients. With the dawn of the 21st century, grant writers have multiplied, and my online classes are constantly full. Yet, the reality of the economy can't be avoided. Grant seeking and contract bidding takes skills and knowledge. The process is highly competitive and isn't getting any easier. This book is for the fearful and for the bold. You can do it, and you can do it well! Winning a grant is a privilege — not a routine event. Show the world that you can use *Grant Writing For Dummies,* 3rd Edition, to overcome the odds of rejection in grant seeking.

Acknowledgments

This book would not have been possible without the encouragement and support of my literary agent, Margot Maley Hutchison at Waterside Productions. I'm also still ever so grateful to Joan Hutchison, Margot's mother-in-law. When I conceived the idea for the first edition of *Grant Writing For Dummies,* it was Joan who helped me connect with Margot.

Next, I'd like to thank the dedicated professionals at Wiley Publishing, Inc., including my team: Tracy Boggier (my Acquisitions Editor), Stephen Clark (my Project Editor), and Jessica Smith (my Copy Editor). Belief and patience go a long way in today's world, so thanks, Team Wiley! I'd also like to thank Donnae Dole, my technical reviewer. Together, this group guided my updating efforts from a mere table of contents to the most comprehensive and best-selling grant writing reference book to date.

Special thanks are also in order for my family. To John Browning, my loving husband of more than four decades, who at this moment has agreed to move again and downsize so I'll have an even more inspirational living environment when I'm writing my projects and books. To my daughter, Lara Scott and her husband, Charles, for their love and faith when times got tough and uncertain during the birth of their twin children. Yes, readers, I'm a grandmother now who has experienced joy and sadness at the same time. My grandson, Ashton William Scott, born on March 24, 2008, only got a glimpse of this world for less than five hours. He is now our littlest, deeply loved angel. My granddaughter, Aaliyah Raine Scott, made her entry some five weeks later as a micro-preemie and has proved to be tough, feisty, and very special. The passage of time has seasoned me as a human being, a grant writer, and an author. I've learned that we must take the sorrowful and joyful moments one at a time and hold our heads high to aim for the best that we can give to others. Don't take anything for granted; learn to embrace each second and live it to the fullest.

Publisher's Acknowledgments

We're proud of this book; please send us your comments through our Dummies online registration form located at `http://dummies.custhelp.com`. For other comments, please contact our Customer Care Department within the U.S. at 877-762-2974, outside the U.S. at 317-572-3993, or fax 317-572-4002.

Some of the people who helped bring this book to market include the following:

Acquisitions, Editorial, and Media Development

Project Editor: Stephen R. Clark

(Previous Edition: Georgette Beatty)

Acquisitions Editor: Tracy Boggier

Copy Editor: Jessica Smith

(Previous Edition: Elizabeth Rea)

Assistant Editor: Erin Calligan Mooney

Editorial Program Coordinator: Joe Niesen

Technical Editor: Donnae Dole

Editorial Manager: Christine Meloy Beck

Editorial Assistants: Jennette ElNaggar, David Lutton

Cover Photos: © iStockphoto

Cartoons: Rich Tennant (`www.the5thwave.com`)

Composition Services

Project Coordinator: Patrick Redmond

Layout and Graphics: Reuben W. Davis, Christine Williams

Proofreaders: Joni Heredia, Caitie Kelly

Indexer: Valerie Haynes Perry

Special Help: Jennifer Tebbe

Publishing and Editorial for Consumer Dummies

Diane Graves Steele, Vice President and Publisher, Consumer Dummies

Kristin Ferguson-Wagstaffe, Product Development Director, Consumer Dummies

Ensley Eikenburg, Associate Publisher, Travel

Kelly Regan, Editorial Director, Travel

Publishing for Technology Dummies

Andy Cummings, Vice President and Publisher, Dummies Technology/General User

Composition Services

Gerry Fahey, Vice President of Production Services

Debbie Stailey, Director of Composition Services

Contents at a Glance

Table of Contents

Part IV: Writing a Competitive Application Narrative 153

Chapter 12: Creating the Documents Outside of the Main Narrative 155

Chapter 13: Building Grant Applicant Credibility................. 169

Chapter 14: Conveying a Hopeless Situation and a Need for Funds................................... 183

Introduction

Everyone is talking about getting a grant! From television infomercials to every Jane and John Doe on the streets, the curiosity factor is high. We've all heard the hype for years and yet there's still a big mystery about what grants are and who can apply for them. Here's your primer: The term *grant* is defined as a monetary gift or award. Or think of it as making someone's dream come true with no strings attached. *Grant writing* is what you're doing when you write a *grant request,* which is also known as a proposal for funding. In essence, you're begging for something you or your organization needs really badly. The catch is that all the begging is done on paper, not in person. Some grantmaking agencies even consider funding requests from individuals for research and artistic-related projects.

I've been perfecting successful grant writing techniques for more than three decades. At the very beginning of my grantseeking efforts, I hit the funding jackpot! I thought anyone who wrote a grant proposal was funded. It wasn't until I received my first rejection that I had a wake-up call about something called *competitive writing.* After a long bout of disbelief, I began analyzing my writing style, format, and content. I searched diligently for flaws or weaknesses. I took notes, and then I began to test new writing approaches. The results of my findings and my application of new writing approaches created a grant writing monster — me! I started writing with a frenzy to test my own tips and new skills. Everything I touched turned to funded grant or contract awards.

My experience of going back to the basics led to the first edition of *Grant Writing For Dummies,* and then it led to major rewriting for the second edition. Now I welcome you to this must-have, newly updated third edition of my bestselling desktop reference book for grantseekers.

About This Book

Grant Writing For Dummies, 3rd Edition, is arranged in a format that's easy to read and understand. And you'll have no trouble finding what you're looking for because of the detailed table of contents and the lengthy doesn't-overlook-any-topic index. I think of the beginning and end of this book as detailed outlines. They're solid and can be counted on when you need to find something quickly. However, obviously you shouldn't overlook all the valuable and well-organized resource information that comes in between the front and back.

When you pick up *Grant Writing For Dummies,* 3rd Edition, you don't find cut and dried — *I need coffee to stay awake and read this* — information. Instead, this book reaches the grant writing finish line way ahead of its competitors. I don't hold back on sharing any of my knowledge. And I don't treat writing winning grant applications and contract bid documents as "niche" or "insider secret" information. This book gives you the immediate advantage and knowledge of my nearly 35 years of experience writing grant proposals for my employers and working as a grant writing consultant. I even add some of Bev's brand of humor to relax you and make the details go down a bit easier. Most importantly, my goal with this book is to help you win more and more grant awards in an increasingly competitive funding environment.

Conventions Used in This Book

To help you make your way through this book, I use the following conventions:

- *Italic* points out new words and defined terms.
- **Boldface** text highlights keywords in bulleted lists and the action part of numbered steps.
- Monofont is used for Web addresses.

When this book was printed, some Web addresses may have needed to break across two lines of text. If that happened, rest assured that I haven't put in any extra characters (such as hyphens) to indicate the break. So, when using one of these Web addresses, just type in exactly what you see in this book, pretending as though the line break doesn't exist.

What You're Not to Read

The sidebars in this book are asides to the topic at hand, and so they aren't critical to getting the hang of the grant writing process. However, they can be interesting and fun to read, so take some time to peruse them when you can.

Foolish Assumptions

As I was writing *Grant Writing For Dummies,* 3rd Edition, I assumed that it would serve as a desktop reference for:

✔ Individuals seeking research and education grant writing sources and approaches.

✔ New grant writers looking to be guided through every step of the process, from understanding the definition of a grant to planning and research and writing and submitting.

✔ Veteran grant writers seeking to increase their funding success rates.

✔ Business owners and contract bid staff who are perplexed at the entire business-to-business procurement process and are looking for detailed step-by-step information on how to compile a winning contract bid document.

In order to be successful at grant writing and contract bid preparation, you must possess good skills in listening, researching, writing, word processing, and critical thinking. Consider complementing your knowledge and skills with information from the following *For Dummies* titles:

✔ *Fundraising For Dummies,* 2nd Edition

✔ *Excel For Dummies*

✔ *Home-Based Business For Dummies,* 2nd Edition

✔ *Nonprofit Kit For Dummies,* 2nd Edition

✔ *English Grammar For Dummies*

How This Book Is Organized

Grant Writing For Dummies, 3rd Edition, is organized into six different parts, with chapters arranged to walk you through the process of planning for, organizing, writing, mailing, and following up on your grant request or contract bid document. The underlying message throughout this book's chapters is creativity and tenacity — to always be fresh in your thinking and writing and to *never, ever* give up if your funding request or contract bid is rejected.

Part I: Finding Your Way with Grant Basics

Part I is all about the basics of grant writing. It answers your questions with enough detail to remove the mystery and reveal the secrets. The chapters in this part answer questions such as: What's the difference between grants and contracts? How do I get started with the planning process? What can I ask for? How do I find contract bidding opportunities? Why is bidding on a contract so difficult? What kinds of money are the feds giving away? What do I write in a funding request? What do foundations and corporations give away, and how do I ask them for funding? How do I manage all this paperwork? What happens when I win a grant award? What's a funding success rate? How do I talk and write in grantlish (in other words, grant jargon)? This part of the book shows you how to plan and carry out winning grant awards and contract bids. So, get ready to roll up your sleeves and get started.

Part II: Identifying Key Grantmakers Worldwide

This part introduces you to worldwide grantmaking organizations, including government, foundation, and corporate grantmakers. I help you with everything from checking out public funding epicenters, wading through Grants. gov, and uncovering private sector funding nuggets to discovering international grantseeking and finding grants for individuals and businesses. Part II shows you where to find the money, from right down the street in your hometown to funders across the oceans. I cover it all.

Part III: Playing and Winning the Grants Game

In this part, I take you around the full circuit of the grants process by showing you how to read a federal grant funding opportunity announcement. I also help you decide whether you're ready to enter the grantseeking competition. You find out about the government peer review process and how to convince peer reviewers to rate your application with the maximum points. Part III also shows you how to practice powerful writing approaches, so you can successfully demonstrate a compelling need for grant funding. Gloom, doom, drama, and trauma all work on the reader's heart and mind in your favor.

Part IV: Writing a Competitive Application Narrative

Every trade has its tricks, and grant writing is no different. So Part IV gives step-by-step guidance on how to prepare each section of your funding request, from the cover letter and abstract to each standard section of grant proposals and contract bids. You no longer need to feel uncertain about spotlighting your organization or presenting your funding needs. Perhaps you've heard a lot of talk about writing an integrated program design; this part shows you how to demonstrate accountability by incorporating the Logic Model design. I wrap up this part with chapters on project staffing, resources, equity, and budgets. The chapters in this part are the solid foundation of the book, and as such, I can assure you that you'll use them over and over for every grant request or contract bid.

Part V: Reaching the Finish Line

In Part V, I lead you through the finish line when it comes to wrapping up your grant proposal or contract bid package. This part contains a helpful checklist to make sure you have everything pulled together, and I help you understand the importance of having a fresh pair of eyes proof and edit your work before submitting it. This part also addresses the electronic submission process and the steps to take after your grant is funded or your contract is awarded. At the end of this part, I give you a bonus: a glance at the Corporate Letter Request. After you become familiar with this short and to the point letter, you'll quickly start receiving products, services, and cash from corporate grantmakers.

Part VI: The Part of Tens

This part of the book presents several collections of ten items; each list is grouped around a particular subject. Every tip in Part VI is intended to help you soar in every skill area related to grant and contract research and writing!

Icons Used in This Book

The little pictures I place in the margins throughout this book are designed to highlight information that's special and important for one reason or another. *Grant Writing For Dummies,* 3rd Edition, uses the following icons:

This icon highlights some extra-special ways to edge out your competition.

Wherever you see this icon you're sure to find a good idea, trick, or shortcut that can save you time and trouble.

This icon points to pieces of information that you shouldn't forget.

Don't skip over paragraphs marked with this icon; it indicates information that can help you avoid disasters.

Where to Go from Here

It's time to get started reading the third edition of *Grant Writing For Dummies.* Some of you may recognize the grant writing terms in this book, but for others most of what's here will be completely new. Either way, the information and examples I use are all designed to help you move forward successfully as a grant writer or contract bidder.

Start by perusing the new and improved table of contents, and then highlight your favorite sections. This book isn't linear — you can start reading anywhere and in any order you like. I suggest you begin with Chapter 1, an overview of this book's tips and skills. Let the games begin!

Part I
Finding Your Way with Grant Basics

The 5th Wave   By Rich Tennant

Philanthropy Officer

"Give me a second and I can give an answer to your grant request right now."

In this part . . .

With the chapters in this part, you discover how to navigate your way through the sea of finding and getting some grant writing bucks. Finding the money is really the second step, however. The first step in grant writing is plotting the dollar trails (for example, determining who you're going to ask for money, choosing how much you'll ask for, and deciding how the funder's criteria and grant amount fit with your own mission and vision).

After you complete your funder research and discover the art of grant speak, you can practice writing and talking with grant terminology.

Chapter 1

Grasping the Basics of Finding and Getting the Bucks

*W*hat makes a great grant writer or contract bidder? A person who's hungry for cash flow and who's willing to roll up her sleeves, dig deep for hard-to-find information, and speak boldly and proudly about her funding needs or contract capabilities. What does it take to get started? First and foremost, you simply need to learn from my knowledge and experience — which I share liberally in this book! Also, you should desire to make a difference in the lives of others. Whether it's a grant-funded intervention or prevention or a contract bid award for delivering an excellent quality of goods or services, you should be ready to give your all.

By using this book daily, you can achieve your highest goals, which probably includes writing and winning almost everything you submit for funding or award consideration. You can even build your funding success rate to 90 percent or higher. And, if you want further one-on-one training, consider enrolling in one of my online classes or attending one of my two-day Grant Writing Boot Camps. For now, in this chapter, I start you down the right path to grant writing gold with the basics of the process.

Exploring the Grant and Contract Basics

Before diving into the wonderful world of grant writing, it's important to understand a few essentials. For instance, it's essential for new grantseekers to know exactly what a grant is. Also, you need to know who qualifies for a grant. Finally, being able to understand what funders want to fund is critical to crafting the right proposal for the right funder. I explain all of this and more in the following sections.

Discovering the definition of a grant

A *grant,* also known as a *cooperative agreement,* is a monetary award given by a *grantor* to a *grantee.* A *grant request* is an advance promise of what you or your organization (the grantee) proposes to do when the grantor fulfills your request for funding. The distinguishing factor between a grant and a cooperative agreement is the degree of federal participation or involvement during the performance of the work activities. When a federal agency program officer participates in funded project activities, it's called a cooperative agreement. When the grant applicant is the sole implementer of project activities, it's called a grant.

Some grant awards come with no strings attached, but many others require you to use the funds in a certain way. Grantors with strings attached to their monies are almost always government grantmaking agencies (local, state, and federal public sector funders). Grantors with literally no strings attached are referred to as *private sector funders.* These usually include corporate and foundation grantmakers.

So what can a grant pay for? A grant award can be used for whatever the funder wants to fund. This means that reading the funding guidelines is critical when it comes to your chance for success. (Refer to Part II for tips on poring over funding guidelines from multiple types of grantmakers.)

Qualifying for a grant

A *grant or cooperative agreement application* is a written request that you use to ask for money from a government agency, a foundation, or a corporation. Most grants go to organizations that have applied to the Internal Revenue Service (IRS) for nonprofit status and have received the IRS's blessing as a 501 (c)(3) organization. However, a few grants are given to individuals as well (see Chapter 7 for details).

Since I've been writing grant applications, I've seen a growing number of grant awards made to cities, villages, townships, counties, and even state agencies. While none of these governmental units are IRS 501 (c)(3) designees, they're still nonprofit in structure and can apply for and receive grant awards from the federal government, foundations, and corporations. Grant awards can even be made to international nonprofits, which are referred to as *non-governmental organizations,* or NGOs. You can read more about funding for NGOs in Chapter 8.

Looking at the simplicity of a proposal

A *proposal* is usually a more free-flowing grant request. A proposal involves you putting down on paper your ideas about your organization and the program you want funded. You can dash off a proposal foolishly, simply writing what pops into your mind at the time. Or you can create a proposal the smart way, using a national or regional *template format* (see "Putting Together and Writing a Winning Request," later in this chapter for more details). Grant proposals (along with grant applications) require planning, organization, good research, and writing skills.

Getting the skinny on for-profit and nonprofit contracts

Think of contracts as cousins to grants — similar but clearly different. A *contract* is a legal instrument reflecting a relationship between the bid-letting agency (government unit or private sector business) and a business. The bid-letting agency is seeking to purchase services or products from that business. The *offeror,* or business seeking to provide the deliverables, must respond to an RFP (Request For Proposal) or RFQ (Request For Quote) in writing and submit it by a deadline.

For-profit businesses apply for and receive contract awards, but nonprofit organizations usually don't. Instead, they apply for and receive grant or cooperative agreement awards (which I explain earlier in this chapter). A grantmaking agency (such as the government, a foundation, or a corporation) can issue an RFP; a business seeking a contractual relationship with another business can issue one as well. An RFP or RFQ is very similar in format to a government grant application.

Planning Rules for the Present and the Future

Rule number one in grant writing is that you don't ask for a grant without first completing a comprehensive planning process that involves your organization (the grant applicant) and its community partners (the stakeholders).

Without planning tools to lay out a visual road map of where your organization needs to head and how it's going to get there, you'll be fighting the same fires daily — never becoming a relaxed and confident grantseeker or agency administrator. You fix this problem by creating a *funding development plan,* which is an internal examination of the organization's strengths, weaknesses, opportunities, and threats. A funding development plan answers questions such as

- ✔ What programs are strong and already have regular funding to keep them going?
- ✔ What new programs need funding?
- ✔ What opportunities exist to find new funding partners?
- ✔ What existing grants will run out before new funding is found?

When you answer these questions, you can begin to look at the multitude of areas where grants are awarded and begin to prioritize the type of funding you need. I write more about funding development plans in Chapter 2.

Understanding How Funders Describe Their Grantmaking Interests

Every potential grant funding agency lists specific types of funding they will and will not award to potential grantseekers. In order to weed out the grants that won't work for your organization, you have to understand the different types of funding that are available. The following list gives you the scoop:

- ✔ **Annual campaigns:** Money to support annual operating expenses, infrastructure improvements, program expansion, and, in some cases, one-time-only expenses (such as a cooling-system replacement).
- ✔ **Building/renovation funds:** Money to build a new facility or renovate an existing facility. These projects are often referred to as *bricks-and-mortar projects.* Building funds are the most difficult to secure; only a small percentage of foundations and corporations award grants for these types of projects.

- ✔ **Capital support:** Money for equipment, buildings, construction, and endowments. These types of large-scale projects aren't quickly funded. It often takes two to three years for total funding to be secured. This type of request is a major undertaking by the applicant organization.

- ✔ **Challenge monies:** These funds act as leverage to secure additional grants from foundations and corporations. They're awarded by funders and are contingent upon your raising additional grant funds from other funding sources. You must use internal organizational funds to meet the challenge grant requirements.

- ✔ **Conferences/seminars:** Money to cover the cost of attending, planning, and/or hosting conferences and seminars. Funding may be used to pay for all the conference expenses, including securing a keynote speaker, travel, printing, advertising, and facility expenses, such as meals.

- ✔ **Consulting services:** You may want to secure the expertise of a consultant or consulting firm to strengthen some aspect of organizational programming. For example, if you bring in a consultant to do a long-range strategic plan or to conduct training for a board of directors, you're paying for consulting services.

- ✔ **Continuing support/continuation grant:** If you've already received a grant award from a funder, you can turn to that funder again and apply for continuing support. However, be aware that many funders only fund an organization one time.

- ✔ **Employee matching gifts:** Many employers match the monetary donations their employees make to nonprofit organizations, often on a ratio of 1:1 or 2:1. If you have board members employed by large corporations, have them check with their human resources departments to see whether their employers have such programs.

- ✔ **Endowments:** A source of long-term, permanent investment income to ensure the continuing presence and financial stability of your nonprofit organization. If your organization is always operating in crisis-management mode, one of your goals should be to develop an endowment fund for long-term viability.

- ✔ **Fellowships:** Money to support graduate and postgraduate students in specific fields. These funds are only awarded to institutions, never to individuals.

- ✔ **General/operating expenses:** Money for general budget line-item expenses. These funds may be used for salaries, fringe benefits, travel, consultants, utilities, equipment, and other expenses necessary to operate grant and contract-funded programs.

- ✔ **Matching funds:** Grant funds that are awarded with the requirement that you must find other grant funding that matches or exceeds the initial grant's matching-fund stipulation. Matching funds are a type of leverage grant. To qualify for a matching funds grant award, the grant applicant must come up with matching funds. The funds can be internal (from the grant applicant organization), from a partner agency, or even from another grant funding agency.

✔ **Program development:** Funding to pay for expenses related to organization growth, the expansion of existing programs, or the development of new programs.

✔ **Research:** Money to support medical and educational research. Monies are usually awarded to the institutions that employ the individuals conducting the research.

✔ **Scholarship funds:** Scholarship awards to individuals. Remember that when funds are awarded directly to an individual, they're considered taxable income (with taxes owed by the recipient).

✔ **Seed money:** Most often, these types of grants are awarded for a pilot program not yet in full-scale operation; hence the term *seed money.* Seed money gets a program underway, but other grant monies are needed to continue the program in its expansion phase.

✔ **Technical (consulting) assistance:** Money to improve your internal program operations. Often, this type of grant is awarded to hire an individual or firm that can provide the needed technical assistance. Alternatively, the funding foundation's personnel may provide the technical assistance. For example, a program officer from a foundation may work on-site with the applicant organization to establish an endowment development fund and start a campaign for endowment monies. In some instances, the funding source identifies a third-party technical assistance provider and pays the third party directly to assist the nonprofit organization.

If you need more help with grant writing terminology, check out Chapter 3, where I cover some "funder talk."

Connecting with Contract Bidding Language

Grant application and contract bid documents have a lot of similarities, but there are still some specific contract bidding terms you need to know when you pick up an RFQ, or Request For Quote. (To find out more about grant application terms, see the earlier section "Understanding How Funders Describe Their Grantmaking Interests.") Knowing the terms used by the bid-letting agency can help you write effective bid responses. The following terms are used by contract bid-letting agencies:

- ✔ **Acceptance:** Acceptance occurs when a bid-letting agency or business accepts the deliverables outlined by the offeror in the bidding document.

- ✔ **Deliverables:** Detailed information about the services or goods the offeror plans to deliver under a contract award.

- ✔ **Financial proposal:** A separate document outside of the contract bid response narrative that outlines the offeror's cost to provide the needed services or goods.

- ✔ **Offeror:** The individual or business bidding on the needed services or goods.

- ✔ **Responsiveness:** When the bid-letting agency examines the offeror's contract bid proposal document to determine whether all the areas in the narrative guidelines have been responded to and at what level.

- ✔ **Request For Proposal (RFP) or Request For Quote (RFQ):** A legally prepared document issued by the bid-letting agency or business requesting a proposal or quote for services or products from qualified vendors.

- ✔ **Services proposal:** A full, written description by the offeror of what services will be provided should a contract be awarded by the bid-letting agency.

- ✔ **Terms and conditions:** These are the circumstances for awarding a contract. They're developed by the bid-letting agency. You may be required to provide proof of liability insurance or to submit a list of demographics for all personnel assigned to the contract work.

Linking Your Needs to a Governmental Source of Funds

I probably receive more than 100 e-mails daily and just as many telephone queries weekly. Everyone wants grants! If you're feeling clueless as to how to proceed finding potential funding for your organization, you simply need to use the Internet. You can search for potential sources that are interested in what your organization needs or business wants to provide in the way of goods and services. Fire up your computer, and then start searching for the monies that may be waiting for you or your organization. One of the largest grantmaking entities is the U.S. government, which is also known as Uncle Sam. If you want to score big in grant awards, start with Sam.

Conducting a funding search leads you to the money. But before you start your search, you need to know what type of grant money (or funder) will pay you to implement your idea, project, or program. I introduce you to your options in the following sections.

Federal government funding: Cashing in with your richest uncle

The first place to look for money is within Uncle Sam's pockets. The federal government is a public funding epicenter. I'm not one to tout the availability of "free" federal grants, but I can tell you that the government does have money for specific types of grant applicants and projects. In Chapter 4, I give you the complete scoop on using the Internet to find government grants.

If you're interested in looking at what the feds have to offer, take some time to look through the Catalog of Federal Domestic Assistance (CFDA), which you can find at www.cfda.gov. The CFDA is the encyclopedia of grant and contract funding programs, so it doesn't tell you about open grant competitions that you can apply for at a particular time. For that information, go to www.grants.gov, which gives you daily funding announcements on money you can apply for *now*.

Heading to the statehouse: Seeking public funds closer to home

Each state receives grant monies from the feds and from tax revenues that are funneled into and out of their general funds. After taking their fair (or unfair) share for administrative overhead, states regrant the money to eligible agencies and organizations in the form of competitive grants or formula grants.

Examples of some state agencies that regrant federal monies are agriculture, commerce, education, health, housing development, natural resources, and transportation. Contact your state legislator at his or her local office or at the state capitol for assistance in identifying grant opportunities within your state. Also consider using the Internet to search for state agencies that award grants and contracts.

The Other Pot of Gold: Considering Foundation and Corporate Funding

Foundation and corporate grantmakers are referred to as *private-sector funders*. The rainfall of private-sector grant money is conservative, but it's also continuously available to grantseekers who meet this type of funder's area of interest.

Where can you find out more about these no-strings-attached grants? You can locate sources by visiting a Foundation Center Cooperating Collections site (usually at a state university library, community foundation, or other nonprofit information center). The Foundation Center's Web address is www. foundationcenter.org.

Examining private and public foundations

Private foundations get their monies from a single source, such as an individual, a family, or a corporation. Think about all the wealthy individuals who have started their own foundations, like the John Templeton Foundation or the Heinz Foundation. You can find hundreds of private foundations in the Foundation Center's online directory.

Public foundations, on the other hand, are supported primarily through donations from the general public. That's a no-brainer, right? They also receive a great deal of their funding from foundation and corporate grants. Again, the Foundation Center's Web site can give you loads of information on these types of foundations. There are lots of public foundations focused on the arts, environment, and faith-based initiatives. Remember, there's no difference in public or private foundations when it comes to grantseeking or grantmaking.

Finding corporate funders

Did you know that many of the biggest businesses in the nation set 5 percent or more of their profits aside for grants? Why is that, you ask? The buzzword of the millennium is *corporate responsibility.*

Corporate responsibility is the approach that a successful business takes when it decides to make a financial commitment to the community where its headquarters are located or where it has operating locations.

Corporations that award grants usually have a Web site link labeled *community, community relations, social responsibility, local initiatives, grants,* or *corporate giving.* Use the Foundation Center's Web site to view some corporations with giving programs, such as American Express (which also has a major foundation) and the United Parcel Service of America, Inc. (better known as simply UPS).

Accessing contract bidding opportunities

Many private and public sector businesses and public agencies seek out vendors to deliver services or goods to them. The type of document these business and agencies solicit competitive contract bids with is referred to by several different names, including Request For Bid (RFB), Request For Quote (RFQ), and Request for Proposal (RFP). If you've been searching your local newspapers and online for contract bidding opportunities to no avail, you need to move into high gear and aggressively subscribe to and screen possible contract bidding opportunities around the United States and beyond.

I have a subscription with www.findrfp.com, and I think it's great. You can choose the types of bids you want to see (keyword subject area) and the geographic locations in which you want to sell your products or services. You can even receive daily e-mail alerts with current bidding opportunities. What's the cost? The monthly subscription is probably around $30. That's right, three ten-dollar bills per month gives you access to hundreds of thousands of dollars worth of contract bids.

Putting Together and Writing a Winning Request

The first step in getting started with grant writing is to recognize the different application formats and when to use them. Some funders require more information than others. In fact, some funders have reams of forms that you can quickly download, save in PDF file form, and open with ease if you have a PDF converter software attached to your word processing software. (I purchased my original converter software online from Nuance, and have since updated it to the most recent version, which you can find at www.scansoft.com.)

Determine the writing format for each funding source that you identify. Call or write each source and ask for its guidelines for submitting a grant application or proposal. Governmental agencies have their own application kits, and you can only submit applications for these agencies at certain times in the year. Foundations and corporations may also have their own formats. If not, you may be instructed to use a regional grant application format. Or you may be required to submit a two- or three-page letter of initial inquiry.

Just remember that if getting grant money were too easy, everyone would already have a grant and there wouldn't be any money left for you! (I cover the entire process of successfully putting together a grant application in Chapters 12 to 17.)

Focusing on the (strict!) review criteria guidelines for government grants

The format for government grant requests varies from agency to agency, but some common threads exist in the highly detailed, structured, military-like regimen that's commonly referred to as an *application package*. These common threads include a standard cover, certification and assurances forms, narrative sections, and the budget narrative and forms. And of course, all types of government grant applications require mandatory attachments or appendixes, such as financial statements, résumés of project staff, and copies of your nonprofit status determination letter from the IRS. (Flip to Chapter 5 for more about the application package.)

Always follow the pagination, order of information, and review criteria guidelines. All government funder grants are awarded on the basis of your meeting their review criteria, which are written and published in each funding agency's grant application guidelines. The review criteria tell you what the peer reviewers will read and rate when they receive your grant application.

As you read through the application guidelines, highlight all narrative writing requirements and look for sections that tell you how the grant reviewers will rate or evaluate each section of the narrative. By formatting and writing to meet the review criteria, you can edge out the competition and increase your funding success rate. In Chapters 9 and 10, I tell you how to prepare and write for the review criteria.

Lean, clean funding machines: Formatting for foundations

Large or small, foundations like to see a cover letter, a regionally or nationally accepted cover sheet or cover form, and a narrative that includes a description of your organization and your request. The attachments are what count with this group of funders. They may ask for the project's evaluation plan, your organization's structure or administration, your finances, and other supporting material.

My favorite private sector (corporations and foundations) grant application format is the one that was developed by the National Network of Grantmakers (NNG). The Network's Web site is no longer active, so you have to search the Internet using a search engine in order to locate a downloadable version of the format. The grant application format, also known as the Common Grant Application (CGA), is accepted by many smaller corporate and foundation grantmakers. To determine whether using the CGA is appropriate in your situation, check the funder's guidelines. Contact the funder directly to obtain the guidelines, or seek information in one of the many available funder directories.

The CGA format has a cover sheet, a two-section narrative, and multiple attachments. I use the CGA format for 90 percent of the foundation grant requests that I write. The format works well because it contains all the essentials. Even if a funder requests a different order of information, you can do a lot of cutting and pasting from a grant application written in the CGA format to create a non-CGA grant request.

Before you start writing in a generic format (like the CGA format) check to see whether the region you operate in requires you to use a different format. The Forum of Regional Associations of Grantmakers, a national network of local leaders and organizations across the United States that support effective charitable giving, can be found on the Internet at www.givingforum.org. Most of the regional groups of foundation grantmakers you can find at this site have designed their own specific grant application formats.

Just get to the point! Contacting corporations

Corporations work with a shorter writing format than the one used by foundation funders. However, corporate grantmakers that don't have their own specific funding request application forms are usually very receptive to the Corporate Letter Request format. Chapter 21 shows you how to use this format to develop a short and effective letter to request goods, services, and even cash!

Sending Your Proposal on Its Merry Way

When you've finished writing your grant proposal, you still have a few more steps to take before you can breathe deeply and really relax. If the funding agency provides an application checklist, use it to make sure your grant application package is complete — in the funder's eyes. If you don't have a funder-provided checklist, create your own and check off each item requested in the grant guidelines. Make sure each section and form is in the order requested in the guidelines. Also, proofread your narrative and other forms several times before considering the application package final. Get help from a colleague or hire a professional proofreader, like I do. Check out Chapter 18 for more about wrapping up your funding request.

Keeping Track of Submitted Requests

After all your funding requests are in the mail, you need to develop a tracking system that will help you keep up with their progress and cue you when the period of silence from funders has been too long. At the federal and state levels, you can even enlist tracking support from your legislative team. However, at the corporate and foundation levels, you're on your own (unless, of course, members of your board of directors have friends and associates on the funder's board of trustees.)

The old school approach is to develop a manual or electronic tracking system to monitor what you've written, who has received it, and the status of your funding request (pending, funded, or rejected). However, the new and easier way to keep track of submitted requests is to purchase grant management or tracking software. Look for lots of popular software packages to meet your needs. You can find out what's available by doing an Internet search using the term "grant management software." Software programs may start at $1,000 and go up to several thousands of dollars.

When it comes to hard-copy organization, I use hanging files for each grant application I write. The hanging file holds individual file folders that contain the following:

- ✔ Application guidelines
- ✔ My copy of the final grant application package
- ✔ Background research
- ✔ Communication notes with funders, clients, and research sources

In Chapter 19, I give you guidelines for following up with government, foundation, and corporate grant applications.

Knowing What to Do When You Win (Or Don't Win) Funds

When you win, you celebrate, right? Well, yes, you celebrate, but you also notify your community partners of your collective success in winning a grant award. You also prepare for the implementation phase now that monies are on the way.

If your grant request or contract wasn't awarded, you have some critical steps to take to determine why your request was denied and when you can resubmit your funding request or contract bid. Here are the steps to follow (also refer to Chapter 20 for more details):

1. **Contact the funding agency or bid-letting agency and ask why your grant application wasn't recommended for funding or why your contract bid wasn't selected.**

   You may have to ask for this feedback in writing so the funders and bid-letting agencies have a paper trail for whom they release information to and why.

2. **When you know where the weakness is in your grant application or contract bid, develop a plan for rewriting.**

   You want to rewrite the weak sections of your narrative and ready it for resubmission to other funders, other contract bid-letting agencies, and even for future resubmission to the same agencies or businesses that rejected the first request. For grants, funders usually allow you to reapply in the next funding cycle (next year). For contracts, you have to wait until the bid-letting agency releases another RFP.

Chapter 2

Mapping Success with a Funding Development Plan

In This Chapter

▶ Developing a road map before your grantseeking trip begins

▶ Examining an example funding development plan

▶ Finding several funding sources to increase your success

Far too often, organizations that are in need of grant or contract monies become frantic and run down the grantseeking track with no real destination in mind. They do this because getting new revenue is critical to program and organization survival. In this situation, the neon bait of a grant funding opportunity announcement beckons, causing all planning rationale to be tossed aside to begin the "Hey, here's some money up for grabs! Let's get this grant now!" chase.

What's wrong with this picture? Simple: You need a map and a plan to successfully reach any destination. Quick decisions that weren't properly thought out can lead to poor fiscal planning, program shutdowns, decreased staff morale, and eventually something known to grant professionals as *grant suicide*. Too much greed, too little planning, and ignorance regarding funding development plans and how they can help guide your organization to grantseeking and funding success are all signs that you're heading in a downward spiral.

But don't worry! This chapter shows you how to avoid grant suicide by guiding you through the steps of proactive planning. The goal is to strengthen your approach to grantseeking. A stronger, more organized approach will help you hit the grant award target more often than the common driving-while-blind approach.

Creating Funding Development Plans to Increase Grantseeking Success

An effective plan isn't just about searching for and printing out a large stack of grant funding opportunities and then saying, "Well, let's start working 24 hours a day to apply for all of this 'free' money!" Instead, planning means developing a road map or written plan — called a *funding development plan* — that includes a systematic approach to grantseeking and grant writing. This type of planning can lead to funded programs that fit and support your organization's mission.

Think about it this way: You would never approve the spending of $100,000 to market your organization's programs and services without a marketing plan. So why would you approach grantseeking and grant writing with your head in the sand? Exactly; you wouldn't!

Planning takes time. And when you're feeling the pressure of quickly gathering funds, taking the time to plan can *feel* like a time waster. But, the truth is that careful planning can help you selectively shape better grants, which will increase your chances of success in the long run. The true time waster is proceeding without planning only to crash repeatedly into dead ends.

Knowing what a successful funding development plan looks like

Before you can begin creating a funding development plan, you have to know what you're striving for. Here are some characteristics of an effective funding plan:

- ✔ It must be written down — just like a long-range strategic plan or a marketing plan would be.

- ✔ It's created to be a daily guide to help your organization make decisions about what programs have funding priority and about the most logical way to fund the programs.

- ✔ It must be updated with progress notes every time you apply for grant funding and every time you know the results of your efforts. For instance, first you need to note whether you're being funded. If so, note the amount of the funding; if not plan to research why your efforts failed.

- ✔ It should be reviewed and revised annually. Why? Funder priorities change annually. For instance, just because a lot of money is available for juvenile justice projects this year doesn't mean that this hot funding area will still be the focus next year.

Your plan must change to reflect what funders want to fund. In other words, your plan isn't just about what your organization wants or needs; it's about what funders want to fund within the parameters of your organization's mission.

✔ It needs to provide certain bits of information, including the name of program or service in need of funding, the amount of monies needed to fund a 12-month operational cycle, and the potential source of grant funding for the program or service. After you've identified potential funders, you add the grant application due dates, the type of initial information that the funder wants to see, and the name of the person who's responsible for preparing the initial information document.

Keep your funding development plan flexible! Funder's change their priorities often, and your target population's needs are likely to change as well. So be willing to review previous evaluation reports or results from funded programs. Pay attention to what works and what doesn't. Update by removing and adding programs and services, and then incorporate these changes into your revised funding development plan.

Starting the plan development process

You'll likely develop your funding plan with your organization's board of directors or with an executive committee (president, vice president, secretary, and treasurer). Or you might develop the plan with the board's designated funding committee (board members and program staff volunteer for this committee).

Typically funding committees aren't short-term commitments. This type of committee meets forever and ever. Why? Your organization's need for dollars never stops; grantseeking is a continual process. Think of a gerbil on a running wheel — it just keeps running and running after some unknown target. At least your funding committee will plan, plot, and then chase the known targets.

I used to suggest that organizations plan a retreat for the board of directors (or whoever is creating the plan) to jump-start the funding development plan development process. However, in today's economy and with everyone working different days and hours, it just isn't practical to think that funds or member availability will allow you to sneak off for a night or two. However, if you have the time and money, feel free to go the retreat route. Just know that you'll get comparable results by simply finding a large room, closing the door, and cranking out your funding development plan. I recently helped a small nonprofit organization create a funding development plan in a board treasurer's dining room. That plan is now being implemented. And to think that it took all of five hours on a Saturday morning!

No matter where you're developing your funding development plan, you have to maintain everyone's focus or else you could waste precious time. To do so, apply the following basic rules when you're ready to start brainstorming and writing your plan:

- ✔ **Make sure that everyone participates.** Explain at the outset that everyone needs to bring something to the table that will assist your organization in identifying priorities for programs and services and finding ways to fund them. It's important for administrators and front line staff to be strongly encouraged to participate in the funding plan's development. After all, those at the top of the organization see programs and services in an entirely different light than the staff working with clients on a day-to-day basis. Everyone's opinion should be incorporated.

- ✔ **Plan your meetings carefully so that you aren't rushed through the process due to time constraints.** Rushing through this process will only cause you to make mistakes and overlook important items. To avoid rushing, remember that the funding committee (or the group that's convened to develop the funding plan) will likely need to meet at least four hours the first time and then for a couple of hours or more monthly thereafter.

  Poll every member to find out the best day and time for everyone to meet. Go with the majority rule theory. If 75 percent of the members can meet on Saturday from 9 a.m. to 12 p.m. and 25 percent can't, choose Saturday morning. And it's perfectly fine to alternate the meeting day and time every other meeting to accommodate the other 25 percent. If you can't alternate days and times, look for replacement committee members who can meet on the selected day and at the set meeting time.

- ✔ **Give homework assignments.** Most times, your meetings won't give you enough time to finish all the tasks that need to be completed. To avoid falling behind, you need to assign funding research tasks to each funding committee member. Give the assignment, set a deadline, and express — with urgency — the need for each committee member to bring his or her completed assignment back on its due date. Using the homework approach enables the meetings to be kept short. Isn't that every working person's goal?

Structuring your plan

Too many nonprofit organizations function in crisis management mode all the time. They frantically write grant proposals to pay for programs and projects that are already in the 11th month of an existing one-year grant award. I often refer to this situation as working on the downside of funding cessation. Everyone is always in a panic, and the threat of layoffs and program closures is a routine fire call. Being *proactive* in grantseeking and grant writing is extremely important because it saves a group from always running in a *reactive* mode.

Laying out a funding development plan is the first step to becoming proactive. (You can read more about the benefits of a good funding plan earlier in this chapter.) The following list describes the parts of an all-purpose funding development plan (in the order in which they should appear):

1. **Mission statement:** Maybe your mission statement creates more confusion than clarity. Take a long look at your existing mission statement and ask yourselves whether it reflects your vision. If not, figure out how you can rewrite the mission statement to make it clear and impactful.

2. **Assessment of funding needs:** Ask yourselves "What programs and services do we want to offer? Where is the funding coming from, internal or external sources?"

3. **Funding goals:** Ask yourselves "How much money do we need to raise from external funding sources for each program or service?"

4. **Funding objectives:** Ask yourselves "What benchmarks do we want to set to assure we reach our funding goals?"

5. **Action plan:** Ask yourselves "What are the annual tasks, over three to five years, that must be completed in order to make our funding development plan a reality?"

6. **Monitoring and evaluation of funding objectives:** Ask yourselves "How can our organization track and prove that the project's measurable objectives were met and at what levels? What are our evaluation tools?"

Check out the later section "Developing a Funding Development Plan in Six Steps" to find out more specifics on these parts of the funding development plan.

After you write your funding development plan, stick to it. Before writing any grant requests, first make sure that the grant fits into your plan. If you're asked to pursue something outside your plan, meet with your administration and other stakeholders and explain that going after every available dollar and making off-track grant requests will come back to haunt you — and them. Be organized, stay focused, and follow your funding plan's road map to success and stability.

For-profits also can benefit from creating a funding development plan. As a small business owner, I know that determining expenditures and identifying how those expenses will be covered are key components in the funding development plan. Think about what new products and services you want to offer and where the funds will come from to launch your new endeavors. You can use the funding plan's structure to capture the funding road map components needed to carry out your plans.

Developing a Funding Development Plan in Six Steps

I find that it's often easier to get a handle on something if I have an example to work off of. So with that in mind, I've put together an example of a funding development plan for a fictional organization that follows the structure outlined in the preceding section. Follow the example as you write your own funding development plan.

Step one: Creating or revising a mission statement

A *mission statement* tells funders your purpose or vision for being a structured nonprofit or for-profit organization. The mission statement should include the name of your organization, its structural status (nonprofit or for-profit), the year it was formed, and its purpose (reason for organization). Here's an example mission statement for Frankenmuth Research Institute:

> *The Frankenmuth Research Institute is a 501 (c)(3) nonprofit private operating foundation that was organized in 2008 by the Frankenmuth Insurance Corporation for the purpose of conducting extensive research on the causes of increasingly high levels of insurance claims for infant car seat injuries.*

Step two: Assessing funding needs

I firmly believe that a full organizational funding assessment is needed in order to help your organization get a clear and accurate picture of where it is now and where you want it to be annually for the next three to five years. You may wonder, "How can we even begin to organize the many areas of need within our organization?" Simple! Take a SWOT at it!

A *SWOT analysis* is a popular organizational funding assessment tool to discover the good, the bad, and the ugly about an organization's status. SWOT stands for strengths, weaknesses, opportunities, and threats. A SWOT analysis looks at each of these elements and determines how each one affects the organization. This method of analysis is an effective tool for turning your agency inside out and seriously dealing with critical issues.

Instead of presenting a specific example of a SWOT in this section, I show you how to use the SWOT method to come up with your own assessment. After all, applied learning is the best way to learn this assessment tool. The following sections guide you through the kinds of questions you ask in SWOT analysis.

Strengths: Patting yourself on the back

This area of the assessment comes first because it bolsters your spirits and starts the planning brainstorming session on a positive note. Questions that identify your organization's strengths as they relate to receiving funding may include the following:

- ✔ What are our financial strengths as an organization?

- ✔ What are some of our premier or stronger programs or services that have high visibility in our target area? List each program by name and include the numbers of clients served. Also make note of how the program is currently funded (if it's funded already). *Remember:* Don't talk about insufficient funding in this section. Stay positive!

- ✔ Who's writing our grants and how much does that arrangement cost? What's the grantwriter's success rate? In other words, what percentage of the grant applications that are written are funded? You should strive for a rate of 50 percent or higher.

- ✔ What funding sources can we count on to continue support for two or more years?

- ✔ Have our board members used their community connections to bring in funding from individuals, businesses, foundations, or government grants? If so, make a list of these connections and note when the connected board members' terms are over.

Weaknesses: Facing the hard truth

The weaknesses area of the assessment helps you objectively identify gaps in services or general grantseeking problems. Questions that identify your organization's weaknesses as they relate to receiving funding may include the following:

✔ What are our financial weaknesses as an organization? If we have programs that are faltering, is that because of insufficient funding or because of shortfalls in the staff's qualifications and abilities?

✔ Are we applying for every grant funding opportunity that fits our mission?

✔ Have we kept track of our past funding successes? Have we fulfilled our grant promises?

✔ Is our success rate for getting grant monies lower than 50 percent? What do we think are the causes of this low rate?

✔ Have we failed to cultivate one-on-one open communications with previous funders and are now unable to reapply for grant funding? If so, why has this happened and how can communications be reopened?

✔ Are board members using their connections in the community to help us identify individual, business, and government funding? If not, why?

Opportunities: Spotting open doors

The opportunities area of the assessment helps you identify possible opportunities that you may have missed thus far. Following are some questions you can ask to identify unexplored paths that may lead to future funding:

✔ Where are similar organizations getting their funding?

✔ Are there possible funders at the local, regional, state, or federal level who aren't familiar with our program?

✔ Are we subscribing to newsletters (both hard copy and electronic) that keep us abreast of any changes that may affect our grantseeking?

Threats: Watching your back

The threats area of the assessment helps you identify any threats that could drastically alter your current funding structure. Use the following sample questions to guide your inquiry:

✔ What funding will be exhausted in the near future, and how will programs be impacted as a result?

✔ Who in our community has taken a negative public position against our agency? In other words, whose toes have we stepped on, and how will that impact our local funding?

✔ Are other organizations doing what we do but doing it better? Why? If other organizations are doing what we do, how are we different?

Step three: Setting funding goals

After you've completed your assessment of funding needs, you're ready to move on to articulating your goals. Your goals should be global and futuristic; they should describe where you want to be when the grant money runs out. Here are some example goals from the Frankenmuth Research Institute:

Goal 1: Secure research grants to assist in fulfilling our mission statement.

Goal 2: Use the research findings to educate the general public (via a safety awareness video), specifically families with young children, about the importance of installing infant car seats properly and checking them repeatedly when seats are removed from and replaced back into the vehicle.

Step four: Determining funding objectives

Your goals can't stand alone. You'll never accomplish anything if your goals aren't supported by objectives. *Objectives* act as benchmarks or reference points; they're measurable steps that must be taken in order to achieve your goals. And every goal must have at least one objective. Here are the objectives of the Frankenmuth Research Institute:

Objective 1a: By the end of 2009, identify at least five national multiyear funders that will each commit to funding 50 percent of the annual industry research budget.

Objective 2a: By the end of 2010, secure 100 percent of the funding needed to develop a 10-minute public education and public service video on infant car seat installation and maintenance.

Objective 2b: By the end of 2012, reduce infant car seat–related fatalities by 5 percent or more in the United States through public education and new car seat manufacturing technologies to warn parents when seats are not installed properly.

Note how the institute's objectives relate to the goals listed in the previous section. Your objectives need to do the same.

Step five: Creating the action plan

In the action plan part of your organization's funding development plan you need to take the funding committee's research findings and sort them into categories of funding for each program or service that was identified as being in need of external funding or grant monies.

The action plan part of your funding plan shows you, your board, and the staff members where the money to support new or expanded programs and services will come from. All your research findings on external grant funding opportunities should be plotted in a working table created with your word processing software. Table 2-1 shows you an example of this type of funding development plan road map.

Table 2-1	Funding Development Plan Road Map	
Funding Activity	*Support Percentages*	*Person(s) Responsible*
Research and development	Federal: 100%	Principal investigator
Video production and distribution	Insurance industry Foundations: 100%	Contracted grant writer
Influencing manufacturers to be proactive	Insurance industry corporations: 100%	Vice president of corporate relations

Step six: Monitoring and evaluating funding objectives

When you write a funding development plan, it's important for the funding committee to discuss how your organization will track and evaluate your funding plan's objectives. In this part of the funding development plan, make sure to mention who will conduct the monitoring and evaluation activities and who will see or review the evaluation findings or reports. Here's an example (using the Frankenmuth Research Institute) of how to word this section of your funding development plan:

> *The board of directors for the Frankenmuth Research Institute will be responsible for convening quarterly to review and monitor the funding development plan's objectives. The principal investigator will prepare written reports on the funding activities for review by the committee. An evaluation report will be prepared for the full board of directors.*

Locating a Wide Range of Funding Sources

Moving from one funding source to many is a logical step in grantseeking. Preparing one grant application or proposal, mailing it to one funding source, and waiting who knows how long for the outcome is like taking the slow road to China. The best way to sustain a high funding success rate is to identify multiple funding sources for each project initiative in your funding development plan. Then submit your grant proposals to all of them.

Is sending out multiple proposals allowed? Of course — it's standard practice as long as you tell all the funders that you plan to approach other sources. Providing each proposal with a simple, one-page attachment labeled "Funding Sources Receiving This Request" is the most ethical way to inform all funders of your strategy. I provide an example of such a document in Chapter 18, where I talk about grant proposal attachments. Some grant applications actually have a section for you to list other sources that you have approached.

In the sections that follow, I explain what you need to know to find a broad range of funding sources.

Digging deep to find sure funding

In order to identify as many potential funding sources as possible for your organization, you need to carefully research the three primary sources of funding: federal funding, foundations, and corporations. The following sections explain what to look for in each of these categories.

As you read information on each funder, you'll see that not all funders (whether federal, foundation, or corporate) want to receive a grant proposal without any forewarning from you, the grant applicant. For many, you need to, in a sense, seek permission to submit a full grant request.

Review each funder's initial approach preference to find what *initial contact* or *approach document* is required. You can find more information regarding these documents in the later section "Testing the waters with a letter of inquiry."

When you're juggling multiple funders, developing a work plan and plotting this information, as I've done in Table 2-2, is a good way to stay organized and on top of everything. (Make sure that the funder number listed on your table matches up with the correct grant proposal.)

Table 2-2	A Table to Keep Track of Multiple Funders		
Funder	**Initial Approach/ Copies**	**Deadline**	**Average Range of Funding**
1	Letter/1	None	Up to $250,000
2	Letter/1	Quarterly	Up to $50,000
3	Proposal/1	None	Up to $50,000
4	Letter/1	May and October	Up to $50,000
5	Letter/1	None	Up to $250,000
6	Letter/1	None	Up to $100,000
7	Letter/1	April and October	Up to $50,000
8	Letter/1	Quarterly	Up to $140,000
9	Letter/1	October 31	Up to $45,000
10	Letter/1	None	Up to $250,000
11	Letter or Proposal/12	September 21	Up to $30,000
12	Letter or Proposal/6	April and October	Up to $100,000
13	Letter/1	None	Up to $250,000
14	Letter/1	None	Up to $100,000
15	Letter/1	Varies	Up to $150,000

Conducting a federal funding search

Keep your funding development plan within close reach when you start your funding search. You'll likely find a lot of potential funding opportunities, and it's wise to read the opportunity and then peruse the plan to make sure the opportunity fits.

You're searching for perfect fits between what you need and what the funder wants to fund. Also keep in mind that many published funding opportunities found on the Internet will have expired. Focus on finding open or current grant funding opportunities first. Then it's okay for you to print out expired notices and contact the grantmaking agency to see whether the funding will be available again in the future.

Thankfully, the federal government aids your federal funding search with its one-stop grant opportunity information Web site, www.grants.gov. This site is the quickest way to conduct a federal funding search.

If you don't have access to the Internet, you can do a hard-copy search for federal funding sources. To do so, you simply visit a public library that serves as a government publication depository and therefore maintains print versions of the *Federal Register*. The *Federal Register* is the official daily publication for rules, proposed rules, and notices of federal agencies and organizations as well as executive orders and other presidential documents. You can find grant opportunity announcements within these notices. However, do note that searching the hard copies has its drawbacks (it's tedious and the info you find could be out of date). So, if you don't have access to the Internet, consider using the computers at the library to connect to the government grant opportunity Web site. A research librarian will be glad to help you if you aren't tech savvy.

After you've logged on to www.grants.gov, click on Find Grant Opportunities at the top of the site's home page. Then click on Basic Search, and type your search terms in the Keyword Search field. Sample keywords include *low-income housing, research, health, after-school programs, museum,* and *library.* Your search should produce a list of federal grant opportunity announcements that contain your keyword(s). Simply click on each one to read the announcement and determine whether it fits your specific funding needs.

You may want to conduct an Internet search at this Web site on a weekly or monthly basis because the federal government releases new grant opportunity announcements daily (except for on federal holidays).

Conducting a foundation or corporate funding search

When you're ready to conduct a foundation or corporate funding search, the place to turn to is the Foundation Center. This center's publications, CD-ROMS, and online databases provide grant seekers, grantmakers, researchers, policymakers, the media, and the general public with up-to-date information on grant funding and other nonprofit-related issues.

To conduct your search, you can either subscribe to the Foundation Center's Online Foundation Directory (varying levels of subscriptions are available, beginning at as little as $19.95 per month). Or you can use the Center's Web site to locate a library near you that has a subscription to FC-Search (the Foundation Center's CD-ROM and by far its largest database with hundreds of thousands of foundation and corporate search entries). To learn more about FC-Search, visit the Foundation Center's Web site at www.foundation center.org.

When you start using the Foundation Center's resources, you'll see several information fields for entering your keywords. Keep it simple. If you're looking for money for homeless housing, in your first search, type in housing and screen the results. For the second search, type in homeless and again screen the results, eliminating duplicate funders found in the first search. I use this search approach, and it yields far more potential grant sources than typing in a search string made of two or more words. (See Chapter 6 for more about foundation and corporate grants.)

To find out more about researching foundation or corporate funding sources located outside the United States, visit Funder's Online, the European Foundation Centre's Web site, at www.fundersonline.org.

Testing the waters with a letter of inquiry

Many foundation funders state in their published guidelines that they prefer the *initial approach* (your first contact with the funder) to be a letter of inquiry rather than a full proposal. This letter allows the funder to make sure that what you're requesting is in its area of interest and range of funding award. Nowadays, practically all foundation funders require a brief letter of inquiry since they're overwhelmed with requests for funding.

The Foundation Center is one source for linking to foundation Web sites to view their funding guidelines. Another way is to use your favorite Internet search engine to locate the funder's Web site.

Often, the published guidelines you find in hard copy funding directories at the public library's reference department do *not* present the funder's most current area of interest. I prefer to use the information found on their Web sites since it is the most current. Some foundation funders have online inquiry forms; others will request a letter of inquiry.

Starting out with a letter can save you time and effort, too. Even though rejections are still rejections, wouldn't you rather be rejected after you write a letter than after you've slaved over a full-length application?

At the top of your letter of inquiry, be sure to type the words *Letter of Inquiry* (refer to Figure 2-1 for an example). It may seem obvious, but with all the paperwork that funders sort through, you're helping them out (and maybe putting them in a better mood to read your stuff) if the first glance at your letter tells them what they're getting.

Frankenmuth Research Institute

LETTER OF INQUIRY

Dr. R. J. Smoltz, Director
Irving Industry Research Support Foundation
12345 W. Northern Lights Way
Buckeye, AZ 85326

Dear Dr. Smoltz:

I am writing on behalf of the Board of Trustees to introduce you to the Frankenmuth Research Institute, a 501 (c)(3) nonprofit private operating foundation that was organized in 2008 by the Frankenmuth Insurance Corporation for the purpose of conducting extensive research on the causes of increasingly high levels of insurance claims for infant car seat injuries. In the past five years, 7,650 infants across North America were either seriously injured or died from improperly installed car seats. In 2007, this number doubled (3,000) from the 2006 number of 1,500 infants injured or killed! *As industry representatives, we are appalled and alarmed. These injuries and deaths are needless!*

The Institute critically needs your financial support **($250,000 project budget)** in order to achieve our goal of producing and distributing a public education video to all media outlets and safety and prevention organizations throughout North America. It is our projection that given the troubling statistics and brief statements from families who have lost infants because of poorly installed infant car seats, that the Institute will achieve the following measurable objective: After one year of media saturation, the public education video will reduce infant car seat-related injuries by 50% or more and fatalities by 35% or more.

As long as no actions are taken to publicize installation and maintenance instructions (prevention), infants will continue to die needlessly. Our research shows that no other highly effective interventions have ever been launched at the magnitude that the Institute is proposing. The Trustees are ready to work with the Institute staff to prepare a full grant proposal for the Irving Industry Research Support Foundation. We await your positive communication and thank you, in advance, for considering a long term financial partnership with the Institute. If, for whatever reason, you are unable to fund our project, we would greatly appreciate your assistance in opening the door and dialogue for the Institute with other potential research funders.

With urgency,

Dr. Theresa Mercy Hines, President & CEO – Board of Trustees
CC: Board of Trustees
Attachments: IRS letter of nonprofit determination and Institute's 2007 annual report

Figure 2-1:
Use this
sample
letter of
inquiry as a
guide when
organizing
your own
letter.

The suggested letter length is one page. Check out the following tips for writing a successful letter of inquiry:

- ✔ All requests for funding must be on grant applicant letterhead. This presentation gives the funder agency a clear visual affirmation of the applicant organization, its location, and how to contact the applicant in writing, by telephone, or by e-mail.

- ✔ Call the funder to verify the gender, name, title, and address of the contact person. After all, to make a professional impression with the letter of inquiry, the contact person's information must be correct.

    Verifying contact information is especially important when you're contacting a funder whose first name is gender ambiguous, such as Terry, Pat, or Kim. Find out whether that person is a Ms., Mrs., Mr., or Dr. Respect titles and use them to reach the right person, the first time!

- ✔ Introduce your organization in the first paragraph. Tell the funding agency who is sending the letter and why.

- ✔ Plant the seeds for your needs by sharing startling facts and statistics about the problem your organization seeks to address with grant funds.

- ✔ Extend an invitation for involvement by asking for the funding agency's investment or partnership in your efforts to provide specific programs and services to the target population.

- ✔ Show the funder your plans by writing global goals that are futuristic yet tell what will change when the grant funds have been spent and are no longer available.

- ✔ Sell, tell, and ask directly for help. For instance, sell the funder on the problem or need that will be addressed with grant funds, tell the story in plain language, and ask for grant funding support.

- ✔ Mention early on the specific monetary amount needed; funders don't have time to guess or hunt all over your request for the amount of money you're requesting.

- ✔ Ask for technical assistance if the funder can't fund your project. Some of the needs identified by your organization may not be monetary needs but rather instructional needs. For example, you might ask the funder to show you how to do a specific task, and then you can combine that knowledge with the resources that you have.

- ✔ Show hope in your closing by signing off with "Waiting to hear from you" or "Hopefully."

- ✔ Make sure the CEO signs the letter of inquiry. This shows that the top administrator for your organization is aware of your request for grant funding.

Receiving full grant invites from multiple funders

Imagine this scenario: You've sent out nearly 50 letters of inquiry and 25 of them result in potential funders who are interested in receiving a full grant proposal from your organization. What do you do now? Panic? Actually, no. It's better to have lots of possible funding opportunities than none.

Not every funder who expresses an interest in receiving a full grant proposal will end up funding your organization. The odds are 1 in 5, which is why you need multiple funding sources for one program or project.

In today's economy, the chances that your organization will receive more grant funds than it needs are slim. The competition is high and the funding pie only has so many slices. So spread your funding development plan net as far as you can by identifying dozens of potential funders and sending them letters of inquiry. Wait, have patience, and see what you catch with your bait. Follow up by providing any additional information requested or by preparing a full grant proposal (the funder will give you directions for what's to be included in this document).

Chapter 3

Adding Winning Words to Your Request for Proposal

In This Chapter

▶ Understanding funder requirements

▶ Securing bidding opportunities

▶ Adding attachments to your funding request

*E*very nonprofit funding source — from corporations and foundations to government agencies — issues guidelines on what and how to write your grant proposal. Even businesses issuing procurement documents issue instructions on who's eligible to apply and what must be written in the submission document. Don't worry. When you know how to cruise through technical instructions and translate a funder's terms into doable tasks, you're on your way to adding winning words to your funding request. Heads up for-profit organizations: You can use this chapter as a tutorial for writing a winning RFP (Request For Proposal) response as well.

Discovering What the Funders Are Talking About

Every set of guidelines issued by the funder has instructions telling you what it wants to see in a competitive funding request. While the order of appearance for the sections can vary from funder to funder, they basically always ask for the following blocks of information, which I cover in this section:

✔ Information about your organization and its qualifications

✔ Information about the specific project for which you're seeking funding

✔ A narrative about what you intend to do with the money if you receive it

As you read through each section of the RFP, you need to be sure that you understand how the funders define their terms. You need to consider whether there's more than one way to interpret what they're asking for. What do you do if you don't understand what they really want? Well, call or e-mail them, of course! When in doubt, ask! When confused, ask!

Whether you're a newcomer to grant writing or a veteran, funders are constantly tweaking their writing requirements. It seems as if some funders try to reduce the number of incoming applications by causing confusion. Technical terms generally scare away most newcomers. So here I orient you to the standard "information is needed here" sections.

The type of RFP for services or products prepared by an agency looking for vendors can contain some of the same narrative sections as grant applications and cooperative agreements (which is another term for a grant).

Speaking of your organization and its qualifications

Any funding source you approach will have questions about your legal name and organizational structure. Although the wording may vary slightly from one application to another, the cover documents and narratives of grant applications and cooperative agreements all ask for the same basic information. Understanding exactly what the application is asking for and knowing how to reply in the right language is critical.

Don't hesitate to call the funding source for assistance if you have questions on any portion of the application. Asking a funder for help won't hurt your chances of getting a grant. In fact, it may even help because you're filling out forms in the best possible way.

Here's the basic applicant information requested by funders:

- ✔ **Legal name of the organization applying:** Be sure to list your organization's *legal* name here. For charitable organizations, associations, and foundations, the legal name is the one that appears on the organization's IRS 501 (c)(3) (charitable designation) or (c)(6) (association or membership designation) letter of nonprofit determination. For cities, townships, villages, county units of government, and public schools, which have a different classification of nonprofit status, the legal name is the incorporated name.

- ✔ **Type of applicant:** Check the box that best describes your organization's forming structure. For example, you can choose from state agency, county, municipal, township, interstate, intermunicipal, special district, independent school district, public college or university, Indian Tribe, individual, private, profit-making organization, and other (which you have to specify).

Is your organization a type of applicant that isn't eligible? Search for a partner (government agency or nonprofit) that can be the lead grant application or RFP responder. Doing so will get dollars into the front door of your organization or business because you'll be incorporated into the funding request as a subcontracting partner. So get ready to negotiate your services and products during the planning and writing period. That way you'll have monies earmarked for you in the funding request's budget narrative and detail.

If an organization is waiting on nonprofit designation, it's common to partner with an established nonprofit to act as the fiscal agent. (An *established nonprofit* is one that has been around for more than three years.)

✔ **Year founded:** Enter the year that your organization incorporated or was created.

✔ **Current operating budget:** Supply the applicant organization's operating budget total for the current fiscal year.

When it comes to money, supply information that portrays the truth and nothing but the truth!

✔ **Employer identification number and DUNS Number:** This portion of the form asks for the seven-digit EIN (employer identification number) assigned to your organization by the Internal Revenue Service. The EIN is also called a *taxpayer reporting number.*

In addition to the EIN, federal grantmaking agencies require that all grant applicants have a nine-digit DUNS Number, an identification number that makes it easier for others to recognize and learn about your organization. You can register for a unique DUNS Number at the Dunn & Bradstreet Web site, `www.dnb.com/US/duns_update`.

The DUNS Number is a unique nine-digit identification sequence that provides unique identifiers of single business entities while linking corporate family structures together.

✔ **Organization's fiscal year:** Indicate the 12-month time frame that your organization considers to be its operating, or fiscal, year. The fiscal year is defined by the organization's bylaws and can correspond with the calendar year or some other period, such as July 1 to June 30.

✔ **Congressional districts:** On a federal grant application, you need to list all the congressional districts in which your organization is located and your grant-funded services will be implemented. You can get this information by calling the public library or surfing the Internet to locate your legislator's Web site — which will contain their district numbers.

Knowing and developing ties with representatives in Washington and at your state capitol is critical. You always need friends in high places. (See Chapter 4 for more about connecting to government officials.)

✔ **Contact person information:** Name the primary contact in your organization for grant or cooperative agreement negotiations, questions, and written correspondence.

Make your contact person an individual who helped write the grant and who's quick enough on his or her feet to answer tough technical questions from the funder, especially by phone.

✔ **Address:** Provide the current street and/or mailing address for the applicant organization.

✔ **Telephone/fax/e-mail information:** List the contact person's telephone and fax numbers (with area code) as well as an e-mail address.

Filling in project-specific blanks with style

Filling in all the blanks on grant application and cooperative agreement cover forms and budget forms is critical! Leaving any field related to applicant agency and project details blank makes you look nonresponsive, and this alone could stop a reviewer from reading any further into your document.

The following sections highlight the blanks you should pay particular attention to so the reviewer doesn't lose interest in your organization.

Creating a project name

List your project name on the cover letter, the cover form, and any other funder-requested documents. People have names. Pets have names. Projects for which you're seeking grant funding must have names, too. (And including your project name on all documents ensures that the paperwork can be easily identified and pulled back together if anything gets separated.)

Project names should be memorable, but stay away from long project names. Here's a great example for a project name: Project ACCESS. What does it stand for? Nothing, it isn't an acronym. This project name could be used for an employment and training program that's accessible to underserved populations or for a program to help senior citizens connect to affordable medical care. Whatever you do, use your imagination and don't use a name that translates into an offensive abbreviation or acronym.

Summarizing your organization's mission

When funders ask for your organization's mission statement, they want to see one sentence that conveys your mission statement. In other words, a mission statement isn't a paragraph or a preamble. It's the vision-driving string of words that tells the world your organization's purpose.

Writing about the purpose of the request

Compose a short, one-sentence statement about how you plan to use the requested funds. All types of grant applications and cooperative agreements require this information to appear on the cover form.

Giving dates for the project

Provide the proposed starting and ending dates of the project. You don't have to figure exact days, just express the project dates according to month and year.

Stating the amount requested

Enter the exact amount (round off to the nearest dollar) you're requesting from the funder. *Tip:* Do your homework by reading the funder's instructions — they will usually contain a funding range or maximum grant award amount number.

Including the total project cost

Include the total cost of the proposed project. Double- and triple-check to make sure that the number you enter here matches the total cost of the project listed in the budget narrative and on the budget forms. (For more about budgets, check out Chapter 17.)

Stating the geographic area served

Describe the location of your project in this order: city, county, state. Some funding is designated for specific states, and some funders even select individual counties within a state for funding projects.

Adding signatures

Most federal government applications are submitted online now, so you'll be typing your initials or the initials of the authorized contact person for your organization into a signature field box.

Telling your story using the right lingo

In order to receive a grant or cooperative agreement award, you must write a concise story explaining why funds are needed and how they will be expended. This story makes up the *narrative,* which is divided into several sections. The chapters in Part IV show you how to pull together a winning narrative for grant applications or cooperative agreements. Here I've listed the sections in the order that they will most likely appear in the funding request guidelines:

✔ **Introduction to/background of the organization:** Write about your organization, when it was founded, its purpose, its mission, and its location.

✔ **History and major accomplishments:** Write about who founded your organization, why it was founded, and major achievements since its founding. Only write about events and accolades that are relevant to the project for which you're requesting grant funds. Otherwise, the funder will become distracted when coming across non-relevant trivia.

✔ **Current programs and activities:** Write about the current initiatives that your organization is involved in. List the programs and activities currently taking place at your organization.

✔ **Description/demographics of your constituency:** Write about the population that your organization provides services to. Include age range, gender, ethnicity, economic status, educational level, and other characteristic descriptors. It's important for the funder to know whom you serve and what's special about your target population.

✔ **Description of community:** Write about your community's makeup. Describe the community by providing a combination of city and county information.

Cite your sources and don't use statistics that are more than five years old.

✔ **Description of work with local groups:** Write about other organizations in your community with which you work, plan events, share end-users, and have affiliations. You probably call these groups *partners*.

✔ **Proposed initiative:** Write about what you plan to do with the grant or cooperative agreement monies. State your intentions simply and directly in one or two sentences. For example, you may write something like "The purpose of this request is to. . . ."

✔ **Problem statement/statement of need:** Write about the problem you will combat with the awarded funds. State the truth about your need, but use compelling words to relay the gloom, doom, drama, and trauma of your situation and why your organization needs the requested funds.

✔ **Program design/plan of action:** Write about the process you'll implement to solve the problem or need. Incorporate proven intervention/prevention or other types of national models (find these on the Internet).

✔ **Goals:** In direct terms, write about what funding support will accomplish for your organization and the target population. Goals are global, visionary statements that create moments of awe for the writer and the reader. (Check out Chapter 15 for more information on goals.)

✔ **SMART objectives:** Write benchmarks for your target population or program that are Specific, Measurable, Attainable, Realistic, and Time bound.

✔ **Activities/strategies:** Write about the activities, tasks, or strategies that you'll implement to reach your goals.

✔ **Timeline:** Incorporate target dates for your objectives and activities/strategies. Note when the objectives will happen and the activities will start and end. A timeline presented in a table looks great to readers.

- ✔ **Impact on problem:** Write about how your proposed action will reduce the problems discussed in the problem statement/statement of need.

- ✔ **Project significance:** Write about the impact the project will have on the target population from a global perspective.

- ✔ **Systemic change:** Write about how the program you plan to develop with funding support will positively change society or rigid and antiquated systems.

- ✔ **Key personnel/staffing:** Write about the staffing needed to carry out the program or project. For each staff person, indicate what percentage of his or her time will be allocated to the project and from which budget (cash match, in-kind, or requested) his or her salary will come from.

- ✔ **Management plan/organizational structure/administration:** Write about who will report to whom and where the built-in assurances of administrative and financial responsibility will be established.

- ✔ **Adequacy of resources:** Write about any financial, physical, and personnel resources your organization already owns or has access to that can be used for program activities.

- ✔ **Equitable access/nondiscriminatory policies for hiring new personnel:** Write about how your program will guarantee access to underrepresented groups, including the physically challenged. Include your organization's nondiscrimination policy.

- ✔ **Performance evaluation plan:** Write about who will conduct the performance evaluation, what it will cover, and the time frame for evaluation activities. Keep in mind that the collection of frequent and unbiased feedback from members of the grant's target population is critical to an accurate performance evaluation.

- ✔ **Dissemination of evaluation findings:** Write about who will receive a copy of the evaluation findings. Dissemination of evaluation materials are important for reporting to current funders and can sway future funding sources when you attach them to grant applications and cooperative agreements.

Searching For and Winning Bidding Opportunities

Looking for bidding opportunities for your for-profit business? Well, you're in luck. Companies and government agencies release thousands of Requests For Proposals (RFPs), Requests for Bids (RFBs), and Requests for Quotes (RFQs) daily.

Bid opportunities are usually announced in the legal section of daily newspapers or in legal news publications. There are also nearly a dozen subscription-based Web sites that provide daily contract bidding opportunity e-mail alerts. When using a search engine to look for RFP alert services, enter this search string: RFP alerts.

Reviewing special sections of an RFP

When you find a bidding opportunity, you must be fluent in contract bid or proposal language (see the preceding sections for the basics of generic language found in most RFPs). You also must be able to quickly research and write your bid response to meet the deadline.

RFPs consist of two parts: a services proposal (scope of services) and a cost proposal. I explain both in the following sections.

Procurement staff at bid-letting agencies often read the services proposals first, and then they rate them based on compliance with the RFP instructions. Then, the cost proposals are reviewed and likely arranged from the lowest bid to the highest bid. A business or offeror scoring high on both its service and cost proposals has a high chance of being awarded a contract.

Services proposal

The services proposal breaks down into two sections: the experience/expertise/reliability section and the method of performance section. In the experience/expertise/reliability section, you tell the procurement staff about the *offeror's* (your organization's) experience and expertise. You present work references and examples of the type of work previously performed by your organization. You also list any current grant, cooperative agreement, or contract awards. (See Chapter 13 for more details on how to write this section.) In the method of performance section, you tell the procurement staff how your organization will perform the services or deliver the goods requested in the bid document. Refer to Chapter 15 to see how to write the accountability and program design paragraphs in the services proposal.

Cost proposal

For the cost proposal, you're instructed to either include the budget detail with the main components of the bid response or package it separately from the narrative sections (outlined in the section "Telling your story using the right lingo," earlier in this chapter). Often, the bid-letting agency requests that the cost proposal be sealed in an envelope separately from the services proposal. (Check out Chapter 17 for more budget-related information.)

Checking and double-checking details

The number-one strategy in winning contract bidding opportunities is to always comply with every requirement. Read the entire bid request document. Then go through it a second time and highlight all technical requirements, including font size, line spacing, page count, and so forth. Something as minor as the wrong font size can cause your bid response to be disqualified for contract consideration. (Jump to Chapter 18 for more on reviewing your completed response.)

 When you submit a bid response, don't make the procurement staff decipher the industry terms or company jargon you use. Place a list of bid response definitions immediately after the table of contents.

Wrapping Up Your Funding Request with Attachments

Additional information about your organization, in the form of *attachments,* follows the grant, cooperative agreement, or RFP narrative. Some of the things you'll likely attach to your grant are outlined in the following list. Keep in mind that each funder has its own instructions on how to order these attachments, so there's no standard order of information.

- ✔ **Budget summary/cost summary:** Fill in the blanks on a standard worksheet listing line items and expense amounts, as required by the grant guidelines or directions. (Flip to Chapter 17 for more about budgets and financial stuff.)

- ✔ **Budget detail/budget narrative/cost justification:** Write a detailed narrative on each proposed expense.

- ✔ **Up-to-date financial statement:** Attach a copy of your most recent financial statement. Whether audited or unaudited, the financial statement should explain any findings of concern.

- ✔ **Proof of tax-exempt status (if applicable):** Proof is a copy of your organization's 501 (c)(3) letter of nonprofit determination from the Internal Revenue Service, with the date on which a certifying agency recognized the status.

- ✔ **Board of directors with affiliations:** This attachment lists the names and community and board positions of the organization's governing body (board of directors, city council members, village trustees, and so on). This document also should mention the lengths of their board terms and amounts of time remaining to be served.

✔ **Letters of commitment:** Ask for letters of commitment from affiliates early in the writing process, and include at least three such letters with all grant applications you send out.

✔ **Annual report:** Include an annual report (brochure, booklet, or newsletter) as an attachment to your grant applications.

✔ **Recent print reviews:** Attach letter-size photocopies of project-related newspaper articles about your organization. Make sure the publication date and name of the newspaper or magazine appear with the article.

✔ **Other documentation:** Submit one-page summaries or complete résumés of key program personnel, as the funding source prefers. Also, if your organization has Memorandums of Agreement or Memorandums of Understanding signed by partner or collaborating agencies, attach these documents last. (Flip to Chapter 9 for more information on these types of documents.)

If the funding source's guidelines indicate that no attachments will be accepted or that any material besides the grant application will be cause for nonreview, omit any of the standard attachments covered in this list.

Part II
Identifying Key Grantmakers Worldwide

The 5th Wave   By Rich Tennant

"Well kid, if your proposal is as good as your cover letter, we may have some funding available."

In this part . . .

This part focuses on researching and qualifying key grantmakers worldwide, including corporations, foundations, and government grantmaking agencies. When writing this part, I thought about all the questions I had when I was first starting out in the grant writing field. I answer a ton of questions you will likely have, such as: What government agencies award grants? How do I read a grant funding opportunity announcement? What's up with foundation and corporate grantmakers? Are there really grants for individuals? Are there any legitimate grants for businesses? What about grants for NGOs (nonprofits that are located outside the United States)?

Chapter 4

Checking Out Public Funding Epicenters

. . . .

In This Chapter

▶ Finding money in state agencies

▶ Comparing direct grants and pass-through grants

▶ Using the CFDA and Grants.gov to find federal dollars

▶ Discovering how to take your best shot at federal grants

. . . .

*E*very time there's an infomercial on television taunting me about "free government grant monies," I'm breathless with frustration. Why? The actors never talk about how to find government grant monies on your own. Instead, they insist that you send them money for their report, which probably contains publically available information.

So, you probably have questions. Where do you start to find this information on your own? And how does money move down from our nation's capitol into your state? Is government grant money really a secret? It's time to bring you up to speed on all types of government grant funding opportunities and how to determine whether your organization or business should move forward with a grant application or cooperative agreement.

This chapter shows you where and how to look for government grant and cooperative agreement programs, especially federal ones. Remember that grants and cooperative agreements are the same thing, but they're given different names by different agencies.

Where's the Money in My State? Calling the State Agencies

Washington, DC, is a funding epicenter. All the country's money seems to flow toward the capitol, and then Congress votes to send it back to the state-level government agencies in one of three forms:

✔ **Formula:** This money is paid based on a preset head count formula.

✔ **Entitlement:** State agencies get these monies because federal legislation entitles them to receive it every fiscal year.

✔ **Competitive grant or cooperative agreement awards:** The state with the best grant applications wins this money.

Some states post all of the state funding and refunding announcement links on one Web page. However, most don't. So you have to be a really great Internet detective to find the monies in your state (not to mention in Washington). You need to surf a bit each day to catch all the new postings for grant funding opportunities.

State grants usually award less money and require just as much paperwork as federal grants. But the odds of winning a grant are better at the state level than at the federal level. The main reason you face better odds is that fewer grant applicants are competing for the state-level monies.

To find grant opportunities at the state level, you should:

✔ **Visit your state government's Web site.** Use a search engine, such as Yahoo! or Google, if you need help locating the address. If you search the site and can't find a listing of all the state's grant opportunities, call the governor's office and ask to be directed to the various agencies that give grants.

✔ **E-mail or call each state agency** responsible for carrying out legislative funding mandates that are relevant to your own funding needs, and be sure to get on its mailing list for grant funding opportunity alerts.

When you receive a state grant funding opportunity alert that you're interested in applying for, look for the Web site link that connects you to the grant application summary and download option. Download the complete grant application (including guidelines) and look for the following information:

✔ **Type of application:** For example, the application may be a hard-copy typed submission or an online electronic submission.

- ✔ **Due date:** Make sure the due date is manageable and gives you enough time to collect topic-related information and write the application.

- ✔ **Who's eligible to apply:** Every grant competition has a section listing the types of grant applicants that are eligible to apply for funds. If your organization's forming structure (local education agency, nonprofit, and so forth) isn't listed, consider partnering with an eligible applicant.

- ✔ **The number of grants to be awarded:** You may have to call the funding agency's contact person to find out the number of available grants; this information often isn't included in state grant application guidelines.

I think that all grant applicants have a fair chance of winning a state agency grant award. I always ask about the number of grants to be awarded so I know how many ways the money will be divided. That information helps me develop a more competitive project budget — staying conservative and on the low end of the average grant range. See Chapter 17 for information on how to put together a winning budget section in your grant or cooperative agreement proposal.

Classifying Types of Federal Grants

Federal grant monies come in two forms:

- ✔ **Direct grants:** With *direct grants,* you apply directly to the federal government.

- ✔ **Pass-through grants:** With *pass-through grants,* your state applies to the federal government for a grant. After receiving the grant, the state then passes the federal monies on to applicants. (Remember that pass-through monies are still considered federal monies even though they're distributed by state agencies.)

Now here's where it gets complicated: Whether in the form of direct or pass-through grants, federal monies are also classified as either *competitive* or *formula.*

In the following sections, I give you the scoop on the pros and cons of direct and pass-through grants, and I discuss the details you need to know about competitive and formula grants.

The encyclopedia of federal grants is the *Catalog of Federal and Domestic Assistance.* This encyclopedia is a directory of all grantmaking programs at the 26 grantmaking agencies. If you're a veteran grant writer, you know that all grant seekers used to depend on the newsprint-type daily publication called the *Federal Register*. The days of thumbing through dozens of irrelevant pages with federal announcements (not just grant funding opportunities) are over! Now if you want to surf federal grant funding opportunities, you simply point your Internet browser to www.grants.gov. (Refer to Chapter 5 for a detailed guide to navigating this site.) Yes, I have embraced technology!

The pros and cons of direct grants

The advantages to applying for a direct grant award, which comes straight from the federal government, include the following:

- **Direct grants have no middlemen and no extra layers of red tape.** You apply directly to the feds for a grant in response to their announcement of the availability of funds.

- **When you compete for a direct grant, you communicate directly with a program officer in a division of a federal agency.** This means one-on-one attention. So be sure to review the application guidelines thoroughly, and then compile all your questions. You can e-mail or call the grantmaking agency's contact person for clarification and answers. Do this upfront so you can clear the way for the topic research and grant or cooperative agreement writing process.

  Avoid being a nuisance! Don't call and make small talk. Have your questions ready before approaching the agency contact, and ask if the individual prefers to have questions e-mailed. Be prepared to take copious notes. If you feel you still lack a clear answer on how to proceed, ask again.

The one major disadvantage to applying for a direct grant award is that they're tough to win. You compete with other grant applicants from the 50 states and all the U.S. territories. If the feds are only planning to award money to five grant applicants, your chances are slim — even with an award-winning funding request.

In fact, you may even be competing with state agencies, which further narrows your chances. Urban and rural poverty pockets receive first priority for most social program funding, such as housing, education, health and human services, and other grantmaking areas earmarked for social issue hot spots. If you aren't proposing services in one of these high-needs geographic funding areas, your chances of winning a federal grant from a competition that gives 5 to 25 extra review points to high needs, census data–supported geographic areas are reduced to almost nothing.

The pros and cons of pass-through grants

The two advantages to applying for pass-through grant funds, which are first won from the federal government by states and are then passed on to individual organizations, are:

✔ **When you apply for pass-through grant funds at the state level, you only compete against other grant applicants in your state.** You encounter considerably less competition than at the federal, direct grant-seeking level.

✔ **Driving to your state capital to make a personal appearance before state agency program staff is relatively easy.** While you're there, get the insider's perspective by asking for a list of grants funded previously. Make sure the list contains the grant recipients and award amounts. And ask for a copy of a successful grant application from a previous competition. Knowing how winners write can boost your chances!

Under the Freedom of Information Act, all government agencies must provide requested public information to the requestor (you, the public). Exceptions to the act are extensive and include national security–related and classified documents. Chapter 20 shows you how to use the Freedom of Information Act to find out why your grant application was not funded.

The only disadvantage to applying for pass-through grants that I'm aware of is that your grant award will be a lot smaller than if you applied directly for a federal grant and received an award. Larger pots of money wait at the direct level, but the heavy competition reduces the odds of your getting those big awards.

Pass-through grant awards are significantly smaller than direct grant awards because the state takes money off the top of each federal grant to cover administrative costs. Then the amount that's left must be divided geographically and politically. For example, grants go to certain areas of a state because those areas haven't won many grant awards recently. They go to other areas because the state senator or representative has a lot of power and influence with a state agency. Wake up, smell the coffee, and realize that politics have influence over grantmaking.

Distinguishing between competitive and formula grants

To win a *competitive grant,* you must compete with other grant applicants for a limited amount of money. A team of peer reviewers (experts and lay people who apply to read and score grant applications) looks at your application and decides how many points you'll receive for each narrative section in the body of the grant request. The applications with the highest scores are recommended for funding. (In Chapter 10, I provide details on the peer review process for grant applications.)

A *formula grant,* on the other hand, is money that's disbursed by a state agency to a grant applicant based on some kind of a preset standard or formula.

A great example for formula monies is a grant for improving recycling efforts. The U.S. Environmental Protection Agency may award a set amount of money to each state and territory for recycling education. "May" is the operative word here. Some grants are formula and some are competitive. It all depends on the agency's budget in any given year — and how they want to award the monies based on Congressional legislative mandates. Suppose you live in a town with 2,500 residents, and the formula grant awards each small or rural community with up to 3,000 residents a formula allocation of $10 per resident. Your community would be in line to receive $25,000 to start or continue a recycling education program.

Browsing the CFDA for Federal Monies

You can find all sorts of information about where the money's at and what it can be used for in the *Catalog of Federal Domestic Assistance* (CFDA). This publication, which contains information about every competitive and formula grant program administered by departments and agencies of the federal government, is available from any public library. Or you can find it online at www.cfda.gov.

When you want to know what funding is out there for you at the federal level, the CFDA is where you start. After you identify grants that you're interested in applying for, you can subscribe to grant announcement alerts published in the *Federal Register.*

When you're looking for federal programs in the CFDA, remember that grant writers must zero in on programs that award *project grants* (also referred to as *cooperative agreements*) — the most plentiful category for local, regional, and national grant seekers. A project grant is funding for a specific period of time. These grant funds must be used to deliver the specific services outlined in the grant application narrative. Project grants include fellowships, scholarships, research grants, training grants, traineeships, experimental and demonstration grants, evaluation grants, planning grants, technical assistance grants, survey grants, construction grants, and unsolicited contractual agreements.

Examining how the CFDA is organized

The CFDA divides programs into nearly two dozen categories and more than 170 subcategories that identify specific areas of interest. Listed here are the basic categories into which programs are grouped:

- ✔ Agriculture
- ✔ Business and Commerce
- ✔ Community Development
- ✔ Consumer Protection
- ✔ Cultural Affairs
- ✔ Disaster Prevention and Relief
- ✔ Education
- ✔ Employment, Labor, and Training
- ✔ Energy
- ✔ Environmental Quality

- ✔ Food and Nutrition
- ✔ Health
- ✔ Housing
- ✔ Income Security and Social Services
- ✔ Information and Statistics
- ✔ Law, Justice, and Legal Services
- ✔ Natural Resources
- ✔ Regional Development
- ✔ Science and Technology
- ✔ Transportation

Understanding what's provided in the CFDA

The entry for each federal program in the CFDA includes general information on the:

- ✔ Federal agency administering the program

- ✔ Five-digit code that identifies the federal grantmaking agency and sub-agency distributing the grant or cooperative agreement funds

- ✔ Authorization upon which the program is based (the federal legislation that created the program)

- ✔ Objectives and goals of the program

- ✔ Types of financial and nonfinancial assistance offered under a program (A grant is financial assistance. Just skip over the nonfinancial talk.)

- ✔ Uses and restrictions placed upon a program

- ✔ Eligibility requirements

✔ Application and award process

✔ Assistance considerations (tells you if there are formula or matching requirements)

✔ Postassistance requirements (gives you the general expectations for grantee reports, audits, and record keeping)

✔ Financial information (tells you the amount of obligations — how much money Congress allocated to this program — for the past, current, and future fiscal years; the federal fiscal year starts October 1 and ends September 30) and estimated average award sizes

✔ Program accomplishments (generic history of what this federal program has done recently to fulfill its mission)

✔ Regulations, guidelines, and literature relevant to a program

✔ Information contacts at the headquarters, regional, and local offices

✔ Related programs based upon program objectives and uses (helps you find other federal programs that award grants in your project's area)

✔ Examples of funded projects (look for funded projects that sound like the project you're seeking grant monies for)

✔ Criteria for selecting proposals

In addition, the CFDA is full of legal terms and numerical references to legislative acts. Entries consist of a numerical code, a program title, and a description. For example, the first part of an entry in the CFDA looks like this:

11.611 Manufacturing Extension Partnership

This first part of the entry breaks down into the

✔ **Numerical code:** Each federal agency has a section, and each section is numbered with a five-digit code. The code labels an agency's programs. The first two digits identify the federal department or agency that administers the program. (*11,* from the previous example, is the U.S. Department of Commerce.) The last three digits are assigned in numerical sequence, beginning with program number 001 through program 999. (For instance, in the previous example, *611* refers to the National Institute of Standards and Technology, a division of Commerce.)

✔ **Program title:** Each program also has a title, which is the descriptive name given to the program. In the example that I give earlier, the title is *Manufacturing Extension Partnership.*

Determining what isn't included in the CDFA

The CDFA doesn't give you the estimated number of awards because you're reading generic information that may not be up-to-date. You can find information on the current estimated number of awards and estimated average award size in the actual grant opportunity announcement on www.grants.gov, the one-stop federal grant information Web site.

Also, note that the CDFA doesn't give specific deadlines for any grantmaking agencies. The CFDA is like a generic encyclopedia. All specific information, such as grant deadlines, is posted in the grant opportunity announcement.

Finding Federal Money on Grants.gov

Every day I get started by opening my e-mail inbox. Why? I've subscribed to the free services offered by Grants.gov (www.grants.gov). By signing up for this free service, you can receive e-mail alerts announcing grant funding opportunities from any of the 26 federal grantmaking agencies. Just log on and subscribe. Choose 1, 2, or more agencies and wait 24 hours to start cruising through the daily list of federal grant announcements.

I depend on Grants.gov to tell me about all of the monies being doled out in our nation's capitol. Here's how Grants.gov can help you find monies for your organization:

- ✔ **You can search, on your own, for current and past grant funding opportunities.** Log on daily and check for postings in your area of interest. A subject search (for example, *housing, legal services,* or *after-school programs*) is the easiest way to narrow down specific grant competitions in your project or program area.

- ✔ **You can register for notification of grant opportunities.** Subscribe to a daily e-mail alert.

- ✔ **You can browse through the Applicant Resources link to look at all sorts of materials.** For example, you can glance through frequently asked questions (FAQs), user guides, animated tutorials, the quarterly *Succeed* e-newsletter, Web cast archives, a software glossary, individual grant resources, and managing grant resources.

You can also apply for grants directly through the Web site. Using Grants. gov, you can

- ✔ **Prepare to apply for grants:** Click the link provided for a grant and read the full announcement. When you find a competition that fits your organization, you can search for the grant opportunity for which you plan to apply and download the grant application package.

- ✔ **Access active grant application packages:** In addition to the required forms, you can also access lists of frequently asked questions (FAQs) regarding each grant. Usually these questions originate at the funding agency's technical assistance conference or Web cast.

- ✔ **Download, complete, and submit grant application packages** online through the e-grant system portal on `www.grants.gov`.

- ✔ **Check the status of an application** submitted via Grants.gov.

For more on federal grant application kits, turn to Chapter 5.

Grants.gov recommends downloading Adobe Reader to seamlessly apply for grants. (Check the current standard version for Grants.gov before you install the software.) Also, note that Grants.gov changes annually, meaning that you'll need to check their e-grant format and submission requirements frequently.

Going For the Gold 101

After you receive a funding alert in your organization's operating area, the clock starts ticking . . . and ticking fast! Most often, you'll have less than 30 calendar days' notice from the time a grant opportunity is published until applications are due at the funding agency. In addition to time-constraint factors, remember that when applying for federal grant monies, you're competing with eligible applicants from the 50 states and the U.S. territories. How do you know when your chances for receiving a grant award are good or not so good? What's the key? I answer these questions in the following sections.

Cautiously calculating your odds of winning

Before you apply for a federal grant, take a minute and focus on the announcement. Identifying the critical points in the federal grant opportunity announcement saves you time and grief later on. Don't even start the writing process until you complete the following four internal, organizational, prequalification steps:

1. **Quickly scan the first few pages to find the *Eligible Applicants* language.**

   Make sure that your organization is eligible to apply for the grant funding. You'll become a skilled speed-reader when you see how long grant application announcements are and figure out how to focus in on the key phrases.

2. **Look for the *Deadline for Transmittal of Applications*.**

   This deadline, listed in the first few pages of the announcement, is when the grant application must be in the hands of the agency issuing the grant announcement. Before you get started, make sure that you or your grant writing team can meet the application deadline.

3. **Identify the *Estimated Average Award Size*.**

   Calculate your anticipated project cost and compare that total sum to the Estimated Average Award, the average grant amount that this federal agency intends to make.

   Suppose you've already started to prepare a draft budget for your project, and it totals $200,000 for the first year. If the average award for the grant you're interested in is only $75,000, where will the rest of your funding come from? See Chapter 2 for how to develop a funding development plan.

4. **Look closely at the *Estimated Number of Awards* to determine the chances of a federal grant being awarded in your state.**

   For example, if only 20 grants will be awarded in a competition, your odds may not be that great. Fifty states plus seven commonwealths and territories mean dozens, even hundreds, of grant applicants from each eligible area. Unless your organization has a one-of-a-kind idea, a fantastic track record when it comes to winning federal grants, and a list of very impressive community, regional, and national partners, the odds that you'll get a grant award aren't good.

When you find that you're ineligible for a grant, you can't meet the deadline, or your chances of getting a federal grant award are negligible, look to other federal agencies that fund in the same area. Also look at other types of grant monies, such as state monies or foundation and corporate monies. Chapter 2 explains how to diversify your grant options.

Schmoozing with elected officials

Searching for federal grant monies without calling your elected legislators really doesn't make much sense. Getting to know these critical contacts on Capitol Hill could make the difference between finding out about a federal funding opportunity before it's published and finding out about it when you have only 15 days (or less!) to write a major grant application.

You elected these individuals to serve *on your behalf* in the nation's capital. Use your leverage. Make a telephone call to the local or regional office for your state's congressional legislators. During your initial phone call, ask for a meeting or simply state your funding needs. Tell legislators that your organization critically needs their support in identifying federal funding.

Also, learn how to impress your elected officials. How? Host annual legislative events (breakfast, lunch, or dinner) where you present an overview of your organization and a wish list for programs and services. Make sure to use a slideshow presentation and give each attendee an information packet covering your presentation content. Feed them, and convince them that your organization has the most need for government funding. You can schmooze with both state and federal elected officials. I helped agencies wine, dine, and win over their elected officials, and then the money door just magically opened for nearly all their government requests.

Chapter 5

Wading through Grants.gov

*W*hy do most grant writers remain in the minor leagues for their entire careers? They fear federal grant applications. Federal grants are the most difficult grants to apply for — more difficult than foundation, corporate, or state and local government grants. Federal grants are known for their short deadlines, technically worded writing and review criteria, and zillions of intimidating forms. But Grants.gov (which is found online at www.grants.gov) makes things a wee bit easier.

When the federal government first launched Grants.gov, it was every grant writer's fear come true. Technology was taking over the submission process, and it wasn't readily accepted nor wanted. The process would be seamless — at least that's what the feds told everyone. But there were many glitches along the way while the online e-grant submission Web site was perfected. Today, it's still a work in progress, but the initial fear that we all had has dissipated.

In this chapter, I take you on a guided tour of the Grants.gov home page, and I give you some pointers on getting your organization registered to apply for federal monies. I also lead you through those confusing grant application forms and the downloading and uploading process for the entire grant application.

As long as you follow the online directions and don't wait until the last minute to upload your grant application, you'll breeze through the once stormy waters of federal e-grant applications.

Homing In On the Grants.gov Home Page

The Grants.gov home page is your gateway to everything you need to know to find federal grants, apply for federal grants, and follow-up on federal grant applications submitted.

The Grants.gov home page looks easy on first glance, but in reality it can be a pain! Most novice grant writers are intimidated by the federal grant writing process. They fear the technical instructions, lengthy writing requirements, and many forms with "I don't have a clue" types of information fields. Even the most fearless grant writer — one who can master the federal grant application research and writing process — is further aghast at the online Grants. gov information retrieval and uploading processes.

So even though the information in this section may seem somewhat repetitive once you actually visit the Grants.gov Web site, I still want to take you on a guided tour. It will prepare you for what you'll see and be expected to provide in order to master the Grants.gov processes. Visit the Web site frequently, expect site changes, and take it one link or step at a time!

To start, grab a drink to soothe your nerves, crank up your computer, and log on to Grants.gov. See how easy this is . . . you're just getting started, and I'm your tour guide. Fasten your seat belt, the tour is beginning!

Getting to know the basics of Grants.gov and eligibility

Grants.gov is a central storehouse for information on more than 1,000 grant programs. It provides access to approximately $400 billion in annual awards. As you can see, there are plenty of grant programs and a ton of money available. Even in slow economy years, grants are still awarded!

Throughout the Grants.gov Website, you'll find tidbits of valuable information that help first-time grant writers familiarize themselves with the basic questions, such as "What is a grant?" and "Who's eligible for one?"

Some of the eligible applicant categories for federal grants are the following: Government organizations, education organizations, public housing organizations, nonprofit organizations, for-profit organizations, small businesses, and individuals.

Delving deeper with other helpful links

The following are some other links that you can see on the Grants.gov home page:

- ✔ **Find Grant Opportunities:** This is where you search for money.

- ✔ **Get Registered:** This is a link to the steps you or your organization must take to access the Grants.gov online application submission system.

- ✔ **Apply for Grants:** When you follow this link, you get an overview of the application process.

- ✔ **Track Your Application:** Here you can track the status of your application once you hit submit.

- ✔ **Applicant Resources:** When you click on this link, you'll find guides, tutorials, frequently asked questions, and links to download the required Grants.gov software. All these materials help you prepare your grant application and submit it in the online e-grant system.

- ✔ **Help:** Here you'll find links to all sorts of documents and downloads to help you navigate Grants.gov and the grant writing process.

- ✔ **Contact Us:** Still clueless? Sometimes I am! This link gives you the inside scoop on how to call, e-mail, or mail Grants.gov. You'll also find a link to submit a complaint or to post a note about grant fraud.

- ✔ **Grant E-Mail Alerts:** Here you can sign up for free notices of grant opportunities at all or selected federal agencies.

Getting Registered to Apply for Grants on Grants.gov

In order to apply for a grant from Grants.gov, you and/or your organization must complete the (not so easy) Grants.gov registration process. You can register as an organization or as an individual. I explain both ways in the following sections.

The registration process can take between three to five business days. It can even take as long as two weeks if all the steps aren't completed on a timely basis. It took me six weeks to register my corporation as a potential grant applicant! So register early to avoid delays!

Registering as an organization

In order to get your organization registered to submit grant applications on the Grants.gov system, you need to follow these steps:

1. **Get a Dun & Bradstreet number (DUNS Number).**

   You can do this online at www.dnb.com/US/duns_update. In fact, there's a link to this Web site on Grants.gov. This registration is free and gives you a common tracking number for doing business with the government (federal, state, and local).

2. **Register with the Central Contractor Registry (also known as the CCR).**

   What is the CCR? It's a secondary Web site that collects all your organization's contact information. The information requested is similar to what you submit in your annual IRS tax return, such as name of organization, address, contact person, and contact person's information including Social Security number. You'll also be asked to upload your banking information (the bank's tracking number and the organization's bank account number). This info is used to facilitate electronic banking between the government and your organization. You didn't think they still sent the check in the mail did you?

3. **Create a username and password with the Grants.gov credential provider.**

   You'll receive a user name and password from a third party credential provider contracted by the government. At that point, you'll be routed back to Grants.gov to complete your registration with the access point information.

4. **Obtain AOR Authorization.**

   This step sounds terribly difficult, but it isn't! The E-Business Point of Contact (or E-Biz POC) at your organization must respond to the registration e-mail from Grants.gov and login at Grants.gov to authorize you as an Authorized Organization Representative (AOR). Your E-Biz POC is the Executive Director or person who manages finances at your organization. Only the AOR can log on and conduct business or grant-related transactions with the federal government.

   At any time, you can track your AOR authorization status by logging in with your username and password that you obtained in Step 3.

Registering as an individual

Individual registration can take up to one business day to complete. If you're going to go it alone, here are the quick steps to follow:

1. **Obtain your Grants.gov username and password.**

   In order to secure your electronic information, Grants.gov uses a credential provider. When you start the individual registration process, you'll be given an ID and password (just like an organization that registers). This secure type of access guarantees that your personal information and grant application will be sent to the appropriate federal grantmaking agency — safely and securely.

   Individuals don't need a DUNS Number to register and submit applications. The Grants.gov system will generate a default value in that field. Registering with the credential provider is a simple process. You can even find a tutorial link on the Grants.gov Web site that guides you through the registration process.

2. **After you've registered with a credential provider, you need to go back to the Grants.gov Web site and enter the username and password provided.**

   After you've logged in at Grants.gov, you'll be asked to provide the *Funding Opportunity Number,* or FON, that's associated with your grant application. This number is the one that's assigned by the federal grantmaking agency to each grant opportunity notice you receive in your free grant alert e-mail.

After you register on Grants.gov as an individual, you can then only apply for federal grant competitions that are open to individuals.

Downloading and Uploading Applications on Grants.gov

Since the arrival of the Grants.gov e-grant system, all the federal grant application forms that you need are available through the Grants.gov Web site. Here are some easy steps to help you maneuver Grants.gov and find an application:

1. **Download your grant application package.**

   To download this package, log on to the Grants.gov home page and click on the Apply for Grants link. There you'll see a link to download your grant application package. You need the Funding Opportunity Number (FON) or the Catalog of Federal and Domestic Assistance (CFDA) number to download. (Chapter 4 gives you the scoop on the CFDA.)

2. **After you find your specific grant funding announcement, you'll be able to download the grant application instructions easily.**

3. **Complete your grant application offline.**

   Instructions on how to open and use the forms in the grant application package are on the cover sheet (the first sheet you view in the down-loaded window view).

4. **Submit the completed grant application.**

   After you click the "Sign and Submit" button on the summary page, your application package will automatically be uploaded to Grants.gov. A con-firmation screen will appear after the upload is complete. You'll see a Grants.gov tracking number as well as the submission's official date and time.

   Record the tracking number. This way you can refer to it if you need to contact Grants.gov or give it to your Congressional officials for tracking your grant application after it's submitted.

5. **Track the status of your submitted grant application package.**

   After your grant application has been submitted, you can check the status by clicking on the Track Your Application link on the home page. Your status can be marked as any of the following:

   Received: The application has been received by Grants.gov, but it's still awaiting validation.

   Validated: The application has been validated by Grants.gov, and it's now available for the agency to download.

   Received by the agency: The agency has confirmed receipt of the application package.

   Agency tracking number assigned: The agency has assigned the application an internal track number. (However, keep in mind that not all agencies assign tracking numbers.)

   Rejected with errors: Because of errors, Grants.gov was unable to process your application. You will receive information by e-mail on how to address the errors and resubmit the application.

Taking a Look at the Many Federal Grant Application Forms

Each federal agency has its own grant application forms and its own guidelines for filling out the forms. Some agencies have fewer than 10 forms, while others have more than 20 forms. Underestimating the importance of the mandatory forms and the importance of filling them out properly could result in the disqualification of your grant application on a technical error.

What federal grant application forms are the most commonly used by the federal grantmaking agencies? Actually all the agencies have standard cover forms, budget forms, and assurances, certifications, and disclosures. The rest of the required forms will vary from agency to agency.

When filling in any form, always read the instructions that come with the online grant application guidelines first. Look for the checklist provided in every grant application announcement. The checklist tells you what to include in your application's upload. This includes mandatory forms, narrative sections, and attachments or appendixes.

Most federal grantmaking agencies make exceptions to the standard Grants. gov application upload requirement and will allow grant applicants to submit a paper application instead. The checklist becomes even more important for hard copy submissions, however, because the forms, narrative, attachments, and appendixes must be assembled in a specific order. Otherwise your application could be rejected on receipt.

The following sections provide an overview of the most common federal grant application forms: cover forms, budget forms, assurance forms, certification forms, and lobbying disclosure forms. Many state funding agencies use similar forms; the required forms are listed in the grant guidelines for each funding competition. These forms are listed in the order in which you're most likely to see them in grant application guidelines.

Cover form

The *cover form* is the top page of all federal grant applications. It's what the feds see when they open your application package. For years, the application cover form has been known as the Application for Federal Assistance Cover Form (see Figure 5-1). The current cover form is four pages when printed out. It has 21 sections and ends with a federal debt delinquency explanation page. Here's a rundown of the sections:

- Section 1: Type of Submission
- Section 2: Type of Application
- Section 3: Date Received
- Section 4: Applicant Identifier
- Sections 5a and 5b: Federal Entity and Federal Award Identifiers
- Sections 6 and 7: For State Agency use only
- Sections 8 and 9: Applicant Information
- Section 10: Name of Federal Agency
- Section 11: CFDA Number and Title
- Section 12: Funding Opportunity Number
- Section 13: Competition Identification Number
- Section 14: Areas Affected by Project
- Section 15: Descriptive Title of Applicant's Project
- Section 16: Congressional Districts
- Section 17: Proposed Project Start and End Dates
- Section 18: Estimated Funding
- Section 19: Application Subject to Review by State Under Executive Order (SPOC pre-review check off)
- Section 20: Applicant Delinquency On Federal Debt
- Section 21: Application Certification and Signatory and Contact Information

Section 8 asks for your organization's DUNS number. This is a unique nine-digit identification sequence issued by Dunn & Bradstreet (www.dnb.com/US/duns_update). The number provides a unique identifier for a single business entity and is required for all federal grant applicants (except those who register as individuals).

Figure 5-1 shows you Pages 1, 2, and 3 of Standard Form 424, the Application for Federal Assistance Cover Form (or just cover form for short).

OMB Number: 4040-0004
Expiration Date: 01/31/2009

Application for Federal Assistance SF-424			Version 02

* 1. Type of Submission:

☐ Preapplication
☐ Application
☐ Changed/Corrected Application

* 2. Type of Application:

☐ New
☐ Continuation
☐ Revision

* If Revision, select appropriate letter(s):

[   ]

* Other (Specify)

[   ]

* 3. Date Received:

[Completed by Grants.gov upon submission.]

4. Applicant Identifier:

[   ]

5a. Federal Entity Identifier:

[   ]

* 5b. Federal Award Identifier:

[   ]

State Use Only:

6. Date Received by State: [   ]   **7. State Application Identifier:** [   ]

8. APPLICANT INFORMATION:

* a. Legal Name: [   ]

* b. Employer/Taxpayer Identification Number (EIN/TIN): [   ]   *** c. Organizational DUNS:** [   ]

d. Address:

* Street1: [   ]
Street2: [   ]
* City: [   ]
County: [   ]
* State: [   ]
Province: [   ]
* Country: [USA: UNITED STATES   ]
* Zip / Postal Code: [   ]

e. Organizational Unit:

Department Name: [   ]   **Division Name:** [   ]

f. Name and contact information of person to be contacted on matters involving this application:

Prefix: [   ]   *** First Name:** [   ]
Middle Name: [   ]
* Last Name: [   ]
Suffix: [   ]

Title: [   ]

Organizational Affiliation: [   ]

* Telephone Number: [   ]   **Fax Number:** [   ]

* Email: [   ]

Figure 5-1:
A blank
cover form.

OMB Number: 4040-0004
Expiration Date: 01/31/2009

Application for Federal Assistance SF-424	Version 02

9. Type of Applicant 1: Select Applicant Type:

Type of Applicant 2: Select Applicant Type:

Type of Applicant 3: Select Applicant Type:

* Other (specify):

* 10. Name of Federal Agency:

NGMS Agency

11. Catalog of Federal Domestic Assistance Number:

CFDA Title:

* 12. Funding Opportunity Number:

MBL-SF424FAMILY-ALLFORMS

* Title:

MBL-SF424Family-AllForms

13. Competition Identification Number:

Title:

14. Areas Affected by Project (Cities, Counties, States, etc.):

* 15. Descriptive Title of Applicant's Project:

Attach supporting documents as specified in agency instructions.

Add Attachments | Delete Attachments | View Attachments

OMB Number: 4040-0004
Expiration Date: 01/31/2009

Application for Federal Assistance SF-424	Version 02

16. Congressional Districts Of:

* a. Applicant [　　　　　]　　　　　　　　　* b. Program/Project [　　　　　]

Attach an additional list of Program/Project Congressional Districts if needed.

[　　　　　]　　[Add Attachment] [Delete Attachment] [View Attachment]

17. Proposed Project:

* a. Start Date: [　　　　　]　　　　　　　　　* b. End Date: [　　　　　]

18. Estimated Funding ($):

* a. Federal [　　　　　]

* b. Applicant [　　　　　]

* c. State [　　　　　]

* d. Local [　　　　　]

* e. Other [　　　　　]

* f. Program Income [　　　　　]

* g. TOTAL [　　　　　]

* 19. Is Application Subject to Review By State Under Executive Order 12372 Process?

☐ a. This application was made available to the State under the Executive Order 12372 Process for review on [　　　　　] .

☐ b. Program is subject to E.O. 12372 but has not been selected by the State for review.

☐ c. Program is not covered by E.O. 12372.

* 20. Is the Applicant Delinquent On Any Federal Debt? (If "Yes", provide explanation.)

☐ Yes　　☐ No　　[Explanation]

21. *By signing this application, I certify (1) to the statements contained in the list of certifications** and (2) that the statements herein are true, complete and accurate to the best of my knowledge. I also provide the required assurances** and agree to comply with any resulting terms if I accept an award. I am aware that any false, fictitious, or fraudulent statements or claims may subject me to criminal, civil, or administrative penalties. (U.S. Code, Title 218, Section 1001)

☐ **** I AGREE**

** The list of certifications and assurances, or an internet site where you may obtain this list, is contained in the announcement or agency specific instructions.

Authorized Representative:

Prefix: [　　　　　]　　　　　　* First Name: [　　　　　　　　　　]

Middle Name: [　　　　　　　　]

* Last Name: [　　　　　　　　　　　　　　]

Suffix: [　　　　　]

* Title: [　　　　　　　　　　　　　　　　]

* Telephone Number: [　　　　　　　]　　　　Fax Number: [　　　　　　　]

* Email: [　　　　　　　　　　　　　　　]

* Signature of Authorized Representative: [Completed by Grants.gov upon submission.]　　* Date Signed: [Completed by Grants.gov upon submission.]

Authorized for Local Reproduction　　　　　　　　　　　　　　　　Standard Form 424 (Revised 10/2005)
Prescribed by OMB Circular A-102

Budget information forms

You'll be filling out a two-page, seven-section set of federal budget forms that's often referred to as *Standard Form 424A, Pages 1 and 2.* The seven sections of this form set are labeled Sections A through G.

✔ **Section A** is where you lay out your budget summary (your federal grant request and your non-federal matching monies).

✔ **Section B** is for detailing the budget categories line item by line item.

When you get to Section B, it's especially important to have read the instructions for these forms because each agency differs in how it wants you to fill in the columns for multiyear federal funding requests.

✔ **Section C** is where you list the source of your non-federal monies (called *non-federal resources*).

✔ **Section D** asks you to forecast your first-year grant funding needs (referred to as *forecasted cash needs*).

✔ **Section E** is where you tell the federal government the total amount of grant funds needed in the second through fifth years of your project. However, fill in this section only if the grant award is for multiple years.

✔ **Section F** is where you explain any amounts requested in the federal portion of your budget that are unusual or unclear to someone outside your agency — such as a federal grant reader (also known as a *peer reviewer*). In this section, you also explain your already negotiated indirect cost rate (contact the Office of Management and Budget, www. whitehouse.gov/omb, to start this lengthy process well before you plan to apply for federal grant funding). Finally, Section F is where you can add any other explanations or comments to explain your rather large or mysterious budget.

✔ **Section G** is where you total Columns C through F.

You can see these forms in Figures 5-2a and 5-2b. Chapter 17 gives you greater insight into the budget line item preparation process.

Assurances form

The federal government wants assurances that your organization — the grant applicant — can meet all of its funding expectations. And it gets these assurances from the aptly named *assurances form*. This is an online form that you add your electronic signature to and submit.

If you have questions regarding this form, you should contact the awarding agency. Also, note that some federal awarding agencies may require you to certify to additional assurances; if that's the case, you'll be notified of how to proceed.

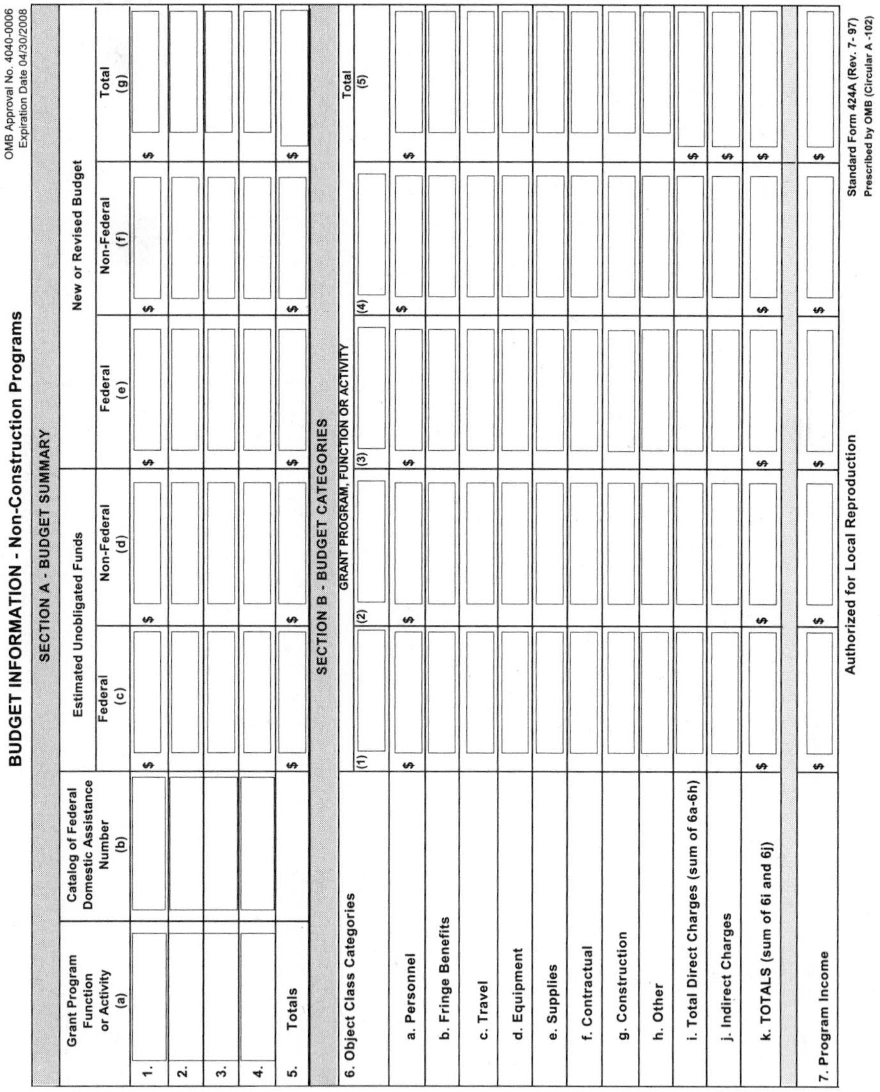

Figure 5-2a:
Sections A and B of the budget information form.

BUDGET INFORMATION - Non-Construction Programs

OMB Approval No. 4040-0006
Expiration Date 04/30/2008

SECTION A - BUDGET SUMMARY

Grant Program Function or Activity (a)	Catalog of Federal Domestic Assistance Number (b)	Estimated Unobligated Funds		New or Revised Budget		
		Federal (c)	Non-Federal (d)	Federal (e)	Non-Federal (f)	Total (g)
1.		$	$	$	$	$
2.						
3.						
4.						
5. Totals		$	$	$	$	$

SECTION B - BUDGET CATEGORIES

6. Object Class Categories	GRANT PROGRAM, FUNCTION OR ACTIVITY				Total (5)
	(1)	(2)	(3)	(4)	
a. Personnel	$	$	$	$	$
b. Fringe Benefits					
c. Travel					
d. Equipment					
e. Supplies					
f. Contractual					
g. Construction					
h. Other					
i. Total Direct Charges (sum of 6a-6h)					
j. Indirect Charges					
k. TOTALS (sum of 6i and 6j)	$	$	$	$	$
7. Program Income	$	$	$	$	$

Authorized for Local Reproduction

Standard Form 424A (Rev. 7- 97)
Prescribed by OMB (Circular A -102)

Figure 5-2b:
Sections C
through F of
the budget
information
form.

SECTION C - NON-FEDERAL RESOURCES

(a) Grant Program	(b) Applicant	(c) State	(d) Other Sources	(e) TOTALS
8.	$	$	$	$
9.				
10.				
11.				
12. TOTAL (sum of lines 8-11)	$	$	$	$

SECTION D - FORECASTED CASH NEEDS

	Total for 1st Year	1st Quarter	2nd Quarter	3rd Quarter	4th Quarter
13. Federal	$	$	$	$	$
14. Non-Federal	$				
15. TOTAL (sum of lines 13 and 14)	$	$	$	$	$

SECTION E - BUDGET ESTIMATES OF FEDERAL FUNDS NEEDED FOR BALANCE OF THE PROJECT

(a) Grant Program	FUTURE FUNDING PERIODS (Years)			
	(b) First	(c) Second	(d) Third	(e) Fourth
16.	$	$	$	$
17.				
18.				
19.				
20. TOTAL (sum of lines 16 - 19)	$	$	$	$

SECTION F - OTHER BUDGET INFORMATION

21. Direct Charges:	22. Indirect Charges:

23. Remarks:

Authorized for Local Reproduction

Standard Form 424A (Rev. 7-97) Page 2

The assurances cover your legal authority to (among other things):

- ✔ Apply for grants
- ✔ Address your commitment to record keeping
- ✔ Provide safeguards for conflict of interest
- ✔ Protect the meeting time frame established in your grant application
- ✔ Comply with multiple federal laws regarding fairness and equity for program staff and participants

By signing the assurances, you're conveying to the government funding agency that your organization will comply with all applicable requirements of all other federal laws, executive orders, regulations, and policies governing this program.

Certification forms

Each federal agency has its own specific certification forms. Basically, *certification forms* inform you of sanctions against fraud, waste, and financial abuse related to federal grant awards. At the time you apply for grant monies, the certification forms require you to acknowledge your understanding of the fact that if you mess up and misspend or mismanage your federal grant award, you won't be allowed to approach any federal agency for grant monies, forever and ever. The feds mean business!

Disclosure of lobbying activity form

A *lobbyist* is an individual or a firm that spends a lot of time on Capitol Hill or at your state capitol schmoozing with elected officials. Lobbyists work for for-profit and nonprofit agencies. They're on a (paid) mission to convince legislators to vote one way or another to benefit their client agencies. Lobbyists apply a lot of pressure, and a lot of money flows as a result.

If you've hired a lobbyist to make sure more federal or state dollars come your way, you must fess up by filling out the Disclosure of Lobbying Activities form.

Chapter 6

Uncovering Private Sector Funding

· ·

In This Chapter

▶ Gathering advice on how to get the grants you want

▶ Discovering where to find private funders

▶ Targeting the best funding source for your project by scanning info fields

▶ Organizing and prioritizing funding source files

· ·

*W*hat exactly is the private sector? Am I talking about the Rockefellers or the Gates' or the Fords? No, I'm talking about corporate and foundation grantmakers whose *endowments* (funds that started each giving entity) came from individuals, families, and for-profit corporations or businesses. These funders are plentiful at the local, state, national, and international levels.

How do you find out who these philanthropic (giving) organizations are and what they like to fund? In this chapter, I take you on a treasure hunt to find out. But rather than hunting gold nuggets, we'll be hunting grantmaker nuggets. Ready, set, turn on your night lights, and let's get started!

Knowing the Secrets of Successful Private Sector Grantseeking

Before you ask a foundation or corporation to hand over money, do your homework. Simply mailing a three- to five-page grant proposal without doing research is asking for a big-time rejection letter — and it's a waste of your time and the grantmaker's time. Here are some things you can do to set yourself apart from the field:

> ✔ Use the Internet to look for Web sites of foundations and corporations. Jump ahead to the section "Mining the Foundation Center's Funding Resources" for a funding search starting point. Set aside at least five 4- to 8-hour days (for an electronic search) to identify all potential foundation and corporate funders for your project.

✔ Subscribe to electronic funding newsletters that contain articles about what types of grants various foundations and corporations fund and that provide information on applying for them. Just a few of the many online newsletters that help you keep up with foundation and corporate giving are the *Philanthropy News Digest* (www.foundationcenter.org/pnd) and the *RFP Bulletin* (www.foundationcenter.org/pnd/rfp/index.jhtml), both of which are produced by The Foundation Center. Another great online newsletter is the GrantStation Insider (www.grantstation.com).

✔ Request grant application guidelines, an annual report (which contains financial information on the funder and usually a section on previous grants funded), and any other print literature that can help you tailor your grant application to the funder's current interest area. Also, while you're on the funder's Web site, look for lists of previous grantees. This list can tell you how much the funder funds, if the fund has funded in your area, and who the funder has funded.

✔ E-mail or call each funder to establish a "real" connection and to inquire about grant writing guideline updates that may not be posted on the funder's Web site yet. If you call, make sure to jot down some notes about the call and the person you speak with. Write down his or her name and title, the date and time of the call, and what was discussed. Having a friend at the funder's office will help if your grant application is rejected and you want the inside scoop on why it was rejected.

✔ Follow to a T all the directions provided by the funding source on how to apply for grants. If you get one item wrong, your proposal can be disqualified — even if everything else is golden.

I would be remiss if I didn't mention some things to avoid when grantseeking. Here's a brief but important list:

✔ Don't rely on outdated funding publications or Web sites for current contact information. Anything older than one year should not be used. Scroll down to the bottom of a Web site's home page to see the date that it was last updated.

✔ Don't buy anything that you can get for free on the Internet or from other sources.

✔ Don't call the funding source with a dozen questions — *self-destruction,* I believe it's called. If you have new questions about instructions or information not found in the grant application guidelines, feel free to call. However, don't call repeatedly with questions that can be answered in the guidelines.

✔ Don't write a grant application or proposal and mail it without having completed extensive research.

✔ Don't broadcast your funding sources to colleagues working for other nonprofits. Keep in mind that you're competing for funding. Learn to treasure, or keep quiet about, your findings, lest others apply as well and lessen your chances of winning.

Remember that only a very small portion of the funding source's monies will be awarded in one geographic area. If your buddy's group gets the cash, you don't. The exception is funding sources that are local and only distribute funds in a specific city, town, county, or state. However, you still should protect the grants you've found, just in case.

Finding Private Funders in All the Right Places

When it comes to grantseeking in the private sector, you have tons of Web sites to screen. Then there are books, books, and more books of potential funding sources. Gone by the wayside are the outdated databases that were sold on CD-ROMs. Some funding database subscription Web sites still market the CDs; however, you will find the most up-to-date information by using the online databases (which are updated daily).

So, to keep you out of the grant seeker's loony bin, this section gives you my favorite hits on the Internet along with a list of some really great publications that carry news on the funders you want to know about. Using these resources is a must and saves you lots of time.

Mining the Foundation Center's funding resources

In the United States, the most affordable nonprofit Web site with the largest database for corporate and foundation funding sources is the Foundation Center's Web site, which you can find at `www.foundationcenter.org`. Headquartered in New York City, the Center has field offices in Atlanta, Cleveland, San Francisco, and Washington, D.C. In addition, the Center also has cooperating collections across the United States and in Puerto Rico.

If you're looking for freebies, *cooperating collections* are free funding information centers in libraries, community foundations, and other nonprofit resource centers. They provide a core collection of the Foundation Center's publications and a variety of supplemental materials and services in areas useful to grantseekers. So if you have a cooperating collection near you, you won't have to pay for a subscription to access the Center's online materials. The advantage of subscribing is that you can have the information you need, when you need it, and at your finger tips — at home or work.

Getting the lowdown on a paid online subscription

The Foundation Center's online directory has multiple paid-subscription levels ranging from basic (10,000 foundations in the database) to professional (over 92,000 detailed profiles). If you decide to pay for a subscription, you'll have access to detailed information on foundation and corporate funders. The pages of info you pull up on these funders are referred to as *funder profiles.*

Look under the Find Funders link, and you'll see the subsection Identify Funding Sources. Under this subsection, you can find links to the Foundation Directory Online and Corporate Giving Online. Get out your credit card if you want to subscribe to these bountiful directories. The minimum subscription for 30 days costs around $20. The maximum subscription for 30 days will set you back around $200.

What do you get for your money? That depends on your subscription level. At the lowest and least expensive level in the Foundation Directory Online, you can peruse 10,000 foundations and more than 70,000 trustees, officers, and donors with 14 search fields plus a key word search. At the highest and most expensive level, your eyes may quickly become tired as you search through more than 92,000 foundations, corporate donors, and public grant-making charities; over 1.3 million recent grant awards; more than 400,000 trustees, officers, and donors; over 441,000 IRS 990 forms. With this level of subscription, you get to search with 39 search fields and a keyword search. Your subscription level is only limited by your credit card limit!

Navigating the IRS Form 990

When I want to know everything about the financial picture of a specific private sector funder, I look at the funder's IRS 990 Form (non-profit tax return) to see all of its assets, major grants awarded, and contact information for its board members in the event I need to ask a board member to be an advocate for my funding request.

The current IRS Form 990 is nine pages and comes in PDF format. It can be downloaded from the Internal Revenue Service (IRS) Web site at www.irs.gov. Sections A through M (Page 1 at the top of the form) request contact and identifying information on the nonprofit organization. After those sections are several parts that require other information.

After you've become a paid subscriber to the Foundation Center's online directory, you can start your funder research in four different ways. You can search by any of the following topics:

- ✔ **Grantmakers:** Your subscription level determines whether you have access to 10,000 grantmakers or more than 90,000. Out of the four topics in this list, I search by the grantmaker most often. It's easy and productive. This type of search allows you to search by

    - Grantmaker name

    - Grantmaker location (state, county, city, metro area, and zip code)

    - Fields of interest

    - Types of support

    - Geographic focus

    - Trustees, officers, and donors

    - Type of grantmaker

    - Total giving

    - Keyword

    With this search, I usually find at least 10 to 20 potential private sector funding sources for each project that I'm working on.

- ✔ **Companies:** This search option is available to professional-level subscribers only. With it, you can search *corporate grantmakers* (businesses that have developed corporate giving programs). When you can't find funders in the Foundation-Only section, it's a good idea to search for grant opportunities in the Companies Section.

- ✔ **Grants:** This option allows you to search by

    - Grantmaker name

    - Recipient name

    - Recipient state/county

    - Recipient city

    - Recipient type

    - Subjects

    - Types of support

    - Keyword

I like the Grants option when I want to know the funders that have awarded grants in a specific county or region. However, this option doesn't give you a detailed profile of the funder.

✔ **Form 990s:** This search option is only available to subscribers at the professional level. Why would you look at an organization's Form 990 anyway? To find out the total number of grants awarded in the grant-maker's most recent *fiscal year* (the 12-month operating period determined when they filed for IRS nonprofit status). Looking at the total number of grants awarded gives you an idea of the funder's financial capacity. If I find a funder only awarding ten grants per year, I view this as a red flag. That usually means there's not too much philanthropy going on there. However, when I see that a funder has awarded 100 grants, I'm ready to be a winner in next year's competition!

If you don't want to fork over the cash to subscribe at the professional level, remember that you can find most IRS Form 990s for nonprofit organizations, including grantmakers, on the subscription-based GuideStar Web site (www.guidestar.org).

Going for hard copy resources

Besides having tons of online info (see the previous section "Getting the low-down on a paid online subscription"), the Foundation Center also has some hard copy publications. Even though these materials aren't free, they still make great desktop references if you write grant proposals in specialized areas. Some of the directory resources include:

✔ Grant guides with information specific to major funding areas. For example, here are some of the major funding areas covered by these guides:

- Arts, culture, and the humanities

- Children and youth

- Elementary and secondary education

- Environmental protection and animal welfare

- Foreign and international programs

- Higher education

- Libraries and information services

- Mental health, addictions, and crisis services

- Minorities

- People with disabilities

- Religion, religious welfare, and religious education

- Women and girls

✔ Print directories of the online funder database are also available. For example, you can order hard copies from the following:

- The Foundation Center Library

- Companion Directory Set

- Classic Directory Set

- U.S. Directory Set

- Comprehensive Directory Set

- Foundation Universe Set

- The International Collection (for you nonprofit governmental organization grantseekers)

Each directory has its own unique and information-filled titles, so cruise the Center's Web site to see full descriptions.

You can buy any of these resources by visiting `www.foundationcenter.org/marketplace`.

Choosing the free route

The following list highlights some online links where you can access free information on the Foundation Center's Web site (`www.foundationcenter.org`):

✔ **The Find Funders Tab:** When you click on this tab, you'll see links that help you find foundations and IRS Form 990s (nonprofit tax returns); track funding trends and requests for proposals; download common grant applications (with download links for each of the Regional Associations of Grantmakers, which are also called RAGS); and decipher statistics on the top funders (corporate and foundation).

✔ **Newsletters Link:** Click this link and you'll find a list of newsletters that you can subscribe to (via e-mail delivery) free of charge. You don't even have to register for online access. You can use the free newsletters to find topic specific Requests for Proposals (RFPs) released by foundation and corporate funders. You can also use the newsletters to keep abreast of what's happening in the world of grantmaking. I have subscriptions for the following:

- **Philanthropy News Digest:** This is the Foundation Center's long-running, award-winning weekly news digest. It tells you what's happening in the world of philanthropy. Staying up-to-date on philanthropy is important because then you know when foundation or corporate contact personnel are leaving or were just hired. You'll also know what each specific funder that's listed in the digest is doing that relates to their grantmaking policies and trends.

- **RFP Bulletin:** This freebie is a weekly roundup of recently announced Requests for Proposals (RFPs) from private, corporate, and government funding sources.

Accessing other online funding resources

While the Foundation Center is my database of preference because of the size of its grantmaker and grantmaking collection, I also use other online funding resources. Here's a brief list of the others I use:

✔ www.grantstation.com: GrantStation.com, a subscription-based Web site, provides members with quick and easy links to all current sources of grant money and tells visitors how to secure available funding. GrantStation's features allow members to find a funder by using the Grantseekers Toolkit, which provides information on new funding opportunities, deadlines, and training for grant writers. This toolkit also allows members to conduct grant research. I particularly enjoy the Grantmaker Updates feature at the bottom of this Web site's home page; the update lists three to five new funding announcements each week.

✔ www.fundsnetservices.com: Fundsnet Services is perhaps the most comprehensive free access Web site of its kind on the Internet today. When you pull up the Fundsnet Services home page, you find so many useful links that you may just have a dizzy spell. Here are some links that I find tremendously helpful: Arts & Culture Grants, Disability Grants, Education Grants, Environment & Conservation Grants, Foundation Directory, Community Foundations, Women Grants, and Computers & Technology. The downside of this free Web site is that some funder links are broken and the information is not updated on the same frequency as the Foundation Center's Online Directory.

Each of the links on this Web site are topic-specific and include click-through features to send you to a funder's Web site to read about grant opportunities firsthand. Fundsnet Services has made Web site navigation easy for grant writers of all levels, beginning to advanced.

✔ www.fortune.com: This free Web site is full of news about the corporate world. I like to use the Fortune 500 lists to quickly find potential, financially healthy corporate grantmakers. I use this Web site to locate the top 500 U.S.-based corporations. The Fortune Web site saves you search time and gives you the companies' rankings where financial assets are concerned. In addition to carrying detailed industry and financial information on U.S.-based corporations, this Web site also has a link to the Global 500, a list of the top 500 corporations around the world.

The downside with Fortune.com is that finding a company's operating locations (where they tend to give grant monies) is more difficult. You have to click through several links, leaving the Fortune.com Web site and searching through the company's Web site to find information on the location of each corporation's headquarters and operating locations. Remember, corporate funders only give grants in the geographical areas in which they have headquarters and operating sites.

If you visit `money.cnn.com/magazines/fortune/fortune500/2008/full_list/index.html`, you can see the full list of Fortune rankings. Click on a company name, and you can see general financial information about the corporation. In order to find out where the company is headquartered and where it operates, you must click on the link to its Web site. A separate page should open, and from there you can look for links such as About Us or Corporate Governance. Finding corporate locations in your state or city takes some clever detective work, but it's well worth your time. You can find multiple corporations that offer grants in your state or community. Again, this is where they practice their social responsibility.

✔ `www.christiangrants.com`: ChristianGrants.com is a subscription-based Web site that has an online directory for churches, ministries, and other grantseekers that looking for monies to start or expand religiously-affiliated programs and projects. This Web site has more than 175 foundations that fund Christian organizations. Church and ministry grant monies are available for building projects, program support, equipment, renovations, youth programs, capital campaigns, outreach ministries, general operating support, mission trips, seed money, and much more.

On ChristianGrants.com there's also an online directory with listings of grantmakers that fund individuals. Individual grant funding is available for scholarships for tuition, missionary work, preaching and ministry, clergy renewal, and evangelism view.

✔ `www.christiangrantsdirectory.org`: ChristianGrantsDirectory.org offers information on hundreds of Christian foundations, nonprofit discounts, and sources of in-kind donations. You can also sign up for a newsletter and RSS feed that provides updates of the latest grant opportunities.

Zeroing In on the Most Important Information Fields of a Funder Profile

After you locate information on a foundation or corporate funding source, you need to quickly scan its profile to determine whether you have a *perfect* match. A perfect match means that your program or project fits the source's funding priorities 100 percent. You can't persuade a funder to change its award guidelines or funding priorities; you're the one who has to do the changing to fit the funder's funding criteria. If you can't change your program or project, that particular funding source isn't the best one for you. In that case, simply keep looking for a better match.

Every online resource and print publication listing funding sources presents the information on the funder in a generalized format referred to as a *profile*. When you look at a funder's profile, you can scan some specific information fields to determine whether reading about this particular funding source is worth your time. Check out the following fields:

- ✓ **Limitations:** Look at the limitations field first. Your organization may be eliminated before it can even get to the starting gate. Does the wording in this section eliminate your program or project? If so, move on to the next funder's profile. If not, move on to the next critical information field. Typical limitations you may see listed in the grantmaker's online profile include:

    - Specific geographic giving area (countries, states, and counties)

    - Restrictions on who they'll fund and what they'll fund

    Most mainstream foundation funders don't award grants for religious purposes, to individuals, or for capital projects (building construction or renovation or major equipment purchases).

- ✓ **Purpose and Activities:** Every foundation and corporate giver has a purpose statement, located at the beginning of the funding profile. Does the funding source's purpose statement reflect your organization's values? Do any of the activities that the funder prefers to fund match activities that your organization is or will be undertaking? If not, read no further. Move on to another funder's information profile. If you can identify with this funder's purpose, move on to the next critical information field.

- ✓ **Fields of Interest:** Does the program area that you're seeking grant funds for match with any of the funding source's fields of interest? Keep in mind that the language you use to describe your program may not be the language the funder uses to list its fields of interest. Think of your program area in broad terms and generic categories.

    For example, say you need grant funding for a program that will tutor and mentor at-risk elementary school students after school and on the weekends. You probably won't find terms such as *tutoring, mentoring, at-risk,* or *after-school* in the funder's fields of interest entry. Rather, you might find terms such as *education (K–12), elementary education, public education, private education,* and *youth programs and services.* The second list is broader than the first.

- ✓ **Types of Support:** What types of activities will this funder pay for? If you're trying to erect a new building and the funder only lists *general operating support, conferences,* and *seed money* under types of support, this funding source may not be the one you want to approach with a construction project.

    Even if this funder isn't willing to support the type of activity that you're currently seeking funds for, save the funder's information if you think it may be willing to support some other aspect of your organization.

✔ **Previous Grants or Grantees:** Have any previous grants been funded in your state? Have any previous grants been for projects similar to yours or in your project area? It's difficult to get a funder to award grant monies in a state where it hasn't previously awarded grants. If a funder has a track record for previous grants in your state or previous grants for projects similar to yours, the door is open to receive your funding request. However, if these aren't the circumstances you face, you may have to e-mail or call the funder to determine whether it's worth your time to proceed with a funding request.

✔ **Amounts of Grants Previously Funded:** Does your guesstimated project budget fit into the range of prior grant awards? Use the funder's prior grantmaking amounts to gauge where your request should fall. You never want to request a grant amount that exceeds the top grant awarded by the funder — that strategy's a bit too risky. If you're looking for $200,000 and the largest grant awarded was $10,000, you may need to find multiple funders for your project.

Prioritizing Your Potential Private Funders and Grant Applications

After you identify the potential private funders that are the best fit for your program, follow these steps:

1. **Contact each funding source (via e-mail, letter, or phone call) and ask to be included in the funder's mailing list.**

   Doing so normally means that you get annual reports, grantmaking guidelines, research, and other information that keeps you up-to-date. Armed with this information, you're ready to take the next step.

2. **Organize your potential foundation and corporate sources by the application due dates.**

   This is a critical step because some private sector funders only have once-yearly competitions. You could be a few weeks or many months away from the annual date for grant submissions. After all your hard work, you don't want to miss an opportunity to get a grant funded because you submitted your application late.

   Develop a good filing system for applications and for funder information in general. Use a separate folder for each funder. You should have massive amounts of information at this point, and keeping everything in order is crucial. Sorting things by due date helps you anticipate how much work you'll have in any given month.

   Even the best laid plans go astray. But sloppily laid plans? Poorly laid plans? These plans are *destined* to go astray. Be as organized as possible to maximize your chances of getting the grants you want.

3. **When you're ready to write, focus on the proposals and applications that have due dates in 60 days or less.**

Get busy! Check out Part IV for all the details on completing an outstanding application.

4. **Single out the foundation and corporate funders who accept generic National Network of Grantmakers or regional common grant format applications anytime during the year.**

These grants are normally fairly easy to write. Because the National Network of Grantmakers (or NNG) template format captures all the most critical grant applicant and project-related information, grant writing veterans have been using this easy five-page narrative format for years. It's the best way to apply for grants from corporations and foundations that accept unsolicited proposals but don't have their own specific grant application formatting guidelines. The NNG Common Grant Application template guides you in the writing process by organizing all the information that the funder needs to know into clearly outlined sections. (For more on the Common Grant Application, see Chapter 1.)

Nearly a decade ago, the NNG developed the Common Grant Application form for their grantmaking members who were willing to accept a more generic grant request template. While the NNG Web site is no longer active, the Common Grant Application Form can be found by using any Internet search engine and typing in "NNG Common Grant Application."

Chapter 7

Finding Individual and Business Grant Opportunities

*F*or the past decade, I've received hundreds of telephone calls and e-mails from people saying they've heard about "free" grant money but don't know where to find it. They want to know whether I can point them in the right direction. Here's what I think happened. They woke up in the middle of the night and saw an infomercial about "free" government grants — free money to buy a house, pay off your bills, start your business, buy a car, and more! When they couldn't find this information the next day, they thought that someone somewhere was withholding the real deal.

This chapter sets the record straight. Yes, selected types of grants are available for individuals and businesses. However, they aren't as plentiful as you'd think, and you have to be able to use your detective skills on the Internet to find legitimate grant-funding opportunities. I get you started in the following pages.

As is the case with all types of grant monies given — whether given by a foundation, corporation, or a government grantmaking agency — strings are attached. From eligibility strings to usage strings to default strings — you'll be filling out paperwork from the start to the finish.

Finding Legitimate Grants for Individuals

According to the Foundation Center Web site (www.foundationcenter.org), the nation's leading print and online authority on philanthropy (grant-making), there are more than 6,200 foundations and charity programs that fund students, artists, researchers, and other individual grantseekers. To make this vast database work for you, you first need to get acquainted with the various types of individual grants that are out there.

Commonly awarded grants for individuals include the following:

- **College scholarships and student loans:** The former doesn't require repayment, but the latter does. Both college scholarships and student loans are awarded to specific financial institutions in the individual's name. Take a look at the College Board's Web site (www.collegeboard.com) for an example. After clicking on the For Students link and then on the Pay for College link, you can click on the Scholarship & Aid link to find helpful scholarship information.

- **Fellowships:** This grant type requires no repayment and may be taxable. However, fellowships are often restricted to specific institutions or fields of study. Some foundations award fellowships directly to individuals; others award them to specific colleges or universities. For an example of a fellowship, visit the John D. and Catherine T. MacArthur Foundation's Web site (www.macfound.org). Click on the MacArthur Fellows link to find out more.

- **Specific funder-directed assistance grants:** These grants are available for patient access programs, discount prescription medication programs, global humanitarian support, and more. Check out the Bristol-Myers Squibb Patient Assistance Foundation's Web site (www.bmspaf.org) for an example. Click on the Apply Now link for an application form.

- **Research grants:** This grant type is reserved for educational and scientific research projects. For an example, take a look at the Web site for the Tides Foundation (www.tides.org). On the home page, click on the Tides Foundation tab and then on the Tides Initiatives link to view the grantmaking program links.

- **First-time homebuyer grants:** Just about every state offers these grants, which are earmarked to help eligible individuals and families purchase a first home with a reduced down payment. Most often, these monies originate from the U.S. Department of Housing and Urban Development and are passed down through your state's housing authority or agency. That agency then subgrants these monies to regional and local housing assistance programs.

Each state's eligibility guidelines vary due to income limits, credit rating requirements, and house pricing limits, so call your state's housing authority before applying. Also, be prepared to take a class on home ownership.

With the exception of grants for first-time homebuyers, the only types of government grants available for individuals are research grants (technology, science, and education). These grants are limited and not as plentiful as foundation grants for individuals, so don't go knocking on Uncle Sam's door and expect the funds to come pouring out.

When you're ready to start your search for individual grants, first decide whether you're going to use the Internet or visit your local public library. If you use the Internet, you can print out your search results and sort them from most likely matches to long shots. Then you can start the process of contacting each funder to obtain specific guidelines and due dates. If you opt to visit your local library and use its printing resources, take plenty of pocket change for copying fees. After all, you'll want to take your findings home for later review.

The competition is heavy for individual grants, so start your search at least one year before you need the funds. Contact the funders for qualification details that may not be posted on their Web sites or up-to-date in their print publications. Then be sure to fill out all the required forms completely and accurately.

Individual grants may be taxable, so check with your accountant and the funding source — unless of course you want to pay taxes on that free money.

Locating Credible Grants for Your Business Start-Up

I'd love to tell you that there are grants raining down on every square inch of the country to help you start your new business. However, this is simply not true. Finding the monies to start a new business has always been an elusive and disappointing process. In the 1970s and 1980s, these monies came from the federal government and were earmarked for Community Development Corporations (also known as CDCs). However, federal help with business start-up monies has all but disappeared.

Having said all that, some grants do exist, both nationally and internationally, that can help you jump-start your new business. The question is: Where are they, and how the heck can you find them? Start by searching the Internet using this term: business plan competitions.

What is a *business plan competition,* anyway? It's when leading universities and other institutional-type funders put out a call for the best business plan models. (In other words, if you enter one of these competitions, you're competing against graduate and post-graduate students.) A panel of business experts reviews each plan and selects the winner(s). The prize can be up to $100,000 for some of the competitions.

Following are some sample listings of legitimate business plan competitions (which I found through `www.smallbusinessnotes.com`):

- ✔ Harvard Business School Business Plan Competition
- ✔ Miller Urban Entrepreneurs Series Business Plan Competition

Try to search the Internet weekly for updated listings and emerging competitions. Be diligent because the early bird gets the worm — or the grand prize to start a new business!

If you're in disbelief about the narrow field of grants for business start-ups, go to the U.S. Small Business Administration's Web site at `www.sba.gov`. There you'll find this disclaimer when searching for grants:

> *Please note that the U.S. Small Business Administration does not offer grants to start or expand small businesses, though it does offer a wide variety of loan programs. While the SBA does offer some grant programs, these are generally designed to expand and enhance organizations that provide small business management, technical, or financial assistance. These grants generally support non-profit organizations, intermediary lending institutions, and state and local governments.*

Don't worry. The U.S. Small Business Administration (SBA) doesn't drop you there like a hot potato. Instead, it gives you links to the other federal grant-making agencies. After you find a federal grantmaking agency that relates to your project idea, move over to Grants.gov to search for that specific agency's grant funding opportunities, current and past. (See Chapter 5 for more on navigating Grants.gov.)

Seeking Business Expansion Monies

Foundations and corporations don't provide grants to help you expand your business (or to help you start your business or pay off existing bills). If you aren't operating in a high-technology area, you're going to have to stay with your day job and start your business on a part-time basis. You may want to consider a loan from your bank as an alternate source of funding.

Or you may prefer to look into the business-expansion funding available through both federal and state governments. The following sections delve into these opportunities in more detail.

Looking into federal expansion funding

The federal government has two types of grants to help you expand your business if you're working on research or a product that it's interested in. The SBA's Office of Technology administers the Small Business Innovation Research (SBIR) Program and the Small Business Technology Transfer (STTR) Program. Through these two competitive programs, the SBA ensures that the nation's small, high tech, innovative businesses are a significant part of the federal government's research and development efforts. Eleven federal departments participate in the SBIR program; five departments participate in the STTR program.

Phase I grants are awarded for as much as $100,000 by federal agencies. These funds must be used for research that will contribute to proving the scientific or technical feasibility of your approach or concept. Phase II grants are awarded for as much as $750,000 by federal agencies and must be used for your further principal research and development activities. *Note:* You must have received a Phase I grant award in order to be eligible to apply for a Phase II grant.

Monitor the SBA's Web site (www.sba.gov) for announcements about technical assistance workshops and conferences around the country. I also recommend fine-tuning your e-mail subscription on Grants.gov (you can read more about this Web site in Chapter 5) by typing in "SBIR" and "STTR" in the keyword search for identifying grant funding opportunity announcements. Doing so allows you to limit your daily e-mail funding alert to only SBIR and STTR grant announcements.

Every state has an SBIR/STTR contact person appointed by the governor's office. After you find an SBIR/STTR grant funding opportunity on Grants. gov, there are two steps you must take immediately, since the deadline for researching and writing your grant application will be less than 60 days. Here's what to do:

1. **Download and print out the application announcement.**

   This announcement will provide information on what will be funded and how to apply.

2. **Call your governor's office to locate the state's SBIR/STTR contact person.**

This individual will be able to connect you with experts in your research and development field who can help strategize your approach for federal funding. He won't be able to write your application for you (that's your job), but he will be able to tell you what the government is interested in funding and the best way to present your specific information in a competitive research and development grant application.

Here's a list of the agencies that award SBIR grants:

- ✔ Department of Agriculture
- ✔ Department of Commerce
- ✔ Department of Defense
- ✔ Department of Education
- ✔ Department of Energy
- ✔ Department of Health and Human Services
- ✔ Department of Homeland Security
- ✔ Department of Transportation
- ✔ Environmental Protection Agency
- ✔ National Aeronautics and Space Administration
- ✔ National Science Foundation

Following are the federal agencies that award STTR grants:

- ✔ Department of Defense
- ✔ Department of Energy
- ✔ Department of Health and Human Services
- ✔ National Aeronautics and Space Administration
- ✔ National Science Foundation

Tracking down your state's business expansion funding opportunities

Every state has some type of economic stimulus fund to help with business and industry expansions. Turn to your state's Department of Commerce as a starting point in your grant-information search. (Some states have changed this historical agency's name to something different, so you may need to call your state capitol's switchboard for the correct agency name.) For example, in Florida, the name of the State Department of Commerce has been changed to Enterprise Florida.

When you call your state agency to discuss your business's expansion needs, make sure to tell them the name of your business, its products or services, the county in which you're located, and why you need to expand (what's the driving force behind growing larger?). Don't waste their time with long-winded statements meant to impress the listener. Also, even if you hit a dead end (meaning there's no funding), thank the listener for his or her time. After all, you can always use a friend in state government!

Here are some examples I found while perusing the Internet looking for business expansion grants:

- In California, a small town's redevelopment agency awarded multiple grants and loans ranging from $7,500 to $10,000 for business expansion, site improvements, property acquisition, and facility improvements to accommodate persons with disabilities (required by the American Disabilities Act).

- In 2007, Enterprise Florida awarded 18 grants to economic development authorities, regional and local chambers of commerce, and other non-profit groups to support international business expansion. Some of the agencies awarded funds from Enterprise Florida may have had plans to regrant a portion of the monies received to businesses that were trying to expand from a national to an international market.

- In Massachusetts, the Massachusetts Technology Collaborative, which administers the Commonwealth's Renewable Energy Trust Fund, offered financial assistance in the form of loans to support renewable energy companies entering or expanding within the manufacturing stage of commercial development.

- In Michigan, the Capital Access Program is one of the Michigan Economic Development Corporation's innovative programs created to assist businesses with capital needs. It uses small amounts of public resources to generate private bank financing, providing small Michigan businesses access to bank financing that may not otherwise be available. Under the Capital Access Program, more than 10,650 loans have been provided to Michigan businesses throughout the past 20 years.

- In Missouri, a state grant funded infrastructure improvements to facilitate the expansion of a custom wood product manufacturer. The company used the $540,000 grant to retain eight employees and create another six new jobs as it doubled the size of its facility to meet increased sales volume.

- In Nebraska, the Department of Economic Development provided $505,000 in Community Development Block Grant (CDBG) funding to a city to help a private company expand beef-packing operations.

- In New York State, Empire State Development, the state's economic development agency, awarded a $200,000 grant to a seed company for business expansion.

These are just a few possibilities. You can find more by firing up your computer and searching for the not-so-well-advertised grant monies available from one or more of your state's grantmaking agencies. Call your governor's office, the local Chamber of Commerce or Economic Development Authority, and even local banks to see whether they have grants, loans, or other funding resources to help you expand your business. After all, an expanded business creates more jobs, puts more payroll into the community's coffers, and contributes to your state's economic stability. Type, click, and call. Consider these words your marching orders!

Chapter 8

Scoping Out International Grants

*I*f you're providing programs and/or services in a national or international arena, you're likely working for a foreign-based Nongovernmental Organization (NGO). NGO status is awarded by foreign governments and defines your organization as a charity that isn't related to any government agency in the country from which you've received NGO approval. Currently, more than 40,000 national NGOs and hundreds of thousands of international NGOs are in existence. NGOs can apply for grant funding from foreign governments, foundations, and corporations, as well as from U.S.-based funding sources. It's the best of both worlds.

Ensuring You're Eligible for International Grants

Read no further if you're writing grants for a U.S.-based nonprofit organization with no programs or activities in other countries. You shouldn't approach funders outside the United States, because funding agencies in other countries have specific funding priorities that are related to programs in their countries of interest.

If you do (or will) have nonprofit programs or activities outside the U.S., you must file for NGO status in every country where your organization currently operates (or plans to operate). Unlike the U.S., where the Internal Revenue Service can grant 501(c)(3) nonprofit status within all 50 states, you must file for NGO status or register with each individual country's national taxation authority. (**Note:** The title of this agency varies from country to country.) After you receive approvals, you can use your NGO letter when seeking grant funding in each specific country.

Get your organizational information together in advance to speed up the NGO approval process. Each country will likely want to see a written description of your organization's purpose and programs, and maybe even multiyear financial data.

After you have your NGO approval letters in hand from each country, make multiple copies or scan them into an electronic file. If you lose this letter or mistakenly attach your only copy to a grant proposal, it may take months or years to obtain another official copy.

Researching International Funding Opportunities Online

You can never quite know when an international funder will go bust. One day it's there, the next it's not. This instability is due to fragile conditions in the countries where these funders operate. The good news, though, is that you can save yourself some time and money by using the Internet to locate funders outside the United States.

In order to make the most of your Internet search for international funding opportunities, you first need to be able to recognize the two main types of foundations:

- **Corporate:** A corporate foundation is a nonprofit entity formed with the profits or proceeds from a company (a corporation).

- **Independent:** An independent foundation isn't affiliated with a corporation. Rather, it was founded by an individual, a group of individuals, or a family.

Most of the formal networks of grantmakers outside the U.S. are organizations that mirror the New York City–based Foundation Center, which was founded in 1956 and is the nation's leading authority on philanthropy. The European Union has the European Foundation Centre, and Canada has Imagine Canada. Both of these information depositories publish details on corporate and independent foundations. I cover the European and Canadian groups, and a few other Web resources for international funding, in the following sections.

The European Foundation Centre

The European Foundation Centre (EFC) is located in Brussels, Belgium, and features an in-depth knowledge base on more than 1,000 foundations and corporate funders that work in and with Europe. To access its searchable Funder Profile Database, you must use euros to purchase a subscription. After you've accessed the home page for the European Foundation Center, click on For Grantseekers and scroll down. You'll see the link to Funders Online. Look for the Funders Online URL in the body of the paragraph under EFC Resources.

Funder profiles are descriptive statements about who a funder is, where they're located, their contact person with title and e-mail or telephone number, funding priorities, grant application processes, and other "all about us" information. By carefully studying a funder's profile, you can determine whether this funder is a perfect match for your project.

In the following sections, I highlight the great bits of info you can find by using the database and provide a sample of a real-life profile so you can see the value of this info for yourself.

Delving into details

So where does all this great data come from, anyway? Funder profiles are based on information collected from Web sites, annual reports, newsletters, grants lists, press releases, and other documents. In short, they're the words of the funders themselves.

Checking out the EFC's hard-copy resources

If you'd rather not browse the Internet for hours on end to find grant funding opportunities in Europe, you'll be pleased to know that the European Foundation Centre (EFC) also provides hard-copy resources. The EFC's various hard-copy funding directories on a range of topic areas are produced from data found on its online Funder Profile Database. Following are some of the main hard-copy EFC publications, along with their publication years:

✔ Independent Funding, 2006

✔ Funding Vocational Training and Employment for People with Disabilities in Europe, 2002

✔ Minorities and Multiculturalism, 2001

✔ Youth Funding in Europe, 2000

Note: The publication prices listed on the EFC Web site (www.efc.be) are in euros. For help with converting dollars into euros and vice versa, check out "Converting Dollars into Foreign Currencies" later in this chapter.

Each funder profile contains the following information about an organization:

- ✔ Name of funder
- ✔ Country where located
- ✔ Primary address and key contact
- ✔ Name in English
- ✔ Mission
- ✔ Background
- ✔ Geographic focus
- ✔ Related organisation
- ✔ Programme areas
- ✔ Types of support
- ✔ Application procedures
- ✔ Restrictions
- ✔ Languages accepted
- ✔ Type of funder
- ✔ Legal status
- ✔ Governance
- ✔ Executive staff
- ✔ Full-time staff
- ✔ Publications
- ✔ Sources of funds
- ✔ Finances
- ✔ Affiliations

Tackling topics of interest

Under the Programme Areas section, every funder profile includes topic-specific information related to its area(s) of focus. Common topic-specific info you'll find includes:

- ✔ Central and Eastern Europe
- ✔ Culture
- ✔ Disabilities and employment
- ✔ Education

- Environment
- HIV/AIDS
- Mediterranean region
- Minorities and multiculturalism
- Transatlantic activities
- Youth

The European Cultural Foundation Web site indicates that individuals as well as organizations can apply for grants and that the application process is simple. On its home page, you'll find a link to Application Forms.

Imagine Canada

Imagine Canada, a subscription-based funding database provider, is the result of a union of two of Canada's leading charitable umbrella organizations: the Canadian Centre for Philanthropy (CCP) and the Coalition of National Voluntary Organizations (NVO).

Its most valuable online resource is the *Canadian Directory to Foundations and Corporations.* With more than 3,100 foundation listings, 150 corporation listings, and 90,000 indexed grants (a large list of grants awarded by the foundations and corporations), the *Directory* is Canada's largest and most accurate bilingual fundraising database. Access to the *Directory* is priced based on your subscription level and your length of time as a subscriber. Annual subscriptions start at $375 and increase based on your access level.

The *Directory* contains the following information on potential funders:

- Address
- Contact person
- Funding interests
- Granting region
- Application procedure and deadline
- Board members
- Previous grant recipients

Profiles are searchable and accessible 24 hours a day to help you find prospects quickly. To subscribe, visit www.imaginecanada.com, click on Engage on the home page, and then click on Subscribe to the Directory on the right-hand side of the next page.

Other Web-based international funding resources

When looking for international grant funding opportunities, you have some additional online resources at your disposal. I use the following resources to scout for international projects in need of funding:

✔ www.foundationcenter.org: This site is the home page for the Foundation Center, where you can find the Foundation Directory Online. Once you're on the Center's home page, you click on Find Funders. Then click on the Foundation Directory Online. There you'll see a Subscribe link. For more on the Foundation Center, see the nearby sidebar "Hard-copy tools from the Foundation Center."

✔ www.internationaldonors.org: Grantmakers Without Borders is a network of individual donors and the trustees and staff of private and public foundations who practice global social change philanthropy. *Global social change philanthropy* is grantmaking rooted in the ideals of justice, equity, peace, democracy, and respect for the natural environment. The site features user-friendly information links. To find listings of foundations and other organizations interested in international grantmaking, click on the Advice for Grantseekers link on the left-hand side of the home page.

✔ www.usig.org: This Web site is maintained by United States International Grantmaking (USIG), which is a project of the Council on Foundations (a membership organization of more than 2,000 grantmaking foundations and giving programs worldwide) in cooperation with the International Center for Not-for-Profit Law (an international network of legal professionals). *Note:* USIG isn't a grantmaking organization and doesn't award grant funds.

Access to the valuable information at this site is free, but you have to register a log-in name and password before you can move beyond the home page. Click on International Grantmaking Basics to view these very important bits of info:

- Basic International Grantmaking Options: This section provides an introduction to international grantmaking and lays out a few basic options available to U.S. funders: grants to U.S. 501(c)(3) organizations, grants to "Friends of" organizations, donor-advised funds, and direct cross-border grants.

- Frequently Asked Questions on Cross-Border International Grantmaking: This section takes a closer look at the legal requirements for private foundations and public charities wanting to make cross-border grants to international (non-U.S.) organizations. There's also a bit of information on anti-terrorism actions and U.S. governmental policies.

Hard-copy tools from the Foundation Center

Want more detailed info than what the Foundation Directory Online provides? Try checking out one of these hard-copy resources, also from the Foundation Center:

✔ *Guide to Funding for International & Foreign Programs:* Features more than 1,500 descriptions of grantmakers that support international relief, conferences, disaster assistance, human rights, civil liberties, community development, education, and more.

✔ *Grants for Foreign & International Programs:* Highlights grants recently awarded for the same funding areas listed in the preceding guide.

✔ *International Grantmaking III: An Update on U.S. Foundation Trends:* Details the latest developments in international giving by U.S. foundations.

Each of these publications can be ordered online by clicking on the Shop link on the Foundation Center's home page.

Preparing to Approach an International Funder

Most international funders (independent foundations and corporations) insist that you contact them via e-mail or telephone to request their grant application guidelines and forms. Some may even query you about your project, asking about location, population served, and what you intend to request from them.

Because the foundation landscape in Europe and the rest of the world is varied, the grant eligibility requirements and monetary differences from one country to the next also differ, making it crucial that you follow the procedures laid out by each foundation. If you don't follow the rules, you don't get the grant — it's that simple!

Do your homework before approaching a funder for support. Being prepared is the key to successful fundraising. Here's a list of a few of the most important steps to take in advance:

1. **Familiarize yourself with the two types of main foundations: independent and corporate.**

   Jump to the section "Researching International Funding Opportunities Online," earlier in this chapter for brief definitions of each type.

2. **Find out the funder's preferred language before you start writing.**

   A German funder may prefer to see applications in English as opposed to German, for example.

If the preferred language isn't English, you may want to consider using a translating service after you've written your letter of inquiry or grant application in English. The quickest way to find a translating service is to conduct a general Internet search. Just type in "Vietnamese translator" or whatever language you need. This type of search will find translators for any language. It always helps to ask for references from the translators as well. That way you get an idea of their work.

3. **Follow the recommended method of initial approach, which should be spelled out in the foundation summary you find during your research.**

   Unless you're directed otherwise, your first contact should be a well-written letter of inquiry (see Chapter 2 for instructions).

Keep in mind that spelling is one of the adjustments you have to make when approaching European-based funding sources. *Program* may become *programme, organization* may become *organisation,* and *center* may become *centre,* just to name a few of the most common spelling quirks.

Converting Dollars into Foreign Currencies

When you're preparing the budget section of your international funding request, write it first (in draft form, of course) using U.S. currency for all the monetary figures. Then prepare a budget page and budget narrative detail using the current currency for the grantmaker's country. (For more about preparing budgets, flip to Chapter 17.)

Figure 8-1 is an example of an online e-grant application template from the Commonwealth Foundation (headquartered in London). Note that in the Programme area and cost section, you're asked to enter your project cost or grant request in GBP Sterling. GBP stands for the British Pound (£).

Following are just a few of the various monetary conversion Web sites out there these days, so let your fingers do the typing to convert U.S. Dollars (USD) to GBP, or any other type of currency desired:

- ✔ www.xe.net/ucc
- ✔ finance.yahoo.com/m3?u
- ✔ www.oanda.com/converter/classic
- ✔ www.x-rates.com/calculator.html

Make sure that your conversion is accurate, or you may be shortchanged if you win the grant.

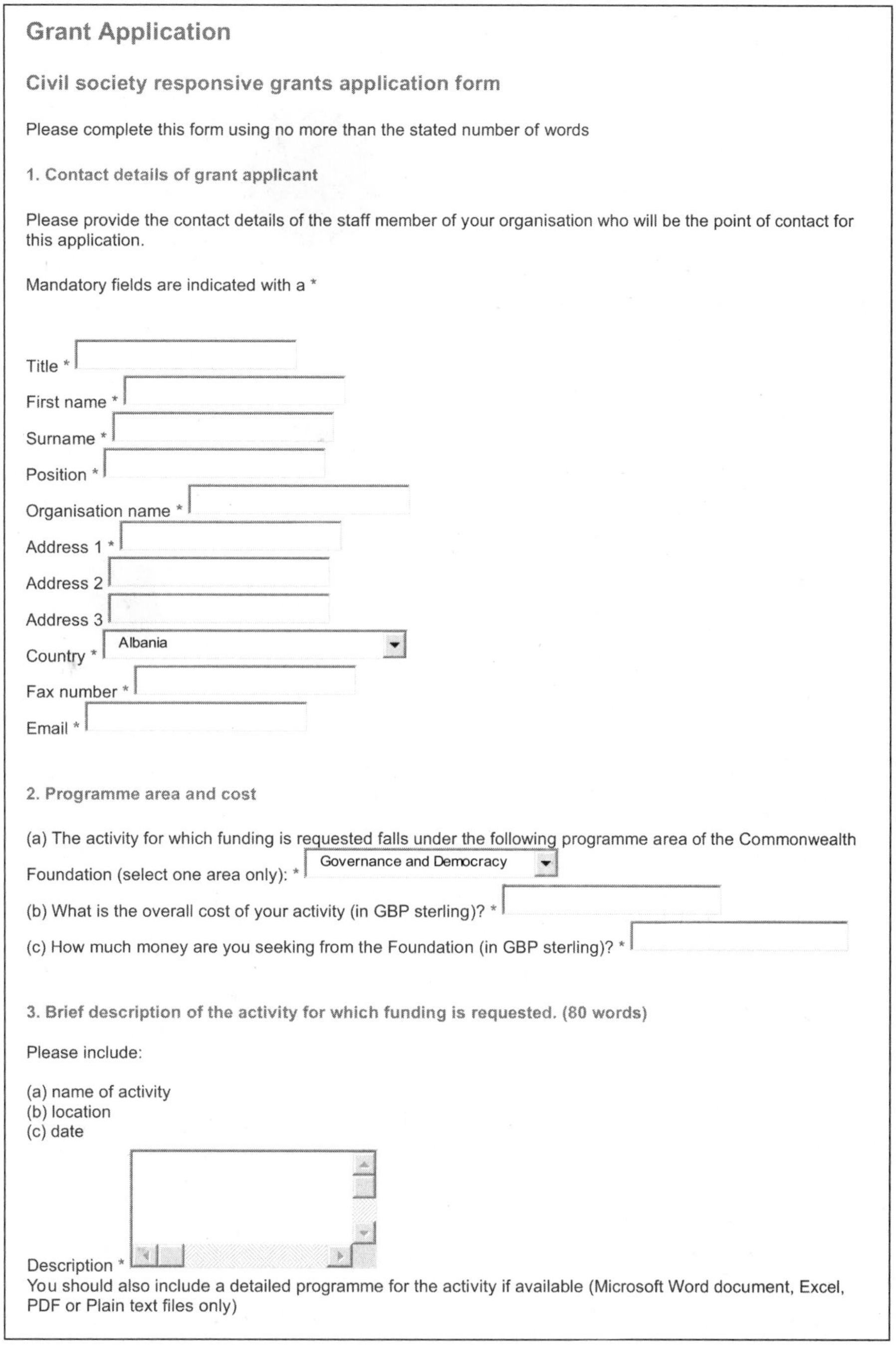

Grant Application

Civil society responsive grants application form

Please complete this form using no more than the stated number of words

1. Contact details of grant applicant

Please provide the contact details of the staff member of your organisation who will be the point of contact for this application.

Mandatory fields are indicated with a *

Title *

First name *

Surname *

Position *

Organisation name *

Address 1 *

Address 2

Address 3

Country * Albania

Fax number *

Email *

2. Programme area and cost

(a) The activity for which funding is requested falls under the following programme area of the Commonwealth Foundation (select one area only): * Governance and Democracy

(b) What is the overall cost of your activity (in GBP sterling)? *

(c) How much money are you seeking from the Foundation (in GBP sterling)? *

3. Brief description of the activity for which funding is requested. (80 words)

Please include:

(a) name of activity
(b) location
(c) date

Description *
You should also include a detailed programme for the activity if available (Microsoft Word document, Excel, PDF or Plain text files only)

Figure 8-1:
An online e-grant application template from a British foundation.

Part III

Playing and Winning the Grants Game

"You know the rules, Cordell. It doesn't count unless it goes in the basket."

In this part . . .

In this part, I tell you how to read federal grant announcements. I provide the skinny on the must-know terms, and I show you how to work the numbers game when it comes to figuring your chances of winning a grant competition. I also cover pre-reviews, peer reviewers, and the secret to writing winning contract bids. In a nutshell, this part shows you how to play the federal grantseeking game with knowledge and skill. Along the way, you can pick up some helpful tips and skills that apply to all types of funding requests.

Chapter 9

Using Your Resources to Win Government Grants and Contracts

*T*his chapter takes a close look at the most important part of a federal grant funding opportunity announcement — the details about the grant competition, including the information that's required to beat out the best of the best. I'm talking about skimming through the funding opportunity announcement first and then eyeballing the review criteria. The *review criteria* is the point-based rating system that a government agency uses to decide whether your grant or cooperative agreement application — section by section — cuts the mustard and is recommended for funding.

All government funding agencies publish guidelines that spell out the type of grant or cooperative agreement application that they expect grant seekers to submit. The guidelines and the review points assigned to each section of the grant or cooperative agreement narrative set the stage for what you must write and establish the point value of a chart-topping response.

Understanding the review criteria can help you determine whether the grant funding opportunity is one you should invest time and effort in pursuing. After all, if you can't fully meet key criteria, there's no reason to go after the grant or the Request for Proposal (RFP). Likewise, if you can meet all the criteria, then following the guidelines closely gives you a much better chance of receiving the points needed for recommendation.

Paying attention to the grant funding opportunity announcement, writing expectation details, and adhering to the formatting guidelines are as important as finding the right funding source and using compelling language. You must read and reread every sentence of a grant funding opportunity announcement before you start. Then you need to get out your magnifying glass and read the grant application guidelines, which includes the peer review or evaluation criterion.

In this chapter, I cover everything you need to know to say yea or nay to a possible grant funding opportunity and to increase your peer review points in order to win the grant funding from the federal government. I also touch on pursuing contract opportunities such as RFPs.

Eyeballing a Federal Grant Funding Announcement

Suppose you receive an e-mail alert on a grant or cooperative agreement opportunity from a federal funding agency, and you think that you have a chance to win the grant. But you don't know where to start or whether the grant's really worth going for. In this section, I walk you through the essentials of determining whether this is the right competition for you. I also give you a quick lesson in "Grantlish," the art of talking about grants, so that you have a better understanding of the review criteria language and terms. (See Chapter 3 for the full scoop on understanding funding terms and requirements.)

Reading funding announcements to decide whether to pursue an opportunity

A new era has arrived. Toss out your copies of old Federal Registers, and don't bother even looking up the cumbersome daily document online. Instead, cruise over to www.grants.gov. It's the must-have online database of all federal grant funding opportunities. You can even subscribe to a few state-level grant funding announcements. (Refer to Chapter 5 for more information on Grants.gov.)

Don't forget, you also need to sign up at Grants.gov for your free e-mail alerts. If you think you have a lot of e-mail now, just wait until you start receiving the Grants.gov daily "here's the money" list. It's detailed and filled with copy and paste Web addresses where you can read full funding announcements — not just a few lines of detail. This site is the beginning of your journey to read about each grant program's application guidelines and the peer review criteria that will determine if you win or lose.

When you receive the e-mail from Grants.gov, you'll see a listing of potential grant funding announcements. Here's an example of an alert entry:

DOT
U.S. Department of Transportation
DOT – Office of Aviation Analysis
FY 2008 Small Community Air Service Development Program Grants
www07.grants.gov/search/search.do?mode=VIEW&oppId=41143

When you copy and paste the Web address included in the announcement into your Internet browser, you'll be directed to a synopsis of the announcement and to a link to the full application document. You can quickly cruise through the summary of the announcement to look for information that can be best called *red stop flags* and *green go flags*. Here are the steps to take when you're cruising through the summary:

1. **Look for the number of grants that will be awarded.**

   For the previous sample synopsis regarding Small Community Air Service Development Program Grants, the expected number of awards is 40. This is a green go flag.

   When would this be a red stop flag? It would be a stop if the funder were going to award fewer than ten grants. Why? Well, look at it this way: There are 50 states, 4 unincorporated organized territories, and 336 federally recognized Indian Tribes. All of these entities are eligible grant applicants who will compete for all Federal grant monies. Do the math! Do you really have a fighting chance at winning one of ten or fewer federal grants when you're going up against multiple eligible grant applicants from states, territories, and Tribes? Probably not!

2. **Determine the grant application deadline.**

   In the sample DOT announcement, the closing date for applications is 66 days from the date of the grant funding opportunity announcement. This is a green go flag. If you're going to successfully research and write a winning government grant application, you need time on your side. Any deadline that's 30 or more days from the date of the grant funding opportunity announcement is definitely appealing.

   If this is your first attempt at a government grant, look for a closing date that allows you at least 30 days for researching and writing. Having less than three weeks to write your first federal grant may be overwhelming unless you can devote 100 percent of your work time to the grant. Normal writing time for a federal grant is 40 to 100 hours, and research can add up to another 20 to 40 hours. So give yourself ample time — even if you're a veteran grant writer.

3. **Find out the total estimated funding available for grant awards.**

In the DOT example, the estimated total program funding is $10 million. Because the expected number of awards is 40, this means that a 12-month grant award could easily average $250,000 each. This is a green go flag! In fact, I am ready to apply for these funds myself.

At this point, you can proceed to the link for the full funding announcement (the application guidelines), or you can continue to read the synopsis for the rest of the story. Remember, the rest of the picture is about who's eligible to apply and what priorities and activities the grant monies will fund.

Knowing whether you're eligible and ready to enter the competition

Before you forge ahead and start to research and write a government grant application, you must first determine whether you're eligible for the competition and whether you're actually ready to start competing. Doing so will help you decide whether you should take the plunge or not.

Determining your eligibility

Are you eligible for that fabulous funding opportunity you just came across? Before you conclude that the grant or cooperative agreement matches your needs, check out the eligibility paragraph in the funding synopsis or full announcement. Make sure that your organization is eligible to apply for these federal funds. Otherwise you'll waste a lot of time working on an application that will no doubt be rejected. Here's a sampling of what you'll see when you look under the *Eligible Applicants* section of the synopsis or full announcement:

1. Eligible Applicants

You may submit (an) application(s) if your organization has any of the following characteristics:

For-profit organizations

Nonprofit organizations

Public or private institutions, such as universities, colleges, hospitals, and laboratories

Units of state government

Units of local government

If your organization is eligible, you've just scored another green go flag! If not, don't give up; look for a potential partnering organization that's eligible to apply, and then contact that organization as soon as possible to see if it's interested in being the grant applicant and fiscal agent. What's your role in this situation? You're considered a subcontracted and funded partner agency. Remember, it's important to scoop up all possible federal grant monies, whether you're eligible or not. After all, there's a way to proceed at full speed in building financial sustainability for your organization.

Making sure you're ready to take the plunge

After you're sure of your eligibility, you have to ask yourself whether your organization is ready to start competing for a specific grant award opportunity. It's also important to decide whether you're willing to fulfill the grant program's purpose after the organization is funded. When you click on the full grant funding announcement link (found in the synopsis), look for the *Purpose of Funding* statement, which tells you exactly what the funding agency plans to fund.

Here are some examples of some really great Purpose of Funding statements:

- ✔ **U.S. Department of Health and Human Services:** "This announcement solicits applications for the Grants to States to Support Oral Health Workforce Activities Program to support a one year cycle for developing a planning report to be used to improve the State's oral health workforce and service delivery infrastructure for the underserved. This program is designed to help States address demonstrated oral health workforce needs."

- ✔ **U.S. Environmental Protection Agency:** "The aim of this funding is to support innovative ideas with the goal of fostering positive change. Projects may include studies, surveys, investigations, demonstrations, training, and public education programs. All demonstration projects must demonstrate applications, technologies, methods or approaches that are new, innovative or experimental."

- ✔ **U.S. Department of Agriculture:** "The purposes of the Rural Youth Development (RYD) program are to: Support programs which address needs of rural youth and involve those youth in design and implementation of their educational activities. RYD funded programs can be delivered in-school and/or during out-of-school time, but should be in the context of connecting the formal classroom to real-life experience and vice versa."

If, after reading through your selected federal funding opportunity Purpose of Funding statements, you find that one or more fits your organization's long-range plan for program development or expansion, you have a green go flag.

If your organization has no experience in any of these programming areas, and you only want to apply for easy money, be aware that your ability to fulfill the purpose on receipt of funding may be limited. This would definitely signal a red stop flag.

When you start writing your *program design* (purpose of funding request, goals, objectives, implementation plan, logic model, management plan, and evaluation plan), remember to incorporate key words and phrases from the grant announcement's Purpose of Funding statement. During the grant review process, this strategy helps peer reviewers clearly make a connection between the purpose of the grant and your needs statement and program design — which should fit like a soft leather glove to the federal language. (See Chapter 15 for more about program design.) This approach of "parroting" the funding agency's own words results in receiving high review points — starting you down the road to getting a funding award! Just make sure that your target population fits the one described in the Purpose of Funding statement.

Recognizing must-know terms

All federal grant and cooperative agreement announcements use two types of terms: general and program-specific. *General terms* are words or phrases that appear in all funding announcements. *Program-specific terms* are words or phrases that are used in connection with a particular program. Knowing both types of terms and using them correctly throughout your grant application increases your review criteria points and your chances of getting grant recommendations.

Getting the gist of general terms

Knowing Grantlish terms, whether general or funder-specific, can help you understand what the funding agency is talking about in the grant or cooperative agreement announcement. If you've only been schooled in oranges and the funding agency writes its entire announcement in apples, you'll be lost if you don't understand the key terms used. Some key terms that you may encounter in grant announcements include the following:

- ✔ **Budget period:** The interval of time into which a multiyear period of assistance (the project or budget funding period) is divided for budgetary and funding purposes. For example, a large percentage of federal grants start on the first day of the federal fiscal year, October 1, and the funding period for grants awarded on October 1 ends on September 31 of the following year.

- ✔ **Nonprofit organization:** Any organization (including a community development corporation) exempt from taxation under Section 501(a) of the Internal Revenue Code.

- ✔ **Project period:** The total time a project is approved for support, including any extensions. This time period can range from 12 months to 60 months.

- ✔ **Third party:** Any individual, organization, or business entity (different from your partners) that isn't the direct recipient of grant funds but will subcontract with the grantee to carry out specified activities in the plan of operation.

- ✔ **Third-party arrangement:** An arrangement in which your agency could be the third party or another agency could be the third party in the grant or cooperative agreement application.

  Check out this example of a third-party arrangement: Say you find a competition that fits your organization, which is a four-year public university that grants degrees in aeronautical science specialties. However, under the eligibility section of this grant opportunity, only two-year community colleges can apply for these funds. So you contact several community colleges in your state, region, and throughout the U.S. to ask whether they plan to apply for these federal funds. You find a potential partner and ask whether you can meet and plan a 2 + 2 transfer program where their students would complete the first two years of general courses and introductory to aeronautics programming at their institution and then transfer to your university for the remainder of their four-year degree program. When you have a working Memoranda of Understanding (MOU) or Memorandum of Agreement (MOA), you're ready to start negotiating your piece of the financial pie — a place in the *Contractual* section of the budget summary and detail. In other words, your university is on its way to become a third-party contractor. Refer to the later section "Gathering partners for your proposal: The more, the merrier" for more on MOUs and MOAs.

- ✔ **Third-party agreement:** A written agreement entered into by the grantee and an organization, individual, or business entity (including a wholly owned subsidiary).

Seeking out specific terms

Every government program, both federal and state, has its own specific terms and definitions. These program-specific terms appear in the grant application guidelines.

Each government agency provides its own definitions of the terms in the grant funding opportunity announcement (see the earlier section "Knowing whether you're eligible and ready to enter the competition"). Use the same terms as those published in the announcement when you write your grant application. By using each agency's terms and its definitions, you meet the basic requirement of the review criteria — showing that you understand the Feds' language.

Gathering partners for your proposal: The more, the merrier

Some funding guidelines give favorable consideration (and thus more review criteria points) to applicants who can get cash or in-kind (noncash) contributions from partner organizations. Here are the two types of partners you might connect with:

- **Community partners** are usually nonprofit organizations or businesses that your program works with on a regular basis to provide services to your constituency. Select community partners when your only need is a letter of support (see Chapter 3).

- **Collaborative partners** are government, social, and human services agencies at local, state, and regional levels that use their resources to help your organization better deliver the services funded by the grant. Select collaborative partners when you need an ongoing working relationship in order to implement the grant-funded activities. Collaborative partners help draft and then sign elaborate Memorandums of Understanding or Agreement (MOUs and MOAs), which are working agreements that spell out the scope of services that will be performed by the partner agency and by the grant applicant (that's you).

  Some funding agencies request that you attach MOUs or MOAs to the funding request in the appendixes. Other funding agencies simply require that the documents be on file with your organization and that they be accessible by the funding agency if monies are awarded. A MOU or MOA is treated like a legal document and should not be developed by a grant writer; this is a task for your executive director or legal staff.

Federal funding agencies prefer to see MOUs or MOAs attached to your funding requests. Letters of support don't carry the weight they used to a decade ago. So, if you're still attaching letters of support instead of MOUs and MOAs, make the switch now.

When looking for a partner, look for an agency that already serves all or part of your target population. For example, an environmental group may not be a good partner if you're trying to secure funding for an adult literacy program. Rather, an agency that focuses on retraining low-skilled, adult workers may be a perfect match. Also, make sure to select partners that have a history and background in your specific grant application area for each grant or cooperative agreement you plan to pursue.

Don't limit yourself to just one partner — the more, the better. One partner will soon tire of your asking for monetary contributions, in-kind services, or repeated letters of support. With many partners, you can pick and choose the ones that have experience in the type of project you're trying to get funded. The same partners you use in one funding application may not be the partners you select for the next application.

Before you meet with a prospective partner, prepare a fact sheet on the grant program's purpose and goals. Fax or mail a copy to each agency you plan to invite onto your team. This way, even before you meet face to face, the other agency can start thinking of ways to collaborate with your organization.

At your first meeting, ask for at least one of the following contributions:

- **Cash-match monies:** A commitment of actual cash in the form of a contribution toward your proposed program's expenses
- **In-kind contributions:** Donated personnel, office space, training space, transportation assistance, supplies, materials, printing services for classroom training use, and other needed items

If you receive a commitment for cash or in-kind contributions before you even write your grant application, you've already chalked up points with reviewers. In the eyes of those who hand out the money, having one or more partners gives you a huge advantage over any grant seeking organization without partners because partners mean that community resources will be maximized to benefit the target population.

Not having any partners could be detrimental to your grant application during the peer review process. I'm a federal peer reviewer, and when I come across a grant or cooperative agreement application with no listed partners, I deduct review points from the program design section. A loss of five or more points in any section can result in your application not making the cut for funding. The typical make-or-break score is 92 points — that is, if you fail to score 92 out of 100 possible points on your funding request, you won't be recommended for federal funding support.

Perusing the Review Criterion Section

When you click on the link in a grant funding opportunity announcement to access the full announcement, you'll see the full-blown grant application guidelines document. Usually this is a PDF file. Scroll down in the document to look for the *Review Criterion* section of the announcement. (This section is also often called the Evaluation Criteria section.)

This section of the document cuts to the chase fast by showing you how each section of the grant application narrative will be rated. The Review Criterion section tells you — to the letter — exactly what the peer reviewers expect to read in a "winning" grant application. It also tells you the total number of possible points that a "winning" narrative section can earn during the peer review process.

Using review point weights to guide your writing

Ninety-nine percent of most government grant application narratives are weighted for a total of 100 possible points. The most comprehensive writing section is the program design section. (See Chapter 15 for more on this important section.).

In the example that follows in this section, note that the largest point section is the Program Design and Methodologies section, which weighs in at 25 points. This means that program design is worth 25 percent of the entire grant application's scoring schematic of 100 points. So you'll want to take more time to research and write this section of your grant application narrative. If the funding agency's formatting instructions tell you that the grant application narrative can't exceed 30 single-spaced pages, you'll want to earmark 25 percent of the 30 pages (7.5 pages) for the Program Design and Methodologies section.

When you know the maximum number of pages that you're allowed to write for the entire grant application narrative, you can take the total points (100 points) and divide them by the points for each section. Translate this into a percent and you'll know how many pages you need to write in each narrative section to fulfill the percent expectation for the number of pages that the peer reviewers expect to see when eyeballing your grant application.

In the following list, I note the maximum number of pages that you should write in each narrative section based on a 30-page narrative limitation. I also provide you with some of the questions that peer reviewers keep in mind when reading your application. Remember, the total possible peer review score for your grant application is 100 points. Here's how it breaks down:

- **Statement of Need, Site Location, and Scope of Project – 15 points (15 percent of 30 pages equals 4.5 pages for this section):** Does the application specify those issues that will be addressed in this project from the list of issues facing the target population? Is it likely that this overall project will address the issues identified? Do they have the likelihood of successful outcomes? Will the target population be involved in the design and implementation of the project? Does the project meet the objectives of the funding and provide sufficient justification for funding the proposal?

- **Outcomes and Indicators – 15 points (15 percent of 30 pages equals 4.5 pages for this section):** Is each outcome articulated? Are the indicators that were selected appropriate to measure the intended outcomes? Are outcomes and indicators written in clear, concise, complete, measurable, and logically arranged statements? Are they sufficiently linked to the goals of the project, based on research, and supported with a reference citation?

✓ **Program Design and Methodologies – 25 points (25 percent of 30 pages equals 7.5 pages for this section):** Will program designs and strategies likely produce the articulated indicators to meet the outcomes established for the project? Are the scope and duration of programs adequate to produce positive outcomes? Will programs link formal and non-formal education? Is the appropriate research base used to support the selected educational design and activities?

✓ **Evaluation Methodologies – 10 points (10 percent of 30 pages equals 3 pages for this section):** Are the evaluation designs and methodologies adequate to measure the extent to which program indicators and outcomes are being met?

✓ **Communication Plan – 5 points (5 percent of 30 pages equals 1.5 pages for this section):** Are there clear and acceptable strategies to communicate the results from this project to stakeholders and the public?

✓ **Project Management – 5 points (5 percent of 30 pages equals 1.5 pages for this section):** Is there evidence of strong and adequate project management, including key staff and their functions, timelines, accounting procedures, reporting, and collaborative efforts with the partner organizations?

✓ **Budget – 5 points (5 percent of 30 pages equals 1.5 pages for this section):** Is there an appropriate amount of money allocated to each key activity/task? Is the total budget allocation adequate to reach project goals?

✓ **Success of Community Projects – 20 points (20 percent of 30 pages equals 6 pages for this section):** Have previously funded projects achieved the target population outcomes? Has community capital investment increased as a result of past projects? Do previous evaluation findings provide sufficient evidence that the outcomes were met? What process was used to obtain feedback from community stakeholders? Was this feedback incorporated into the final evaluation reports?

Earning bonus points by creating a cost-effective program

You can get an edge on the competition by proposing a cost-effective program. Here's how the government defines *cost-effective:* Your cost to serve each program participant is less than the maximum allowed cost-per-participant. Your cost to serve is calculated by dividing the number of persons your program will serve into the total amount of federal funds requested. The resulting number must be at or under the maximum allowable federal amount. In some federal grant competitions, five review criteria points can be earned for having a cost-effective project. Similarly, five points can be deducted from the total 100 points for not having a cost-effective project.

Researching Your Request

Knowing the grant's or cooperative agreement's intent or focus sets the direction for the type of research you must do in order to write a high-scoring competitive grant application. For example, if the monies are intended to open employment and training centers in the Mississippi Delta region, then you need to research demographics on the unemployed and underemployed in the counties along the Mississippi Delta.

Using the Internet, you can get a jump-start on your grant or cooperative agreement application by searching for existing programs in the area of the competition. In the Mississippi Delta example, you would conduct an Internet search (using a search engine) for all existing employment and training programs. You would review what they offer, who they provide services for, and how successful their intervention model is in reducing unemployment and poverty in the Mississippi Delta. Remember, tons of programs are out there. Your job is to decide which programs look like the kind you want to propose in your funding request.

Start researching the target population's demographics in your state and region — those counties or parishes that make up your Metropolitan Statistical Area (MSA). Call state and local agencies that provide services to the targeted groups and ask for reports that provide demographics on this target population.

After I collect all my research, I sort it into stacks according to the types of information it is. I have one stack for statistics or demographics, another stack for model programs, and another stack for evaluations of model programs. With this arrangement, I can start writing my grant or cooperative agreement application narrative and pull research from one stack at a time. (See Chapter 10 for how to pull all your research together for the funding application.)

Finding Third-Party Evaluators Early in the Grant Writing Process

Writing an application for a federal grant or cooperative agreement requires making new friends in your community — not only community partners (covered earlier in this chapter) but also community specialists such as evaluators. You can always score higher review points by using an *outside evaluator,* who's basically a person or organization that can operate in an objective mode and give you factual, nonemotional feedback on your grant-funded goals and objectives.

As a federal grant reviewer, I'm more likely to award high review points for the evaluation plan when a third-party evaluator is proposed. Even though evaluators are paid from grant funds, I know that they will call the shots as they see them when it comes to helping grant applicants develop data collection tools, collect and interpret data, and compile comprehensive evaluation reports for funders and other stakeholders. (I talk about the evaluation process in depth in Chapter 15.)

The following folks make excellent outside evaluators:

- ✔ Retired college or university faculty. Often, these individuals have participated in the grant writing process and have even helped their college or university development offices design evaluations for government grant applications.

- ✔ Retired government personnel who have worked in an administrative capacity in a finance department.

- ✔ Evaluation consultants. These people normally have years of experience just in the field of evaluation.

  Try calling your local community foundation for consultant recommendations. Community foundations often use evaluation consultants to assist in evaluating their own programs.

As far as timing's concerned, I think it's essential to bring in an evaluator when you're sitting down with your staff and your community partners to plan what will be proposed in the grant or cooperative agreement application.

Running an online search for outside evaluators is also helpful, but you may not locate an evaluator close to home. It's okay to use an evaluator who doesn't live in your city or town as long as he or she is familiar with the area.

Understanding RFP Review Criteria for Contract Bids

If you own a business and plan to start bidding on contract opportunities, you need to familiarize yourself with the standard review criteria language for contract bidding documents.

The language in contract bidding documents often is intimidating to businesses that are vying for a public or private sector contract to provide services or goods. (I tend to refer to this language as *legalese*.)

When a company issues an opportunity to bid on a contract, which is often referred to as an RFP (Request For Proposal) or RFQ (Request for Quote), you must be able to quickly scan the technical proposal and cost proposal requirements to determine whether your business can deliver the requested services or goods. These bidding opportunity announcements, which contain all the instructions for submitting your contract bidding document, don't just magically appear on your desk. You have to aggressively search the classified advertising sections of your local and regional newspapers and look for the legal announcements section, which is where companies place their RFP or RFQ announcements.

You're looking for announcements that match your products or services, and when you find one, you need to call the agency or business to request a copy of the actual RFP or RFQ. Any government agency or business issuing an RFP or RFQ likes to keep close track of who requests copies. After you're on an agency's mailing list, you may automatically receive notices of future RFPs and RFQs.

Here's an example of a legal advertisement announcing an RFP:

Legal Advertisement
Request for Proposal (RFP) for Wetlands and Water Quality
Engineering Services
Solicitation #: DOT 08014

The Department of Transportation (DOT) is seeking expressions of interest from consulting firms to provide on-call services to provide professional engineering services related to wetland and water quality services for transportation projects. The selected team will be required to have a comprehensive understanding of wetland and water quality services relative to highway, multi-modal transportation projects, and a thorough knowledge of Federal Highway Administration guidelines and DOT's policies and procedures. During the course of the contract, work will be solicited only as the need arises.

For RFP package, contact: DOT Procurement Officer, Lara Scott at 555-555-5555.

Closing date for bids: November 21 at 5 p.m. EST.

As you peruse a hard copy of the full RFP or RFQ document, highlight the sections listed below and read them several times to ensure that you understand what the bid-letting agency is asking for and what you have to return in your RFP or RFQ bid package to meet the agency's review criteria and ultimately qualify for a contract award. The following RFP and RFQ sections are listed in the order that you're likely to see them in the RFP or RFQ document:

✔ **Cover Form:** Contains the name and contact information of the soliciting agency; the solicitation number (an internal bid-letting agency number issued for internal record-keeping purposes), issue date, due date, and time due; and whether or not it's a set-aside contract. (Government agencies earmark, or set aside, a portion of their annual contracts for businesses that are small, disadvantaged, or owned by minorities or women.)

✔ **Supplies or Services & Price and Costs:** Spells out, in excruciating detail, the types of products or services that the solicitor (RFP or RFQ-issuing agency) is seeking to purchase and the price or cost parameters the solicitor must work within.

✔ **Statement of Work:** Tells you the work tasks to be performed. This section contains numerically ordered tasks and *deliverables* (time frames for when each task must be completed). Depending on the soliciting agency, you may find multiple deliverables for one task.

✔ **Cost Proposal:** Tells you how the bid-letting agency plans to pay for services. For example, the cost proposal section may lay out advance payments each month or cost reimbursement payments after your invoice and expenses receipts have been received, reviewed, and approved by the bid-letting agency.

✔ **Deliveries or Performance:** Spells out the length of the contract.

✔ **Level of Effort:** Tells how many hours of service are expected during the contract award period.

✔ **Instructions, Conditions, and Notices to Offerors:** Explains the conditions that your company or agency is obligated to fulfill if you're given a contract award. This section scares away most potential bidders because it's a lot of small print typing full of legalese!

✔ **Evaluation Factors for Award:** Tells you how the solicitor rates or evaluates each section of the RFP or RFQ narrative response.

Use this section as a guide when you write your narrative response (see Chapter 10 for more on writing to meet the peer review criteria). For the sections with higher point values, you garner greater solicitor attention when your narrative uses buzzwords taken from the RFP or RFQ guidelines language.

Chapter 10

Writing to Convince Peer Reviewers to Give You the Maximum Points

. . . .

In This Chapter

▶ Formatting your application properly

▶ Understanding the peer review process

▶ Discovering the best ways to read guidelines and write your application

▶ Taking advantage of federal publications

▶ Becoming a peer reviewer

. . . .

Consider the grant writing process: You first receive an e-mail alert from Grants.gov and find a grant opportunity announcement matching your program's funding needs. Then you carefully screen the funding competition and determine that your organization is eligible to apply, that the number of grants awarded is more than ten, and that the average grant award is more than sufficient to cover your proposed project's cost. (See Chapter 9 for more on this step.) By this time, your partner organizations also are on board, and the third-party evaluator has agreed to be included in the grant request.

Now that everything's falling into place, you're ready to start writing your grant application narrative. This chapter details the writing process based on standard government agency review criteria. Remember that writing to meet a grant application's review criteria is as important as identifying the right funding source and preparing your response.

The basics of review criteria apply to all types of grant guidelines. Because government guidelines are the most rigid, I use them as my example throughout this chapter. Trust me: You can write *anything* if you can write government

grant application narratives (also called cooperative agreements) and Request For Proposal, or RFP, narratives (also known as contract bids made by a business, which is also referred to as a for-profit).

Succeeding in the Technical Review Process with the Right Formatting

When you first submit a grant application or RFP response to a federal agency for funding consideration, your application goes through a *technical review process* (or simply *pre-review*). This pre-review includes checking to see whether you've completed and signed all the required forms. The pre-review process also verifies your compliance with formatting instructions and checks the page length of your narrative. Many government grant and cooperative agreement applications as well as RFPs have narrative length restrictions, such as no more than 20 double-spaced pages. If you fail to pass one of the pre-review mandatory checks, your application doesn't move from the pre-review phase to the peer review phase.

The lesson here is to always read the grant application or RFP guidelines, and then be sure to follow the instructions for forms and formatting — to the letter!

Formatting criteria for grant applications

When you first read a grant or cooperative agreement opportunity announcement (refer to Chapter 9 for more on these announcements), some basic information points can give you quick cues about how to set up your word processing software to correctly format the narrative.

As you read through the formatting instructions, find out what spacing is required, what type and size of font must be used, and whether pagination begins with the first form and ends with the last page in the appendixes or is limited to the narrative section of the request. The quicker you find these answers, the sooner you can get started with the writing process!

As part of the pre-review elimination process, funding agency program staff members first check your application to see that you followed the criteria exactly as it's laid out. If you failed to follow the formatting instructions, your grant application will not advance to the peer reviewers.

In addition to the formatting requirements, there may be specific programmatic requirements. To be sure of the requirements, check the actual funding announcement before preparing your application.

The following are formatting requirements excerpted from a Substance Abuse and Mental Health Services Administration document. You can find the latest full version of the document by going to `samhsa.gov/grants/apply.aspx` and scrolling through the page. As you can see from these excerpts (there's a lot more in the document), the requirements are very specific:

> *Type size in the Project Narrative cannot exceed an average of 15 characters per inch, as measured on the physical page. (Type size in charts, tables, graphs, and footnotes will not be considered in determining compliance.)*

> *Text in the Project Narrative cannot exceed 6 lines per vertical inch. Paper must be white paper and 8.5 inches by 11.0 inches in size.*

> *Applications would meet this requirement by using all margins (left, right, top, and bottom) of at least one inch each, and adhering to the page limit for the Project Narrative stated in the specific funding announcement.*

> *Should an application not conform to these margin or page limits, the funding agency will use the following method to determine compliance: The total area of the Project Narrative (excluding margins, but including charts, tables, graphs and footnotes) cannot exceed 58.5 square inches multiplied by the page limit. This number represents the full page less margins, multiplied by the total number of allowed pages.*

> *Space will be measured on the physical page. Space left blank within the Project Narrative (excluding margins) is considered part of the Project Narrative, in determining compliance.*

> *Pages should be typed single-spaced in black ink, with one column per page. Pages should not have printing on both sides.*

> *Please number pages consecutively from beginning to end so that information can be located easily during review of the application. The cover page should be page 1, the abstract page should be page 2, and the table of contents page should be page 3.*

> *The page limits for Appendices stated in the specific funding announcement should not be exceeded.*

Formatting criteria for contract bids

When you first open a contract bid package, you may feel overwhelmed by the forms and instructions. Remember to tackle the "first reading" process one page at a time. After you note the due date and time, look for formatting criteria. Do you have to fill in the bid-letting agency's forms, or can you re-create its forms with your word processor? Is there a particular font that you must type your response in, and are there restrictions on the font size? Make written notes on all technical requirements related to formatting. You can even highlight the specific formatting instructions or put sticky notes on the formatting-related pages in the RFP instructions.

Timing is everything!

Some contract bids must be received before a certain time on a specific day. For example, RFP instructions may tell you to submit your *sealed bid* (a bid sealed in a separate envelope inside the mailing envelope and marked with the RFP number and due date) by noon on July 10. If you rely on the regular mail and the mail delivery arrives at 12:30 p.m. at the bid-letting agency, you're out of luck! Use courier delivery services and make sure to get your bid in at least a full day before the due date.

The following is an example of the type of criteria you see in an RFP. As part of the pre-review elimination process, reviewers check to see that you follow the criteria exactly.

Content and form of contract bid

1. Contract bids submitted to the state in a format other than the one requested will not progress beyond the initial technical review process.

2. The numerical outline for the bidding document, the titles/subtitles of the document, and the bidding organization will appear on the top right-hand corner of each page.

3. Page numbers must be consecutive beginning with the Table of Contents and ending with the Certifications and Assurances.

4. A written response is required for each item. Failure to answer any of the items will have an impact upon an applicant's score.

5. The Technical Proposal and the Cost Proposal are separate documents and must be prepared and submitted separately. Failure to do so will result in an immediate rejection of the bidder's proposal.

Getting the Skinny on the Peer Review

After you pass the pre-review (and I know you will!), your application or contract bid is given to either a peer review panel (for grants and cooperative agreements) or a purchasing manager (for contract bids).

In the sections that follow, I give you all the info you need to know about the review process for grant and cooperative agreement applications and for contract bids.

Scoring grant applications

A peer review panel usually includes three experts from around the country who work in the field that the grant competition is directed to. It's called *peer review* because you're accepted or rejected by your peers, not by a government program officer. Each reviewer gives a numerical score to each application reviewed; in most instances, the scoring of your narrative is based on a total of 100 points. Explanatory statements on a formal rating form support the numerical score; for each section of the application's review criteria (criteria that was published in the Grants.gov announcement), reviewers describe your application's major strengths and weaknesses.

Some government agencies assign more than 100 points to the narrative sections of grant applications. Read every word in the guidelines so you know what to shoot for. You may need to write extra response sections to be considered eligible for the additional review points.

I can see you waving your hand, about to ask "How many pages do I have to write?" As a general guide, plan to write one page for every five review points assigned to each narrative section. (In the grant application or cooperative agreement guidelines, the section titled *Review Criteria* tells you how many review points are assigned to each section of the narrative.) For example, if the program design section carries 25 points, you should write five pages for that narrative. And remember to stay within the total narrative page limits. (See Chapter 9 for the inside scoop on peer review points.)

Normally, your grant application needs to score in the high 90s to make the cut (meaning you're recommended for the grant award instead of rejected based on low scores from the three reviewers).

You may be asking what happens when two grant reviewers in the peer review rate you highly (92 or above) and the third reviewer rates you below the cutoff score for an award. Well, after each reviewer independently scores your application, they get together (over the telephone or in person) and discuss and defend their scores. The general rule is that all three reviewers must come within ten points of each other in order for an application to go one way or the other; often, after discussion, application scores change, sometimes in your favor and sometimes not.

The length of time from the moment you submit your grant application for funding consideration to the time you receive notification of funding can range from three to six months, depending on the program and the number of applications it receives.

Judging contract bids

For contract bids, your fate is in the hands of the agency's Purchasing or Procurement Department. Most likely a purchasing manager or procurement officer is assigned to review your bid. The lowest bid doesn't always win the contract, so use fair and *profitable* pricing for your services or products. It's important to submit a bid that emits a high quality of services and goods from a reliable potential vendor (your company). The price is secondary when another bidder has shabby services and goods and a blue light special price. The latter proposal screams "buyer beware"!

Each agency has its own specific criteria for evaluating and awarding contract bids. Most RFPs don't have specific review points, though. Instead, look for *evaluation factors,* which tell you how the contract will be evaluated for completeness.

Here's an excerpt from an RFP Statement of Intent (the bid-letting agency intends to award contracts for the delivery of services) that shows you the breakdown of evaluation factors and percentage values for each factor:

> ***EVALUATION FACTORS*** *will be based on the following criteria in descending order of importance:*
>
> *1. Specialized experience and technical competence in the type of work required under this contract (30%)*
>
> *2. Professional qualifications necessary for satisfactory performance of required services (30%)*
>
> *3. Past performance on public/private industry contracts in terms of cost control, quality of work and compliance with performance schedules (15%)*
>
> *4. Capacity to accomplish the work in the required time (15%)*
>
> *5. Location in the general geographical area of the project and knowledge of the locality of the project (10%)*

With contract bids, the purchasing manager or procurement officer makes the final decision. Contract bids are selected based on:

✔ **Technical proposal**

- Experience and background of the bidder or offeror

- Complete and thorough scope of services section

- Complete narrative responses to all other sections of the RFP narrative

- All forms filled in and signed, as instructed

- Supporting documentation attached, as instructed

✓ **Cost proposal**

- Cost-effectiveness of amount needed to deliver the services or goods

- Accuracy of the budget line items and totals

Writing a successful RFP response means your company wins a contract award from a government agency or business. After you're notified that your bid was selected, you may be required to enter into negotiations with the awarding agency. At this time, the scope of services or goods to be delivered may be changed, or the payment for the services or goods may be lessened.

Nothing's set in stone — it's up to the purchasing manager or procurement officer as to whether your company will receive a contract award. Hang in there and don't give up. You know you're on the way to a major contract award when you're invited to sit down and talk "best and final" offers with the awarding agency. (See Chapter 3 for definitions of standard contract terms.)

Reading and Writing the Government Way

Read *all* guidelines for government grant applications, cooperative agreements, and RFPs. Then read them again. In fact, I suggest you read them three times, focusing on different aspects with each review:

1. The first time through the guidelines, check for due dates, number of awards, average size of grants, and eligible applicants.

2. The second time through, look at the technical requirements. By *technical requirements,* I mean whether the grant competition requires that you submit your grant application to a state agency for preapproval before the final submission due date.

3. During the third review, read for narrative content requirements. The following sections walk you through the narrative content requirements for government funding applications (grants and cooperative agreements) and contract bids so that you can understand what you should look for in content requirements.

Your government funding request or contract bid response (also called RFP narrative) should contain a lot of words and phrases that you cull from the grant application or RFP guidelines. Plan to use these terms in almost every section of your grant narrative; doing so shows that you're familiar with the guidelines and that your program is in line with the grant or contract.

Making your needs clearly known

One of the major sections in government grant narratives, and in most RFP documents, is the *needs statement,* which is usually an explanation of the problem you hope to address if you receive the grant or contract. Normally, when you're writing a grant or cooperative agreement application, this section is worth about 20 of the 100 points possible that can be granted by a review committee. (Jump to Chapter 14 for information on how to structure your needs statement.)

The needs statement is the place not only to write about your own research findings on the target population but also to bring in facts and figures from regional and national research. (See Chapter 9 for details on how to gather all the information you need before you start writing this part of your application.) To win all the points allocated to this section, follow these tips:

✔ When it comes to federal grant and cooperative agreement applications, write about every problem you can unearth. Be sure to address what the problem is, when it started, and how you know it's a problem.

✔ Always include results from recent community needs assessments. Doing so shows the funder that you're basing your problem statement or needs statement on valid findings about your target population or community.

✔ Refer to the current lack of services or programs in your area.

✔ Don't talk in generalities — use facts, statistics, quotes, and citations.

✔ Cite all your sources, and stay current — don't use anything more than five years old.

✔ Show that you know what you're talking about by comparing your problems to similar problems in other communities of your size.

In your needs statement, describe a large black hole of gloom and doom if that's what you see based on the facts. You're not exaggerating with the information you include in this section; you're simply writing to meet the review criteria, and you're addressing each point covered in the program's or agency's goals. For more on communicating needs, see Chapter 14.

Putting project design in a funder's own terms

Another major section in a funding request narrative is what's often referred to as the *plan of operation.* This section usually addresses the project design. In grant applications and cooperative agreement narratives, this section is usually weighted at 35 or 40 points in the review criteria. (However, remember that RFPs and contract bidding documents usually don't have review points.)

In order to receive the most points possible, the project design must be sound and must contain program elements directly linked to the achievement of project objectives. Therefore, you need to write in a way that uses the language of the government agency or contract-awarding agency's own objectives. (See Chapter 15 for more about program design.)

In other words, the project design section includes your proposed project's goals and objectives, which should reflect those of the government or contracting agency. Give back to the government agency or contract-awarding agency reviewers the same language that's used in the application or RFP announcement and in the guidelines for grant/RFP review criteria.

Always write measurable objectives that state who will be impacted, where they will be impacted, at what rate (in a percent), and by when (a specific time frame). Language concerning a time frame is optional in the objectives only when the grant application guidelines ask for a separate timeline section.

The objective stated in a grant announcement or RFP is like a big finger pointing in the direction that you need to write in order to win a grant or contract award. The objective shouts out to you, "Write me, write me!" For more about goals and objectives, flip to Chapter 15.

Communicating your evaluation plan

A sound *evaluation plan,* the next major part of your narrative, is essential to winning big review points. This section can be scored from 5 to 15 points. When writing about the evaluation of your project, you explain how you propose to answer key questions about how effectively the grant-funded project was implemented or how efficiently the contracted services were delivered. You must provide a clear plan for answering the following key questions:

- ✔ How will the results of your evaluation be shared with stakeholders?
- ✔ What data collection tools will you use to measure qualitative and quantitative data?
- ✔ What's the frequency of the data collection processes?
- ✔ What qualitative and quantitative measures will you collect data on?
- ✔ Who will conduct the evaluation?

If you brought in your third-party evaluator during the planning stages of your project or service, she's on board as a member of the narrative writing team. The evaluator can write the entire evaluation plan section because she should be an expert in gleaning a program design and quickly developing research-driven evaluation plans. Spending some of your agency's dollars to secure this individual early on is the best strategy because you want to receive all the points in this section. Head to Chapter 15 for more specific information and tips on evaluations.

Showing that you're capable

The project management and overall organizational capability section of your grant application or cooperative agreement narrative usually carries the same weight as the problem or needs statement — 20 points. (Remember, RFP narratives to win contract bids rarely have review points.) In this section, you're expected to write about your capacity to successfully operate and support a government-funded grant project or manage a contract award.

In a well-constructed *project management statement,* you cite your organization's capability and relevant experience in developing and operating programs that deal with problems similar to those addressed by the proposed project or service. You should also cite the organization's experience in operating programs in cooperation with other community organizations.

Also remember to identify your program's executive leaders in the project management section. Briefly describe their involvement in the proposed project or service, and provide assurance of their commitment to the successful implementation of that project or service.

Keep in mind that all key personnel (the persons responsible for the project's implementation) should have extensive experience in programs and services like the one you're proposing. You score more points during the review process if you can name actual staff members instead of relying on the standard "yet-to-be hired" statement. **Note:** Don't forget to identify your third-party evaluator upfront. And be prepared to include a copy of her full résumé in your appendixes, if requested.

To further your claims regarding project management, include documentation that briefly summarizes similar projects undertaken by your organization, and note the extent to which your objectives were achieved. Also, note and justify the priority that this project or service will have within your organization, including the facilities and resources that are available to carry out your plans.

Losing even one or two points in this section can hurt you when the total score is tallied.

Connecting numbers to words

Your budget forms and detailed narrative must show the grant reviewer or procurement officer/purchasing manager (for RFP narratives) that your costs are reasonable, allowable, and worth the result you seek. In grants and cooperative agreements, this section is usually worth the remaining review criteria points, ranging from five to ten points.

In most government grant and cooperative agreement competitions and RFP opportunities, you're asked to provide, with your budget narrative, a detailed budget work sheet for each year of the project period. You also need to include an explanation of the basis for computation of all costs.

Add up your budget, and then add it up again. Make sure each expense is directly related to an activity that's necessary to reach the project's objectives. Don't introduce any costs here that you haven't addressed in your main proposal, cooperative agreement, or RFP narrative.

When you read the guidelines for preparing the budget, look closely for any language about construction costs. Most government grants won't cover new construction, but they will allow program-related renovations. RFPs usually have construction exclusions, as well.

When in doubt about the guidelines and how they relate to your budget, call and ask the government agency's program officer (for grants) or the procurement officer (for RFPs). These calls — even if they seem trivial — can establish a relationship that could be beneficial to your grant getting funded or your contract being awarded. See Chapter 17 for more about budget presentation.

Scoring Higher with Some Help from the Feds

Most government agencies that award grants or contracts produce publications that can give you a leg up on writing all types of grant applications and RFP narratives. These valuable resources can be obtained from each government agency's information clearinghouse. Check out agency Web sites for links labeled "Resources" or "Publications." You may encounter any of the following publications, which can be of great help:

- **Bulletins:** These summarize recent findings from government program initiatives. Designed for use as references, they may contain graphic elements such as tables, charts, graphs, and photographs. You can re-create some of the most current and relevant graphics in your needs statement or program design.

- **Fact sheets:** Fact sheets highlight, in one to two pages, key points and sources of further information on government programs and initiatives. You can cite the most recent facts (never more than five years old) in your needs statement.

✔ **Journals:** These highlight innovative programs or carry articles on critical issues and trends. You can cite some of the model programs at the beginning of your program design section to show how you're modeling your project on a successful program. You can also use any critical issues or trends covered in journals in your needs statement.

✔ **Reports:** These documents contain comprehensive research and evaluation findings; provide detailed descriptions of innovative programs implemented at the national, state, and local levels; and present statistical analysis, trends, or other data on selected topics. Reports may include explanations of case studies, field studies, and other strategies used for assessing program success and replication. Some reports provide training curriculums and lesson plans as well. You can cite research on evaluation findings in your needs statement. Innovative programs that are considered models can be cited in your program design section to build the basis for proposing your own program model.

✔ **Summaries:** Summaries describe key research and evaluation findings that may affect future policies and practices. Summaries highlight funded programs implemented at the national, state, or local level that may serve as models for other jurisdictions. These publications are generally 30 to 90 pages in length and usually include appendixes and lists of resources and additional readings. You can cite research on evaluation findings in your needs statement. Innovative programs that are considered models can be cited in your program design section to build the basis for proposing your own program model.

I stock up on every print publication I can get my hands on. Grant writing is so easy when you have the information you need (and the information you didn't even know you needed) at your fingertips. Even when I use the Internet to let my fingers do the walking, I print out my research findings so I have a hard copy for use now and for future reference. Learn to work smarter, not harder!

Connecting to the Peer Review Process by Becoming a Peer Reviewer

Before you jump the gun and start writing your grant application narrative, I want to share an insider secret with you about how to connect mentally and skill-wise to the peer review process: You can search for and sign up to become a government peer reviewer, which is also known as a grant reader. Yes, you! Use your favorite search engine and type in this search string: *Call for peer reviewer.* One of the federal agencies that's constantly looking for peer reviewers is the U.S. Department of Health and Human Services.

Desirable peer reviewer characteristics include the following:

✓ Experience with writing grant applications in the grant funding topic area

✓ Formal education in the grant funding topic area

✓ Volunteer experience in the grant funding topic area

✓ Work experience in the grant funding topic area

Here are the benefits of participating in the government peer review process:

✓ **You get paid!** Yes, even the government recognizes that your time is valuable. Compensation ranges from $100 to $300 per day. Often you're required to make a multiday commitment. When I participated in the peer review process, I was in Washington, DC, for seven days (two of which were traveling days).

✓ **You gain valuable experience as a grant reader.** You get to see, first hand, how other grant writers write, incorporate compelling graphics, and present research-based evidence of their need for the grant funding and how that funding will impact the target population. In other words, you're going to be paid to train yourself to be a better grant writer!

✓ **You have the opportunity to network with other peer reviewers from throughout the United States and its territories.** During the day, you'll be isolated while you read grant applications and write your list of strengths and weaknesses about each section of each narrative. When you're done with your daily individual reviewing process (usually, you'll read up to ten grant applications per day), you then meet with two or more other peer reviewers who read the same set of grant applications that you did. It's during this team peer review process (where you must come to a consensus on the final scoring for each application) that you meet many types of individuals who are "connected."

What do I mean by people who are connected? I mean people who are experts in the grant funding field. These same people can become your best friends when you need a third-party evaluator (or a referral for one) or when you need a copy of a successful grant application they've written for this particular funding agency.

Sometimes, if the peer review database is already full, you may not be contacted for months — even a year or longer. But don't give up! Continue to e-mail the agency's peer reviewer database contact person and indicate your enthusiasm about being invited to participate in the peer review process. You may have to update your resume and the peer review application every year, so make a note on your annual calendar now!

Chapter 11

Magnetizing Funders with Powerful Writing

*A*nyone can write in a cut and dried (aka boring) style. However, when it comes to winning competitive grants and contracts, the term paper approach to writing will only result in immediate rejection by funders. So, do you need an advanced degree in creative writing? No. Do you need to head back to school to master the winning words? No, again. What you need is this book and, most importantly, this chapter.

In this chapter, I share with you some vivid words and sentences that are sure to jump-start your creative side. This is where I share the *best of the best from Bev* with my faithful readers. I think you'll find yourself returning to these pages over and over — every time you write. Sit back and get ready to discover the real definition of *wordsmithing*.

Choosing the Right Words to Write a Winning Application

If you've read other chapters in this book, you know that I give you tons of action steps for every point in the grant seeking and grant writing processes. But for this chapter, I want you to throw out those "get to the point" ideas about writing. Reprogram your brain with passion, creativity, and emotion.

In the beginning, being creative and pulling words from the sky will seem difficult and awkward. Give yourself some time and practice and in no time you'll be writing like Dr. Bev Browning! To help you settle into the writing process, the following sections offer you three easy-to-follow steps.

Action Step 1: Lay out who and where

No one sends money to strangers in unknown places. (After all, would you?) This rule also applies to grantseekers, who often spend pages writing about what they need and only one small sentence about the grant applicant organization's location and its unique characteristics.

You need to tell the reviewers who you are and where you are — with passion and flavor. Sound like fluff? Contrary, my friend! Just remember that money comes from the heart, not from the brain. Grants are made based on your tugging on the hearts of the peer reviewers (see Chapters 9 and 10 for more on the peer reviewers and their criteria). Their minds are only used to read your grant application. Their hearts, on the other hand, make the fund 'em or reject 'em decisions.

The following are a handful of compelling examples that will shoot the reviewers in their hearts with Cupid's arrows. Hopefully, these examples will kick-start your journey of exploring creative writing and using words that work!

> *A small and struggling nonprofit organization that was founded at the beginning of this millennium . . .*
>
> *One of 50 state-level chapters seeking to grasp the many miles we encompass and individuals we strive to serve . . .*
>
> *Located in the nucleus of the Ozark Mountain's art community . . .*
>
> *Adjacent to three of America's historical landmarks . . .*
>
> *Sitting amidst a tall sea of pristine forestry . . .*
>
> *A new IRS-approved 501(c)(3) nonprofit private operating foundation located in the heartland of America's natural state . . .*
>
> *While only 75 miles from the Metroplex, our small organization serves many in this rural, isolated, and economically deprived pocket of poverty . . .*

While these examples may seem like they're going overboard in description, they're the types of paragraph starters that make the grant readers want to read more! (See Chapter 13 for how to pull together the description of the organization.)

Action Step 2: Play up the bad stuff

If the sun is shining and everything is fine inside and outside of your organization, you really don't need any grant monies, right? This is how the grant readers view what you write. If you only write about the good things happening, you don't really have a justification or need for outside funding. I know it may be difficult for the really positive folks out there, but when writing an application, you need to do the following:

✔ Focus on the negative

✔ Talk about the organization's gaps or needs

✔ Convey or communicate how dire the situation is for your target population

Flip to Chapter 14 for a tour through doom, gloom, drama, and trauma.

I want you to write about your endless situation, but I don't want you to go overboard. To be safe, select only 10 to 15 of the terms that follow to build your "frantic" sentences.

Alienate, abandon, abashment, abbreviated, abortive, adjudicate, aghast, aimless,

Backbone, backfire, barren, baseless, benign, besiege, betray, beyond, bland, blast, blatant, bottom, boundary

Capitulate, categorical, ceaseless, censor, challenge, cheapen, choke, clash, close-minded, collateral, commonplace, compound, concealed

Danger, deadly, decadence, decay, decline, defection, demoralize, depressive, despairing

Economical, egression, eject, elongated, emaciated, emergency, endless, endure, entangle

The next group of words literally calls out to grant readers consciously and subconsciously. Use these words to grab and keep the attention of grant readers.

Fade, fallacious, fallacy, fallible, faltering, fault, feckless, fend, feverish, fictitious, final

Germane, glaring, gloom, glum, gradual, grasping, grave, gulf, gut

Habitually, hallow, halfhearted, hamper, haphazard, harbor, harden, hardly, harrowing, harshly

Icy, idleness, illimitable, immoral, impassible, immutable, impenetrable, imperfect, impractical

Jagged, jolt, judicious, jurisdiction, justification, juxtaposed

Keen, kick, kill, knifelike, knock-down-and-drag-out

Lacerated, lackadaisical, lambaste, lapse, lash, latitude, levity

Your words must "walk" and "talk" to grant readers. Even if you're writing a contract bid, you need magnetizing words. The following strong words can give you the winning edge every time.

Madness, maggot, makeshift, malign, mandate, matchless, medial, migratory

Nameless, near-at-hand, neglectful, never-ending, nigh, nonetheless

Object, obviate, oftentimes, ominous, once and again, one-sidedness, outcry

Painful, pallid, paradigm, parallel, paralyze, paramount, pariah, partiality, precarious, propensity

Quagmire, queasy, quit, quizzical

Rabid, ration, rattle, ravage, recluse, reevaluate, relinquish, remedy, remiss

Writing with words that "walk" and "talk" means you have to start and keep thinking outside of the box. Granted, this isn't the way you usually load up your paragraphs with words, but it's time to start winning all of your grant requests and contract bids.

Sacrifice, safety, sanction, scant, scatter, search, seedy, seemingly, separation, seriously, shallow

Tacit, tantamount, tarnish, temperate, thwart, tight-fisted, timeworn

Unaccompanied, unadvisable, unbiased, undescribable, unthinkable

Vacancy, vacillating, vague, value, vanish, variance, vegetate

Waive, wallop, waning, wastethrift, watchful, wayfaring, weakling, weary

Yearning, yielding, yet, yonder

Zealous, zenith

Don't underestimate the power of the written word. Using powerful words to paint a picture of where the problem is geographically located is especially important when you're approaching potential funders who aren't located in or near your community. However, when you use new words in a grant application, make sure you know the meanings and connotations of them so you don't end up using them in the wrong ways.

Action Step 3: Use a thesaurus

Don't be shy about using a thesaurus to bring your thoughts to life in a way that conveys true and serious *need*. Keep a thesaurus on your desk to help you select impactive words when writing about your organization and the problems it faces.

A thesaurus is a wonderful tool to help you expand your vocabulary and ultimately become a better writer, but if you're new to vocabulary expansion, be careful to avoid words that aren't slightly mainstream. In an attempt to sound smart, you may scare off reviewers who won't bother to haul out a dictionary in order to read your proposal.

Pulling out a Few Tricks to Win Grant Monies

The opening section of your application for funding is all about you. The focus is on the problem *you* want to solve, where *you* are located, what *you* have done as an organization, and what *you* are doing now. This section is a key ingredient of your winning grant, cooperative agreement, or contract bid recipe.

Grant request narratives and responses to Requests for Proposals (RFPs) practically shadow each other in content and format. The examples in the following sections illustrate well-written content about the applicant or bidder — excerpted from real grant or cooperative agreement requests and RFP response narratives that won real funding. The names and places have been changed to protect the privacy of the winners. I include comments to explain why these examples are so effective. (Refer to Chapter 13 for more on how to effectively showcase your organization in an application.)

Take advantage of your word processor's formatting tools. Bold, underline, and italicize key words and phrases. It's even okay to put some critical language in red type. (Flip to the later section "Keeping your reader on track" for more on how to format your writing.)

You just want to lace your narrative with unique formatting; don't go overboard. There's nothing worse for the reader than trying to read all bold, italicized, or underlined text.

Using groups of three

Research shows that groups of three are effective in getting your audience to remember an important point. The *groups of three* tactic is a way to make a memorable impression with the words you choose. The words that stick in our minds forever usually come in groups of three. For example: blood, sweat, and tears; reading, writing, and arithmetic; and red, white, and blue. An example of this tactic applied to grant writing terms would look like this:

> *The American Association of the Benefit Examiners (AABE) works with third-party insurance providers to determine the average expenditure per patient. The services provided allow insurance companies to calculate the level of benefits to offer in each category of health care benefits. The ultimate selling tools to insurance providers are **cost-saving, cost effective, and cost-wise** advice and expertise from the AABE.*

In this case, the grant readers or contract bid decision makers have been given a rhythm of words that will be embedded in their minds.

Demonstrating soft cash assets

In the following excerpt, the bolded phrases strongly suggest that the organization isn't begging for grant, cooperative agreement, or contract monies with both hands out, but rather it has some resources or strengths already in place to build upon — a very good situation to be in. The grant, cooperative agreement, or contract review team is more likely to bestow review points on an organization that already has some assets — not just cobwebs — in its corner.

> *The Grant Writing Training Foundation has minimal fiscal resources; however, our newly formed nonprofit does have other assets.* ***The 12-member Board of Directors willingly volunteers for monthly board meetings, weekly committee-level meetings, and for fundraising events.*** *The Foundation is headquartered in an* ***1,800 sq. ft. home on a residential street. The home has been donated by the Town of Buckeye's Community Development Agency.***

In this next example, I show you how to switch hats and write similar language for a contract bidding document (where you're responding to an RFP):

> *The Genesee Corporation has the following assets that are not being requested for expense reimbursement in this contract bid:* ***24,000 sq. ft. corporate and warehouse center; over $100,000 in communications equipment, and a fleet of 40 commercial vehicles.***

Making a point with emotion

When you write about your need or the need of your target population, you must stick to the facts. However, there are no hard and fast rules when it comes to how you present those facts. Write with the understanding that you increase your chances of winning grant awards, cooperative agreements, and RFPs by touching the hearts of the individuals making the funding decisions. Remember, I don't want you to go overboard, but I do want you to make an impression by using emotion-filled phrases.

The bolded text in the following example highlights powerful phrases that you can use in your grant or cooperative agreement applications and RFPs to describe any isolated class of people. The imagery of escaping something moves the reviewer to a new level of emotion. The reviewer isn't just reading dry text with facts and statistics. Emotion generates higher review points and the beginning of a recommendation for funding.

This is a fact-driven emotional statement for a $100,000 request:

> *The project targets individuals 18 to 65 years old. 18.8 percent of the population between 18 and 65 years old live **below the federal poverty line;** 13.3 percent of individuals 65 or over also live below the poverty line. Approximately 9 percent of residents have a physical disability; 15 percent have sought mental health services. The proposed project will address the community problems of **chronic underemployment and unemployment** by helping clients create and implement employability plans. The targeted area has not developed sufficiently to spawn large-scale, high-wage employers. Jobs at prevailing livable wages are **beyond the reach of many who grew up in poor and struggling families and who truly believe and accept that as their fate.** Sadly, cultural ignorance on the part of local and regional units of government has caused the target population to be **overlooked and become transparent!** The target population has experienced **sporadic unemployment because they were employed by seasonal employers.***

I used to save my emotional verbiage for foundation and corporate funding requests and for private sector contract bids. However, those days have passed. You won't lose review points with a government funding agency or a public sector contract bid-letting agency when you draw their attention to the need by beefing up the verbiage. As a federal grant reviewer, I expect to see magnetizing and emotional language supporting the facts.

Keeping the reader on track

When you get the attention of the person making the funding decision, you don't want to lose it. Here are my general writing rules for keeping your reader on track, with eyes glued to your writing:

- ✔ Use lots of headings.
- ✔ Use numbered and bulleted lists.
- ✔ Keep paragraphs short, incorporating no more than 5 to 7 sentences in each paragraph.
- ✔ Use a 12-point Times New Roman font (preferred by 80 percent of grant-making agencies).
- ✔ Stick with one font to avoid a jumbled appearance.
- ✔ Avoid using all capital letters.
- ✔ Underline sparingly.
- ✔ Use boldface or italics to emphasize key words and phrases.

Applying Specific Steps When Writing Your Program Design Section

When you write the program design section of your grant application, cooperative agreement, or RFP narrative, remember that the point is to explain what you want to do with the grant, agreement, or contract monies.

The program design includes a description of your program, goals, objectives, and activities. It also includes an implementation timeline, a management plan, and finally an evaluation plan. Note that while some grantmakers request separate management and evaluation plan sections, these sections are still considered critical components of the overall program design. (See Chapter 15 for the full scoop on laying out the plan of action.) You also need to define the population you serve, the partnerships you have with other agencies in your community, and the changes you plan to make. The program design section is the main event, so weigh every word carefully, and make sure that your sentences work together like magic.

The following sections present three important steps to follow when writing the program design. I use excerpts from a winning grant application to show you how to apply each of the three steps.

Step 1: Use power-packed words to describe your program

Use words and phrases such as *provide, prepare, empowering catalyst, strengthening, continuum,* and *taking the lead.* They point to the fact that your organization takes action. Here's an example that uses these descriptive words and phrases:

> *The Mary Mack Board of Directors has just completed nine months of capacity-building training under the Capital Compassion Campaign. As a sub-grantee, our role is to provide diligent oversight to the ongoing operation of the Community Employment Project. Our board is prepared to help the project become an empowering catalyst in the Far West Valley. The first step in strengthening the project is to enter into an agreement with other social services agencies in order to form a continuum of services for low-income clients. Our organization will also take the lead in grant seeking and grant writing for other small to mid-size nonprofits in the target region.*

Step 2: Present your goals and objectives in the proper terms

Remember, you want to wow funding request readers. To do so, make an impressionable point by writing your goals in visionary terms. Use words such as *decrease, deliver, develop, establish, improve, increase, produce,* and *provide.* These words point to meeting a level of performance.

Check out the following sample goals:

> *Goal 1: Upgrade employment skills of 75 working poor individuals.*
>
> *Goal 2: Support self-sufficiency efforts for the working poor by providing an integrated social services network that enables individuals to identify and aggressively address barriers to professional and personal self-improvement.*

Similarly, you should write your objectives using the S.M.A.R.T. structure, which means that your objectives are specific, measurable, attainable, realistic, and time bound. In the following examples, each objective is aligned with the goal that it addresses.

> *SMART Objective 1a: By the end of Year 1, individuals enrolled in the Community Employment Project will increase their job upgrade skills by 50 percent or more upon completion of vocational, basic education, and on-the-job training components.*
>
> *SMART Objective 2a: By the end of Year 1, 90 percent or more of individuals enrolled in the Community Employment Project will complete 100 hours of comprehensive job and life-enhancing counseling with licensed social workers and mental health professionals.*

Step 3: Finish your story by writing about longevity and future plans

Use words and phrases such as *external, internal, local fundraising, creating future funding partners, inviting more external funding sources to the organization's table of partners, seeking to identify more investors in our stakeholders,* and *continuing grant-funded activities after the funding is gone.* These words and phrases don't just point to something; they rocket off the page and say, "We're planning for the future of this organization, and we're asking for your help, but we have a plan for keeping this program alive after we spend your money."

All types of funders want assurances that when you finish spending all their money, the show or program will go on. No funder wants the efforts started with their investment or contract award to suddenly shut down at the end of the grant or contract funding period.

In your Program Design and Evaluation section, you must write a paragraph to address the funder's concerns, which arise during the funding request review stage.

This paragraph from the Community Employment Project's grant request lays out the organization's financial plan for its project's future.

The Community Employment Project (CEP) has recently been designed as the Town of Jackrabbit's faith-based intermediary agent. This means that all grant applications written by the Town will designate CEP as a fiscal agent or grant applicant depending on the funding agency's applicant eligibility guidelines. This means that CEP will be given, at a minimum, a 10 percent administrative oversight fee for every funded application. Based on 2007 grant submissions by the Town, CEP could receive $250,000 in the next year and even more thereafter. These monies will enable CEP to continue providing critically needed employment and training services in Jackrabbit.

Part IV
Writing a Competitive Application Narrative

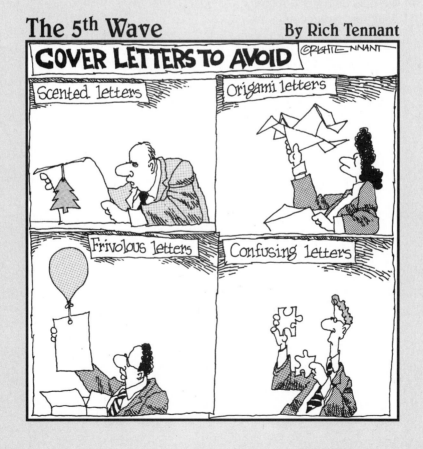

The 5th Wave   By Rich Tennant

COVER LETTERS TO AVOID

Scented letters

Origami letters

Frivolous letters

Confusing letters

In this part . . .

In this part, you find out how to make what's on the outside count! You get comfortable with writing all sorts of award-winning documents, from magnetic cover letters to succinct abstracts and executive summaries.

Part IV is the foundation to building your grant- and contract bid–seeking house. In fact, this part delivers the best of Bev's best! I show you how to present your organization's or business's grant applicant credibility, convey a hopeless situation, lay out the plan for implanting grant-funded projects, demonstrate that you have resources to compliment the grant funds, and develop an accurate and reasonable budget section.

Chapter 12

Creating the Documents Outside of the Main Narrative

*B*ack in the old days, every type of request that you submitted to a funder required a cover letter. I even typed cover letters for federal grant applications. Well, those days are long gone — at least for government grant applications. However, there are a handful of foundation and corporate grantmakers that still require cover letters with grant proposals. What do you write in these cover letters? How long should they be? Should they be formal or informal? I answer these questions in this chapter.

I also introduce you to some of the standard information gathering forms and other pre-narrative sections you can expect to see. Remember that every funding source, private (foundation and corporation) and public (government agencies) has different grant proposal formatting and submission requirements. With so many types of funding applications floating around, determining what goes where can be confusing. That's why I explain it all for you in this chapter.

By order of appearance, the upfront stuff (the items that come before the grant application narrative) should be the following (note that not all the pieces apply in every case):

✔ Cover letter (only for foundation and corporate requests; only provide a cover letter for a Request for Proposal, or RFP, or cooperative agreement when the guidelines instruct you to do so)

> ✔ Common grant application form (only for foundation and corporate requests when the funder doesn't have its own specific application form or format)
>
> ✔ Application for Federal Assistance (only for federal grant applications)
>
> ✔ Abstract or Executive Summary (appropriate for all types of funders; required when requested)
>
> ✔ Notice of Request for Proposal Cover Form (only for RFP or contract bidding documents)
>
> ✔ Table of contents (generally for federal and state grant applications)

Federal guidelines for using a cooperative agreement (as distinct from a contract or grant) are basically the same as those for a grant except that the funding agency expects to be substantially involved with the recipient of the research funds in carrying out the funded activities. So, follow the guidelines and work closely with the funding agency's contact person to pose technical questions.

Making the Cover Letter Factual and Personal

Today, I use cover letters only on foundation and corporate requests, not on federal or state grant or cooperative agreement applications. Government funders want you to provide only the parts they ask for, and they rarely, if ever, ask for a cover letter. Foundations and corporations, on the other hand, usually expect to see a cover letter.

Your cover letter should be brief, it should get to the point, and it shouldn't regurgitate the information that's in the grant application (government funding request) or proposal (foundation or corporate funding request). When a funder opens your request for assistance, the cover letter should provide the first inkling of how well you understand the person to whom you've addressed the letter (that's the funder). Figure 12-1 gives you the basic format of a cover letter.

Write the cover letter last, after you've completed the entire funding request and when you're in a reflective mood. As you consider your great achievement (the finished funding request), let the creative, right side of your brain kick in and connect your feelings of accomplishment to the person who will help make your plans come true.

Heads up, contract bidders: RFP guidelines vary, so read the checklist requirements to determine whether you need to add a cover letter to your application.

Grant Proposal Cover Letter

Sunshine Equine Research, Inc.
24444 W. Sunshine Trail
Sunshine, NV 88888
(702) 888-8888 (voice)
(702) 888-8888 (fax)

January 2, 2009

Mrs. You R. Rich
Funding Manager – Equine Programs
Horses Our Us Fund
777 W. Lucky Bucks Way
Money, FL 77777

Dear Mrs. Rich:

May this cover letter serve as your introduction to Sunshine Equine Research (SER), Inc., based in Sunshine, Nevada. As the Executive Director and Ranch Manager, I humbly submit our grant proposal for your review. We are requesting $25,000 from the Horses Our Us Fund to repair broken and rusted fencing around the 10-acre *"waiting to go to horse heaven"* section of our research center's ranch. Each year, nearly 400 horses that are abused and neglected are brought to SER for recovery care. Many of the horses arrive in varying states of health and often die within 90 days of arriving. Nationally, research by the American Veterinarian Association (2008) indicates that our approach to equine research is the most humane offered. No research is conducted until after a horse has died, and all research contributes to advancing equine medicines for future generations of thoroughbreds.

SER is a 501(c)(3) private operating foundation that was created in 2000 by Sir Ranch a Lot, Sr., on his retirement from the thoroughbred racing industry. Our purpose is to advance research on what causes illness and foal deformities among thoroughbred racing horses. SER and the Horses R Us Fund have some things in common. What might those things be? We both have a love for horses, and we're both dedicated to advancing equine research.

Your investment in SER will make the difference in our securing these *special boarders* — rather than losing them to the desert where they have, in the past, lost their way and died a cruel death in the 120-plus degree sun.

Hoping,

Rusty

Russell J. Lot, Executive Director and Ranch Manager

ENCLOSURE

Figure 12-1:
A fully developed cover letter leaves the funder feeling connected to the applicant.

Follow these handy tips when you write your own cover letters:

- ✔ **Use the same date that the complete grant application will be sent to the funding source.** You want to create documents that are consistent, so the dates on cover letters and accompanying cover forms should be the same.

- ✔ **Open with the contact person's name and title, followed by the funding source name, address, city, state, and zip code.** Remember to double-check the contact information with a telephone call or e-mail to the funder.

- ✔ **Greet the contact person with "Dear" plus the personal title, as in Mr., Ms., Mrs., Messrs., followed by the last name.** This is your first point of introduction to a potential funder, so a personal title must be used. Call ahead to make sure that the personal title is correct. I once used Ms. for a female program director who preferred to be addressed with "Miss." The request was denied because I did not do my homework on her correct personal title.

- ✔ **Keep the first paragraph short and focused.** Start by introducing your organization (use its legal name), and then introduce yourself and give your job title (Executive Director, Development Officer, and so forth). Finally, get to the point. Tell the funder how much money you're requesting and why the monies are needed by your organization. Write a sentence or two about what your organization does. Validate your existence by adding at least one sentence that includes research-based evidence that there is a need for what your organization does.

- ✔ **Write a second paragraph that's brief and to the point.** Include no more than three sentences stating your organization's corporate structure status and the date it was founded. Then tell the funder your organization's purpose and how it aligns with the funder's mission or funding priority.

- ✔ **Wrap up your cover letter with a final, summarizing paragraph.** Share a closing thought or reflection about what this funding partnership can mean for the future of your project's target audience.

- ✔ **Use a standard closing, such as "Sincerely" or "With hope."** It's important to sound both thankful (using "sincerely") and optimistic (using "with hope") as you close your request for funds.

- ✔ **Sign your first name only; doing so invites an informal, long-term relationship.** Below your signature, type your first name, middle initial, last name, and job title.

- ✔ **At the bottom of the letter, include the note "ENCLOSURE" (in all caps).** This note indicates that a grant proposal is included in the same packet. The capital letters signal that the grant proposal is important.

Use the letter in Figure 12-1 as a guide when you write your cover letter. Chapter 11 details how to craft exciting, vivid language throughout your application.

Completing Common Grant Application Cover Forms

Many groups of grantmakers, from foundations to corporations, have created their own customized common grant application forms and formats. These types of commonly developed and used forms and formats can be found on the Foundation Center's Web site, www.foundationcenter.org. (See Chapter 6 for more on the Foundation Center.)

No one group of funders is using the exact same formatting or forms. So, in this section, I give you the most commonly requested information fields that you can expect to see with any of the state-level applications and the Regional Association of Grantmakers common grant applications.

The following are the most commonly requested cover form information fields that may be required for the varying common grant application formats:

- ✔ **Organization name, tax-exempt status, year organization was founded, date of application, address, telephone number, fax number, director, and contact person and title:** These items give the funding source straight information about your eligibility to apply for funds.

- ✔ **Grant request:** The funding source wants to know how much money you're asking for before it even reads the full proposal. The amount listed here is the first clue to the funder that you're counting on it to provide 100 percent of your project support.

This doesn't mean that you're only requesting the total amount needed from one funder; you still send your customized common grant application proposal package to other funders that are willing to accept this format. Having more than one potential funder lined up increases your chances of receiving the full amount needed.

- ✔ **Period grant will cover:** Most foundation and corporate funders award grant monies for only one year. Some will fund you for multiple years, but they don't represent the norm among private sector funders.

- ✔ **Type of request:** Typically, the funders want to know if you're requesting general support (money to pay the day-to-day bills), start-up funds (just beginning operations), technical assistance (training, accounting aid, or some other type of specialized consulting), and so on. See Chapter 1 for your grant language choices when it comes to the type of funds requested.

✓ **Project title:** I personally like for every funding request to have a project or program title. A title gives your request personality. Remember to be consistent in the use of your title. It should be the same from the cover letter to the cover form to the grant proposal.

✓ **Total project budget:** The amount you enter here is the total cost to implement your program. Include the value of your in-kind and cash contributions in addition to the amount needed from the funder. (See Chapter 17 for budget terms and definitions.)

✓ **Total organizational budget:** This is the amount of your organization's total operating budget for the current fiscal year.

✓ **Start date of fiscal year:** The *fiscal year* is the date that your organization's financial year begins. For example, your fiscal year may begin on January 1, September 1, or July 1. Check with your financial staff to determine your start date.

✓ **Summarize the organization's mission:** The word "summarize" is key here. If you have a long mission statement, give the abbreviated version. Remember that usually the entire cover form fits on one page.

✓ **Summary of project or grant request:** Don't fill out this field until you've written the grant application narrative. Then you cut and paste into this section the sentences that most effectively summarize your project.

Just the Facts: Filling In Federal Cover Forms

Since the arrival of Grants.gov and the online federal grant application e-grant submission system, it's no longer necessary to fill out grant application cover forms the old way (typing or scanning them).

The new and improved electronic Grant Application Cover Form (also known as Form 424) has expanded from one page to four pages. Here I walk you through the sections you can expect to see when you're filling it in online. I tell you exactly what the government wants you to include.

Here are the sections you'll find on Page 1 of the Application for Federal Assistance SF-424:

✓ **Section 1: Type of Submission.** Your options for this section are "Pre-application," "Application," or "Changed/Corrected Application."

✓ **Section 2: Type of Application.** Your options for this section are "New," "Continuation," or "Revision."

✔ **Section 3: Date Received.** This section will be completed by Grants.gov upon submission.

✔ **Section 4: Applicant Identifier.** Enter the entity identifier number (assigned by the federal agency) or your application control number (usually issued by Grants.gov when you submit the application). You likely won't have a number to enter here if your application isn't a revised or continuation application.

✔ **Section 5a: Federal Entity Identifier.** This section is similar to Section 4. If you're a new applicant, this section will remain blank.

✔ **Section 5b: Federal Award Identifier.** Leave this section blank if you're a new applicant. If you aren't a new applicant, you will have been given this number by the federal funding agency.

✔ **Section 6: Date Received by State.** This section is for state use only.

✔ **Section 7: State Application Identifier.** This section is for state use only.

✔ **Section 8: Application Information.** This is a clear and to the point section about your organization. You enter the legal name, employer/taxpayer identification number (EIN/TIN), DUNS number (see Chapter 3), address, department and division names, and name and contact information of the person to be contacted regarding matters involving your grant application.

Here are the sections you'll find on Page 2 of the Application for Federal Assistance SF-424:

✔ **Section 9: Type of Applicant.** In this section, you'll see a drop-down window where you can select from the following options: nonprofit, for-profit, institution of higher education, local education agency, state education agency, state agency, and just about every other eligible applicant citatory that you read about in the grant application's summary and guidelines. (See Chapter 9 for more on the summary and guidelines.)

✔ **Section 10: Name of Federal Agency.** In this section, you type in the name of the federal funding agency that you're submitting your grant application to for review (and hopefully recommendation for funding) by the peer review team.

✔ **Section 11: Catalog of Federal Domestic Assistance Number.** You'll find this number in the Grant Funding Opportunity Announcement Summary. Remember, this is a five-digit number.

✔ **Section 12: Funding Opportunity Number.** You find this number in the Grant Funding Opportunity Announcement Summary. This number can vary in the number of digits. In this section, you also need to type in the title of the funding competition.

✔ **Section 13: Competition Identification Number.** You find this number in the Grant Funding Opportunity Announcement Summary. You also need to type in the title of the competition in this section.

✔ **Section 14: Areas Affected by Project (Cities, Counties, States, etc.).** Don't just list the city, county, and state where your organization is located; list the cities, counties, and states where you provide services and where your target population is located.

✔ **Section 15: Descriptive Title of Applicants Project.** This is the section where you spotlight the fantastic name you've selected for your grant-funded project. After all, every project in need of grant funding must have a "can't forget this" name! Stumped? See Chapter 3.

Here are the sections you'll find on Page 3 of the Application for Federal Assistance SF-424:

✔ **Section 16: Congressional Districts.** Don't know your districts very well? Call your nearest public library and ask. Remember to include all the districts that your target population resides in, not just the one where your organization is located.

✔ **Section 17: Proposed Project.** In this section, you enter your project's start date and end date.

✔ **Section 18: Estimated Funding.** Here you enter the federal request amount, your own local contribution, and any other expected contributions. For example: state, local, other revenues as well as potential program income (fees to clients) amounts. You also have to total the amounts.

✔ **Section 19: Is Application Subject to Review by State under Executive Order 12372 Process?** If so, you have three options for responding: you're eligible, and you submitted it on the date you'll enter; you didn't submit your grant application for state review; your state doesn't have a pre-review requirement for federal grants submitted from organizations located there.

How do you know which option is right for you? Go to www.whitehouse.gov/omb/grants/spoc.html. At this site, you can see whether your state is on the list that requires a pre-review on all federal grant applications. As of 2008, only 22 states and five U.S. territories had designated Single Points of Contact (SPOC). A SPOC is appointed by the governor as the designated individual or agency who has the authority to pre-review your grant application request and submit comments, including recommendations, to the federal funding agency. Failing to adhere to the SPOC review requirement can result in your grant application not progressing from the technical review process to the peer review process.

✔ **Section 20: Is the Applicant Delinquent On Any Federal Debt?** It's either yes or no. If it's yes, you'll have a lot of explaining to do!

✔ **Section 21: Signatory box.** In this box, you simply type in the name of your authorized contact person or their initials. Each federal grantmaking agency provides specific instructions on what they want you to enter into this information field.

Here's the section you find on Page 4 of the Application for Federal Assistance SF-424:

✔ **Section 22: Applicant Federal Debt Delinquency Information.** Page 4 is only applicable if you have delinquent federal debt. This page houses your lengthy 4,000-character explanation of your debt.

Crafting the Abstract or Executive Summary

The *abstract* or *executive summary* is a brief, one-page overview of what the grant reviewer will find in the full grant application. Brevity is important (this section should be no longer than one page unless the guidelines indicate the need for a two page summary), so your abstract or summary should be written (or assembled) after the grant application narrative has been entirely written. Why? By then you should have all the wordy explanations out of your system!

You can create an abstract or executive summary by pulling the most significant sentences from each key writing section in the grant narrative and doing a quick cut and paste. Refer to Figure 12-2 for an example of an executive summary. Take key sentences from the following areas, and keep them in the same order in the abstract or executive summary as they appear in the narrative:

✔ **Proposed initiative:** Here you enter the name of your project or program and the full name of the funding competition you're applying to for grant consideration.

✔ **Introduction of target population:** Copy and paste a sentence or two about who you're planning to target and serve with grant monies.

✔ **Goals:** Copy and paste your goals from the project design section of your proposal narrative.

✓ **Program Measurements and Performance Targets (also known as objectives):** Copy and paste your objectives and performance targets from the project design section of your proposal narrative.

✓ **Plan of action:** Copy and paste the key activities that comprise the program's implementation process.

Grant Application Executive Summary

Proposed Initiative: Jobs For Innovation (JFI) is applying for U.S. Department of Labor funding for its proposed Hollywood School To Career Partnership.

Target Population: The target population for the Hollywood Youth Entrepreneurial Program (YEP) will be **30** TANF-eligible youth, ages 15 to 19, who are placed in juvenile aftercare services or are at risk of dropping out of high school or entering the juvenile justice system.

Program Goal: The goal of the program will be to facilitate the continuing education of these youth and develop their basic workplace skills by exposing them to entrepreneurial training and work experience in cooperating Hollywood businesses.

Entrepreneurial/Educational Program Measurements	LTI Performance Targets
1. Percentage of youth who remained in and/or completed high school or continue working toward GED/additional vocational education training	50% or more
2. Percentage of youth who participate in job readiness or technical skills training	75% or more
3. Percentage of youth who participate in part-time and/or summer employment	50% or more
4. Percentage of youth who receive classroom instruction in the practices and principles of entrepreneurship	100%
5. Percentage of youth who create self-sustaining businesses with potential to expand	25% or more
6. Percentage of participants who left or were dismissed before completion of training	25% or less
7. Percentage of youth who did not re-enter the juvenile justice or corrections system	25% or more six months post exit
8. Percentage of youth who do not become single adolescent parents during the program participation period	68% or more

Plan of Action: Jobs For Innovation (JFI) will work with Hollywood High School to develop a two-semester entrepreneurial training course using the *Get a Job Now* curriculum package. The Hollywood School To Career Partnership will orient teachers and JFI YEP staff with the curriculum. Endorsed and used by Partnership sites, the curriculum helps students enrolled in vocational skills training courses/programs experience business firsthand. Students put lessons to use in running individual or class ventures. The curriculum teaches students how to keep financial records, facilitates their interviews with local entrepreneurs, and guides them in outlining a business plan. Career skills students gain include: business introductions, win-win negotiations, sales presentations, advertising, financial record keeping, tracking stocks, and filling out job applications. This training course, open to YEP participants enrolled in grades 9–12, will be a prevocational course for in-school students. In-school students will have already completed remedial core curriculum coursework that equates to basic skills training. They will be placed in employer-provided work-based learning, work-based mentoring, and job shadowing evenings (from 3 p.m. to 6 p.m.), weekends, school holidays and vacations, and during the summer months. JFI will also organize an after school drop-in Job Club for in-school students at the YEP site. Students will be required to attend Job Club at least twice weekly in the first semester. In the second semester, JFI will develop an after school YEP peer support group, so participants can aid and encourage each other. JFI will work with the Hollywood School To Career Partnership, JFI's existing secure and non-secure juvenile program residents, Hollywood Housing Authority, Hollywood Hispanic Civic Association, Village of Hollywood Hills, Kiwanis International, Mercedes County Youth Board, the Hollywood Chamber of Commerce, Hollywood School District, and the "Worst to First"/Serve America Program to coordinate existing services to the target population and to maximize YEP program resources.

Figure 12-2:
The abstract or executive summary draws critical details from different parts of the narrative.

Developing the Table of Contents

Whether you include a table of contents depends on the grant application guidelines. Rigidly structured guidelines typically call for a table of contents, particularly if the narrative is long (more than ten pages) or if you're asked to provide several attachments or appendixes.

The table of contents shouldn't include the abstract or executive summary because those parts almost always precede the table of contents. Exceptions to this rule are applications from state or federal agencies that stipulate a format in which the table of contents comes before the abstract or executive summary. Grant guidelines and writing formats vary from one agency to another and even within departments in an agency, so be sure to read the grant application guidelines and follow the format listed in the reviewer's criteria (see Chapters 9 and 10 for details on review criteria).

Figure 12-3 provides you with an example of a federal grant application table of contents. Note that

✔ Only the main sections of the grant application are listed.

✔ Appendixes are listed and numbered.

✔ Federal or state mandated forms and attachments or appendixes are listed.

Including mandated forms in your table of contents lets the government know that you included them in the application. If a form disappears during the review process, at least the grant reviewer can affirm that it was included in the original application.

Great Neck Compassion Capital Fund (CCF)
Communities Empowering Youth (CEY) Program

TABLE OF CONTENTS

Figure 12-3:
Example of a complete table of contents for a federal grant application.

Section	Page(s)
Project Summary/Abstract	2
Objectives and Needs for Assistance	3-9
Results or Benefits Expected	10 – 13
Approach	13 - 18
Organizational Profiles	18 - 22
Budget and Budget Justification	22 - 28
Appendices:	
Certifications	
Assurances	
Resumes and job descriptions	
Memoranda of Understanding	
Letters of Commitment	
State Agency Comments for Pre-Application Review Requirements	
Copy of Intervention Curriculum Proposed in Grant Application	

Examining the RFP Opening Instructions for Contract Bids

Every contract bid-letting agency has its own version of the Notice of Request for Proposal cover letter or page. See Figure 12-4 for an example. The RFP's opening instructions typically provide this type of information:

- ✔ The solicitation number. This number is assigned by the procurement agency (the department or division releasing the RFP for bidding purposes).

- ✔ The RFP title. This title is noted on the first page of the bidding instructions.

- ✔ The contract award time frame.

- ✔ The fact that there will not be a Pre-Bid Conference for the procurement.

- ✔ Instructions for when and where to submit your bidding documents.

- ✔ Set-asides for federally-designated businesses.

- ✔ The name of the procurement officer. The RFP's opening instructions close with that person's name.

- ✔ The name of the agency requesting the contracted or proposed services. You can find the name at the top of the letterhead or on the first page of the RFP's opening instructions.

- ✔ The announcement for the preproposal conference, if there is one. This information will appear in the first few pages of most RFPs.

- ✔ A paragraph instructing you to contact the solicitation contact person with questions about the RFP.

- ✔ Information regarding the competitive sealed proposal submission process. A specific state government code is also cited.

Notice of Request for Proposal		Healthcare Group of Arizona
SOLICITATION NO.: **YH05-0010**	PAGE 1	761 East Jefferson, MD 5700
Offeror: _____	OF 59	Phoenix, Arizona 85034

Solicitation Contact Person:

Gary L. Callahan
Contracts and Purchasing Section
761 E. Jefferson, MD5700
Phoenix, Arizona 85034

Telephone: (602) 417-4038
Telefax: (602) 417-5907
E-Mail: glcallah@ahcccs.state.az.us
Issue Date: October 8, 2009

LOCATION: **HEALTHCARE GROUP OF ARIZONA (HCG) a division of AHCCCSA**
Contracts and Purchasing Section (First Floor)
761 E. Jefferson, MD5700
Phoenix, Arizona 85034

DESCRIPTION: _____ **THIRD PARTY ADMINISTRATION**

PROPOSAL DUE DATE: _____ **November 10, 2009** _____ AT 3:00 P.M. MST

Pre-Proposal Conference: A Pre-Proposal Conference has not been scheduled.

QUESTIONS CONCERNING THIS SOLICITATION SHALL BE SUBMITTED TO THE SOLICITATION CONTACT PERSON NAMED ABOVE, IN WRITING EITHER VIA TELEFAX OR E-MAIL (PREFERRED).

In accordance with A.R.S. § 41-2534, which is incorporated herein by reference, competitive sealed proposals will be received at the above specified location, until the time and date cited. Proposals received by the correct time and date will be opened and the name of each offeror will be publicly read.

Proposals must be in the actual possession of the Contracts & Purchasing Section on or prior to the time and date and at the location indicated above.

Late proposals shall not be considered.

Proposals must be submitted in a sealed envelope or package with the Solicitation Number and the offeror's name and address clearly indicated on the envelope or package. All proposals must be completed in ink or typewritten. Additional instructions for preparing a proposal are included in this solicitation document.

Persons with a disability may request a reasonable accommodation, such as a sign language interpreter, by contacting the appropriate Procurement Agency. Requests should be made as early as possible to allow time to arrange the accommodation. A person requiring special accommodations may contact the solicitation contact person responsible for this procurement as identified above.

OFFERORS ARE STRONGLY ENCOURAGED TO CAREFULLY READ THE ENTIRE SOLICITATION.

Figure 12-4: Example of a Notice of Request For Proposal (RFP) cover form.

Chapter 13

Building Grant Applicant Credibility

....

....

*W*hen your organization decides to apply for its first grant monies, it's critical that you know about your organization and show (in your writing) that it's capable and credible in the eyes of the grant funders. The section of the grant application narrative that houses this information, whether upfront, in the middle, or at the end of the narrative writing format, communicates who you are, where you are, and what you do as an organization.

When you write your opening paragraphs, keep in mind the way you would behave when meeting someone for the first time. The cordial thing to do is to engage in general chitchat about what you do for a living. Well, it's no different when you're introducing your organization on paper to the funding source — you have to cover the formalities of who, what, where, and how. (Chapter 12 tells you what to put in the application prior to the opening narrative.) Note that for foundation and corporate funding requests, the section of your narrative in which you describe your organization shouldn't exceed two typed, single-spaced pages in length.

In this chapter, you find out how to build your organization's background, programs, and affiliations into compelling introductory paragraphs. These opening sections convince the grant reader that you're financially and operationally capable to receive and manage grant monies.

A little trivia and a lot of facts create the kind of reader interest every successful grant writer shoots for. The longer you can keep readers' attention, the better your chances are of getting recommended for a grant award. I include a full-length grant application in the appendix at the end of the book. Be sure to check it out before you write.

Discovering the Details of Funding Source Writing Instructions

In most cases, the funding source's narrative writing instructions will point you in the right direction for what to include in the capability section of the application. Some funders title this section *Organizational Background* or *History*. Others label it *Grant Applicant Capability* or *Organizational Capability*. Regardless of what the funder calls this section, when introducing your organization, be sure to divide the information into different parts for easy digestion by the grant reviewer.

For example, you might include these different parts: Background (history and accomplishments), Programs and Activities (current services), Constituency Demographics (information about your service population) and Community Affiliations (local, regional, and state partners).

Here are some examples of the types of narrative section writing instructions you may see in your application guidelines:

> ***Community Foundation guidelines for writing organizational information (maximum of 150 words):*** *Describe your organization, its history and background, accomplishments and qualifications, services provided, and how it benefits the residents of the community. Include the number of people served, and then illustrate the increase in service, whether to people or in expansion of programs. Show us the track record of past work. If the agency is relatively new, talk about the track record to date.*

> ***U.S. Department of Labor Employment and Training Administration guidelines for writing organizational capacity narrative:*** *To satisfy the criterion, applicants must describe their proposed project management structure, including, where appropriate, the identification of a proposed project manager, a discussion of the proposed staffing pattern, and the qualifications and experience of key staff members. Applicants must also show evidence of the use of data systems to track outcomes in a timely and accurate manner. The applicant must include a description of organizational capacity and of the organization's track record in projects similar to those described in the proposal and/or similar to related activities of the primary partners. This section is worth 10 points.*

See Chapters 9 and 10 for more details on review points and criteria.

Laying the Organizational Capability Foundation

When writing the organizational capability section of your application, you need to tell the grant reader, clearly and concisely, just enough information about your organization's experience and accomplishments to pique her interest and keep her reading word for word. Remember that you're just introducing yourself, and it's not polite to start jabbering about the money you need or the problems you have.

In the first few sentences, the grant reader wants to see

✔ The full legal name of your organization

✔ The year the organization was founded, by whom, and for what purpose

If you don't know the appropriate answers, ask a veteran employee or a long-time board member. Sometimes, the history of an organization is written up in its annual report or in an anniversary issue of its newsletter. Keep researching and asking others until you strike gold.

✔ The location of the organization's headquarters and any other operating sites (name, city, county, state)

✔ The mission statement (use the abbreviated version)

✔ The organization's most important achievements that are related to the activities covered in the grant application

If you're seeking, for example, grant funds for a new after-school program, don't mention unrelated accomplishments, such as the school football team's winning record or the cabinet full of medals from the school's swim team. Taking the grant reader down a dead-end road with unrelated information is a fatal flaw, and it can result in your application not being read or funded.

Complete the organizational capability section by writing about important milestones in the organization's history. Even though your organization may have dozens of milestones, use bulleted, abbreviated statements to share only the top three to five milestones. And use a casual voice to make the list more inviting. Your organization's milestones may look something like this:

✔ Beginning in 2000, Pacific Rim Injury has established its role with government ministries and national committees working on education and training issues related to child traffic injuries.

✔ Since early 2006, we have worked with the Pacific Rim Ministries of Education and Training and the International Traffic Safety Committee to develop active learning techniques for traffic safety education for primary school children in the Pacific Rim.

> ✔ Last year, Pacific Rim Injury worked with Pacific Rim government agencies to identify the extent of motorbike injuries that claim the lives of young riders, especially primary school–age children, and to develop milestone interventions to protect the Rim's children when riding motorbikes.
>
> ✔ This year, Pacific Rim Injury's CEO coauthored the safety manual "Child Standard for Motorbikes and Mopeds," which was adopted by 100 percent of the Pacific Rim governments.

When you're writing the organizational capability section of the proposal narrative for a foundation or corporate funder, be sure to use language that works its way into the grant reader's heart and mind. The added impact always helps push your grant request down the funding path.

In the example that follows, I make the text inviting by putting a face on the organization's history. (See Chapter 11 for more about using colorful language in your writing.)

> *Romanian-born conductor Valentin Radu formed Vox Ama Deus in 1987, in Philadelphia, in order to revive appreciation and understanding of music of the 14th through 17th centuries from such masters as Palestrina, Monteverdi, Victoria, and Schutz. Vox Ama Deus presents voice and instrumental music of the Renaissance, Baroque, and Classical periods.*
>
> *Vox Ama Deus consists of two performance groups: the Ama Deus Ensemble, with 40 voices and an orchestra of appropriate period or modern instruments; and Vox Renaissance Consort, with 12 to 16 costumed professional singers who perform music of the High Renaissance both a cappella and with period instrument accompaniment.*

When writing the organizational capabilities section, I like to use customized bullets to draw attention to the grant applicant's attributes. For example, you could use musical notes to highlight Vox Ama Deus' strengths.

In order to get your grant application funded, you must be able to take the mundane and make it interesting to the grant reader. Your story must be magnetizing to all who read it, from your community partners to potential funders. After years of experimenting, I'm thoroughly convinced that telling and *selling* your organization's story is critical when funders are at the point of making a decision to fund or not to fund. You must write to hit them where their hearts are! This approach has pushed my *funding success rate* (the percentage of grants funded out of all the grants I write on an annual basis) from 50 percent to 90–95 percent.

Strong, emotional writing works best with foundation and corporate grant applications, but you need to adopt a different writing style for government applications.

When you describe your organization's history in a government grant application, follow these tips to rack up the review points:

✔ Use a cut-and-dried writing style — only write what's asked for, no more, no less.

✔ Stick with the cold, hard facts.

✔ Don't write the history and accomplishments section in first person (using such pronouns as I, our, and my). Instead, use the third-person writing approach. When you write in third person, you're writing as if you're on the outside of the grant applicant organization and looking back in with a third-party perspective. Your reference to your organization must be from a formal and straightforward approach. Here are two examples that allow you to compare first- and third-person writing styles:

• **First person:** *Our organization was founded in 2007 and is located in Montgomery, Alabama. Last year, our staff handed out food boxes to 4,967 individuals and families whose household incomes were 30 percent below the federal poverty rate. My 200 volunteers worked a total of 5,423 hours to meet our demand for food supplements.*

• **Third person:** *The organization was founded in 2007 and is located in Montgomery, Alabama. Last year, its staff handed out food boxes to 4,967 individuals and families whose household incomes were 30 percent below the federal poverty rate. The organization's 200 volunteers worked a total of 5,423 hours to meet the demand for food supplements.*

✔ Sterilize the writing content by avoiding emotional terms. Don't talk about anyone's feelings!

Describing Your Programs with Flair

Use the program section of your opening narrative to write about the day-to-day happenings at your organization. Describe the programs that you currently provide to your constituency (also called the *target population*), not what you plan to provide when your grant request is funded. (You can read more about target populations later in this chapter.) If you work for a smaller organization, you probably have only one or two programs. However, keep in mind that having fewer programs doesn't decrease your chances of winning a grant award. Grants are available for organizations of all sizes and shapes. Remember, it's all in the writing.

The grant reader is looking for you to briefly

- ✔ Give the name of the program and state how long it has existed (focus on long lasting and successful programs).
- ✔ Tell who the program serves (youth, adults, women, the elderly, physically challenged individuals, or whoever).
- ✔ Describe how your target population benefits from the program.

The following is an abbreviated version of a current programs section from a United Way grant application.

> *Brief Description of VOSS: Valley Outreach for Social Services (VOSS) was founded in 2007 by a core group of concerned and community-oriented far–West Valley residents in the state of California. The organization's mission is to build relationships within our communities by offering programs that provide support, education, and counseling in a variety of initiatives to enable each person and/or family to achieve a self-building relationship. To achieve this mission, VOSS has developed two core community intervention and prevention service tiers:* **Community Outreach Programs** *and* **The Wellness Center.**
>
> *Community Outreach Programs: Food distribution to the needy; clothes closet for welfare to work individuals; utility fund for individuals residing in households below 150 percent of the Federal Poverty Level; basic life skills training (youth and adults); job placement assistance (youth and adults); helping individuals develop new life skills and knowledge; individual and family life-crisis prevention; and an Adopt a Block Program.*
>
> *The Wellness Center: Alcohol and drug rehabilitation and prevention onsite support group; adult and child abuse prevention counseling referrals; sexual abuse prevention counseling referrals; medical screening and assistance referrals; and prisoner reentry assistance (emergency housing assistance and life skills readjustment counseling and training).*

Don't make the mistake of pulling the language for this section from a previously written grant (such as last year's failed attempt). Always use fresh, up-to-date programs and activities information. Grant readers are very intuitive and can pick up on outdated, out-of-place information.

Defining the Target Population

The target population section is the place to write about the people you serve. If you're serving certain organizations, you write about the organizations. If you're writing a grant for an animal shelter, you write about the animals.

Give just enough detail to aid the reader in understanding where your operating dollars end up — for use with the poor, the blind, the unemployed, the high school dropouts, the homeless, or the terminally ill, for instance. To make this section as accurate as possible, do your homework. Pull old evaluation reports from previously funded grants, and review reports given to your board members — both types of documents should detail exactly who benefits from your organization's services.

The grant reader wants to see:

- ✔ Characteristics of your target population (age range, gender, ethnicity, education level, and income level)

- ✔ Numbers served by each program (make a table that covers the past five years)

- ✔ Changes in the target population that may relate to why you're asking for grant funds

Clearly define your target population. You must convey to funders that you're serving a constituency that falls within their funding parameters. Also, be sure to cite the source of your demographics!

When you write the target population section, use boldface and italics to make words describing the population stand out for the grant reader. In the following example, I introduce the grant reviewer to a faith-based nonprofit organization serving inner city residents. Because I want the reader to understand the importance of the funding request, I use a lot of boldface to make phrases stick in the reviewer's mind. This request was for a Board of Director's capacity building grant application.

> ***Brief description of the community to be served and engaged in SPF process:*** *The community targeted to be served and engaged in the SPF process is located in an **area known as Central-South Phoenix** (CSP). The general boundaries are Central Avenue on the east, I-17 freeway on the west, Jackson Street on the north, and I-17 on the south. Zip codes in the targeted area are: 85003, 85004, 85006, 85007, 85009, 85031, 85032, and*

*85041. **Cultures in this area are tied strongly to ethnic ancestry.** The hybrid mix of **new immigrants from Mexico and multiple generations of minorities as well as nonminorities has bred many risk factors** that contribute to the need for the SPF process in the targeted area.*

Relevant demographic information:** The total population of the City of Phoenix is 1,512,986. **The targeted area, CSP, has at least 10 distinct neighborhoods with 201,462 residents.** Racial makeup is 66.2 percent Hispanic; 19.5 percent White; 11.2 percent African American; and 1.5 percent Native American. Thirty percent (60,400) of residents are ages 18 and younger; 43.7 percent of youth are female. **The targeted census tracts have a 40 percent poverty rate — the highest in the city. Sixty percent of residents are high school dropouts, and 80 percent of adults are unemployed.

Collaborating to win: Partnerships that rock

Among today's grantmakers, both in the private sector (foundation and corporate) and public sector (government), all expect grant applicants to have already formed partnerships with local, regional, state, and national agencies. This means you can't go it alone anymore or keep all of the grant award pie for yourself. Partners have expectations and operate in a reciprocal frame of mind.

What's a *partnership?* It's a continuum of relationships that foster the sharing of resources, responsibility, and accountability in undertaking activities within a community. As you can imagine, there are both pros and cons of involving your organization in a partnership.

As for the pros, partnerships do all of the following:

✔ Create new opportunities

✔ Initiate trust at the local level

✔ Expand your organization's marketing/target population area

✔ Expand your service image

✔ Help maximize your financial assets to a grantmaker by adding external leveraging and/or matching resources

✔ Improve your risk management abilities during a crisis

✔ Increase your competitive advantage in the grant seeking arena

✔ Provide access to broader financial and human resources

Inevitably, where there are pros, there are cons. When it comes to partnerships, the cons are mostly related to what the partners expect. They expect all of the following:

✔ A piece of the "grant" or "contract" pie

✔ An equal voice and vote in group decisions

✔ Reciprocal benefits from your organization (letters of support, MOU's, grant alert sharing, and more)

Usually, I advise grant writers to refrain from putting any needs statement language in the section of the proposal narrative that contains a description of the organization. However, I break this rule when I'm writing about any projects serving children — specifically, a target population under the age of 18. For children's services programs, I drop hints of need every chance I can. This helps reach out and touch the hearts of the grant or cooperative agreement readers, whether foundation, corporate, state, or federal. I even use this technique in RFP narratives. It really works!

Writing About Your Collaboration with Partners

In the partnerships section of your organization description narrative, write about your organization's local, regional, and national partnerships. What organizations do you team with to provide your program's services? What organizations have asked you to write letters of support for their grant applications? What groups have historically supported you? If you find that this section of your narrative is a bit slim, Chapter 9 gives you more information about establishing community partners to give your grant application the competitive edge.

When writing about your partnerships, list the partner's full name and its role in relation to your organization. Whether you're writing a corporate or foundation funding request or a government funding request, the information you provide in your narrative on partnerships will be the same: who, where, and what role the partner plays.

As you write about your partnerships, don't include an organization that you're considering partnering with without first talking to a representative about what you're doing and asking permission to include the organization in your proposal. It doesn't reflect well on you if the funder calls your "partner" and that organization has no clue as to who you are and no knowledge of a partnership.

Partners are like friends: You get to know them inside and out, and you complement each other in the delivery of like or unlike services. For example, say you operate a group home for mentally and physically challenged adults. In that case, you need to depend on the Get 'Em There Transportation Service to take your clients to and from medical appointments.

When it comes time to review the partnership section of your funding application, the grant reader looks for evidence of:

- ✔ Collaborative efforts with multiple partners to maximize the use of grant funds through the coordination of services to the target population (see the previous section for the lowdown on target populations)

- ✔ Partners that commit cash to reduce the amount of grant funding you need

- ✔ Partners that contribute personnel, space, equipment, supplies, and other valuable items to reduce the amount of grant funding needed

Your grant guidelines may call for your partnership information to appear at the beginning of the narrative, before the history and accomplishments. However, the partnerships could just as easily be placed after the problem statement or as an attachment. Read your grant application directions carefully before you start writing. The great thing about modern technology, however, is that little tool called *cut and paste.* You can move anything anywhere after it's written.

In the following example, I briefly introduce a grant applicant's partners and their roles in helping the applicant organization coordinate its services. Note that I write in third person. Also, note that the partners who contribute cash should be mentioned simply as *cash contributors* in your narrative. (See Chapter 17 for how to incorporate matching funds from your organization and its partners into the project budget summary and narrative detail.)

> *Saving Sisters works closely with local community, faith, and nonprofit organizations to develop a collective response to the complex issues facing this community. Currently, the agency works in collaboration with the following partners: Keys Community Center (space and volunteers); Grace Temple (space, administrative oversight, and volunteers); Children First (technical assistance); the Hope VI Project (our organization is a subgrantee and receives $40,000 annually from this partner); City of Lovedale (collaborative public events); and Mercury Gardens (transportation assistance). Participating organizations in the Strategic Prevention Framework will engage in recruitment, resource sharing, information distribution, training, and services intervention.*

If you prefer, you can present this same information in a small table instead of a paragraph. After all, graphics and tables throughout your narrative give the grant reader a break from reading straight text. Remember that grant readers may have to read dozens of grant requests each week. You can give them a much-needed respite from standard sentences and win them over by using a table effectively.

When I'm writing a short (five pages or less) proposal for corporation or foundation funding sources, I only create a table to spotlight the grant applicant organization's partnerships when I have sufficient room on the second page to accommodate the entire table. Remember, you have four subsections to squeeze into two pages. Revert to using a narrative to describe your partnerships when a table format puts you over the page limit.

If you decide to use a table format to present the organizations with which you have a partnership, define their partnership role and include the value of their contributions. See Figure 13-1 for an example of how to present partnerships in a table format.

Town of Beulah Main Street Revitalization Project
Community Partners

Figure 13-1:
Information about your collaboration with local groups looks lean and clean in a table.

Partners	Roles	Value of Contribution
12-member Board of Directors	Management oversight	400 hours annually @ $20/hr.
Town of Beulah Council	Legislative oversight	200 hours annually @ $20/hr.
State Department of Historic Preservation	Funding agency and technical assistance	Awarded the Main Street Program with a $100,000 grant
Beulah Historical Society	Project management oversight	100 hours annually @ $20/hr.
Leadership Beulah	Project site volunteers	400 hours annually @ $20/hr.
Beulah Public Works Department	Project site labor	600 hours annually @ $50/hr.
Beulah Chamber of Commerce	Space and refreshments for board meetings	36 hours annually @ $25/hr.

Presenting the Required Elements for Contract Bids

When you respond to an RFP (Request For Proposal), you position your company to win a contract bid. Pursuing contracted services on a regular basis can strengthen and grow your business. In the first section of your services proposal, you're asked to write about your organization's experience, expertise, and reliability. Although this section of the services proposal is similar to the description of the organization section in a grant or cooperative agreement request, it does differ in format. To keep on top of what's required in the experience, expertise, and reliability section of a services proposal, the following information and examples show you

✔ How the bid-letting agency words its information request

✔ How to write a compelling narrative that convinces the agency that your business can deliver the services required

Making sure you understand the guidelines

All RFPs are written differently, depending on the contract bid-letting agency's standard template (developed internally by the procurement staff). Be on the lookout for this type of organizational information language in the guidelines and writing instructions of RFP documents:

> *Give a summary that details the Offeror's experience, expertise, and number of years in providing the service.*

To figure out the expected length of the summary, follow the page limitation instructions. And don't forget that *offeror* refers to the bidding agency — that's you!

Conveying the qualifications of your company

The experience, reliability, and expertise section of your services proposal should be divided into the following categories:

- ✔ **Bidder:** Type your company's full legal name (the name you used to incorporate your business).

- ✔ **Mission Statement:** Provide the complete mission statement for your company.

- ✔ **Areas of Expertise:** List the areas of experience for your business, and don't forget to include the corresponding years or time frames for those experiences.

- ✔ **Track Record for Winning and Managing Contracts with Positive Client Outcomes/Collaborative Partners:** Present your narrative or create a table showing the previous contracts your business has been awarded (specifically list the agencies or businesses, which are also referred to as your collaborative partners) and the outcomes (list the numbers of individuals served or the number of products sold).

- ✔ **Background of Bidder:** Provide information on your company's background. For example, note when your company was formed. Make sure to provide details to validate the impact or effectiveness of the program, product, or service that you're proposing in this services proposal.

- ✔ **Current Service Levels:** Include the names of your services, programs, and products along with the current levels for their provisions.

Always use a formal tone when writing services proposals. Use the third-person writing tips I cover in the earlier section "Laying the Organizational Capability Foundation." To make an impact on the bidding proposal reviewer, I bold, italicize, and underline key terms in my services proposals.

Here's a sample of a winning response for the experience, reliability, and expertise section of a services proposal:

> *Bidder: New Directions Chamber of Commerce.*
>
> *Mission Statement: To provide members with the highest quality and level of customer service in order to promote their presence, products, and goods to the Ramona Valley region.*
>
> *Areas of Expertise: Thirty years as a formally organized Chamber of Commerce. The combined staff of six full-time individuals has more than 64 years of business and public sector experience.*
>
> *Track Record for Winning and Managing Contracts with Positive Client Outcomes/Collaborative Partners: The New Directions Chamber of Commerce has been bidding on and winning competitive state and federal contract awards since 1985. To date, the Chamber has received and prudently managed more than $6 million in outside revenues, not including membership dues.*
>
> *Background of Bidder: The New Directions Chamber of Commerce was formed when the county's population grew to 75,000 persons. At the time, in 1978, Ramona Valley had a total of 700 small- to mid-size businesses. Fertile land for agribusiness and low cost utilities drew hundreds of more businesses here. In 2000, there were 1,200 businesses of all sizes, including three Fortune 500 corporations. In 2008, this number increased to 2,500 businesses, 39 national franchises, and 12 Fortune 500 corporations. All of the past and new businesses are members of the New Directions Chamber of Commerce. Total revenues from membership dues exceed $1 million annually.*
>
> *Current Service Levels: The Chamber has the following services and membership participation levels: general membership (2,500); business-to-business network (1,800); monthly membership luncheon (400 to 500 is the average attendance); and annual Sister City visit (25 members are selected to attend by a regional panel of trip application reviewers).*

You can also use a table for this information. Figure 13-2 is an example of how a simple table can convey your organization's capability.

New Directions Chamber of Commerce
Contract Bid Awards and Client Outcomes

Bid Awarding Agency/ Collaborative Partners	Amount of Award/Year	Client Outcomes
State Department of Commerce	$100,000/1985	Trained 25 large corporations in economic development action steps — local economy increased by 10% in 12 months.
U.S. Department of Transportation	$500,000/1995	Three-year award to train transportation vendors in federal grant seeking and grant award reporting protocol. Resulted in six vendors winning contract awards of more than $5 million.
Merry Mack Foundation	$250,000/2005	Planned and carried out international exchange where 20 Chamber members traveled to our Sister City in Japan. Trip resulted in $2.5 million in import/export contracts and a reciprocal visit in 2006.
U.S. Agency for International Development Administration	$1,000,000/2007	Created economic development curriculum for 12 third-world countries, and worked with the American University to provide distance learning training in multiple languages. More than 600 microbusiness enterprises participated in the program and generated over $1 billion in new revenues in the first 12 months following training.

Figure 13-2:
A table showing an organization's capability.

Chapter 14

Conveying a Hopeless Situation and a Need for Funds

In This Chapter

▶ Explaining the problem that grant funds will solve

▶ Using graphics to drive your point home

▶ Including the right info in a contract bid's problem statement

So you've been looking for grant and contract monies for weeks — maybe months. You've also been reading lots of grant funding opportunities and subscribing to e-mail alerts on potential grant monies. And when you finished writing the Organizational Capability or Background section of your application, you stopped to take a deep breath. I'm glad you did! Recharge yourself and prepare to proceed at full speed in this chapter.

This chapter is all about the *needs statement* (which is also referred to as the *problem statement*). It tells the grant reviewer that you know what you're talking about. It oozes gloom, doom, drama, and trauma. You must get your point across in the most effective, attention-drawing, memorable way that you can. How do you do that? By writing from your heart (where your emotional center lies) and by telling the story of how bad things really are for your target population.

Gather the facts, read them, and highlight the most compelling or startling statistics, events, life stories, situations, and so forth. Then think about what it would be like if you were reading about yourself, your family, or your close friends. You would feel sad, disheartened, even disconnected from society's mainstream. Keep those feelings fresh and you're ready to write a compelling statement!

Making the Problem Come to Life with the Problem Statement

When you're writing your problem statement, remember this: *Grant writing is like storytelling.* Like all great stories, your problem statement must be compelling, magnetizing, entertaining, and believable. With all that emotion floating around, you'll really be in need of a break, right? Don't worry. I try to inject some humor when discussing the more difficult sections of the grant application narrative. Hopefully the comic relief will lighten your *getting started* stress.

Finding pertinent information

Every good problem statement is like a well-written story. And every well-written story is filled with compelling details that bring the narrative to life in the mind of the reader. So, to write your story, you need to gather all the available data from your organization's own materials. Then you can fill in the gaps with additional research.

Start off by looking for current statistics on your services and programs. Try looking at board of director meeting minutes, copies of annual reports (usually gathered by the program staff and presented to the board in the first quarter of your organization's fiscal year). Also, become the Sherlock Holmes you always wanted to be and search out copies of old grant applications. Whether these applications were funded or not, they still contain critical statistics and other problem statement information.

After you've found all the available statistics, use the Internet to fill in any information gaps. You can search for missing information about your identified need and additional data on your target population.

You conduct an Internet search in hopes of finding the following problem-related information:

- ✔ Similar problem area trends in other communities with characteristics like yours (rural, urban, increases or declines in population)

- ✔ Emerging demographics on the magnitude of the problem (Congressional testimonies, research findings by experts and graduate students, and newly issued press releases from government agencies or government watchdogs)

- ✔ Solutions to the problem (even though you don't go over solutions to the problem in the problem statement section of your proposal)

To find up-to-date and relevant information, I recommend that you run a general search on a major search engine. A general search results in hundreds of local, regional, and national government Web site links. This approach is much easier than trying to find the Internet address for a specific information site. For example, if your organization works with the elderly to help them with home-based health care needs, you can enter the phrase "elderly home-based care statistics" in your favorite Web browser. You're likely to find a lot of relevant information on the Web site of your state's Area Agency on Aging office or on the U.S. Department of Health and Human Services Web site.

When I'm visualizing and writing my problem statements, I like to have stacks of current problem-related information in front of me for review. I look at information provided by the grant application organization, and I study my own Internet research findings. I sort all this information by topic (for example, health care, dementia, home security, trends in preventable injuries, home alone fatalities for the elderly, and more). Then I simply put the topical stacks into chronological order (by year, with the most recent year on top).

The more information you have on your topic, the easier it is to write a winning statement of need. With the right preparation, you aren't grasping for straws or generalizing; instead, you're able to give the grant reader true, hard, grant-getting facts. And by including citations for data sources and names of noteworthy researchers, you show the grant reader that your information is accurate and reputable.

Putting potent writing tips to use

The grant reader expects a good problem statement to answer the following questions:

- ✔ How and when did you identify the problem?

- ✔ Do you have a thorough understanding of the problem at the local, regional, and national levels?

- ✔ Do you cite statistics and research conducted by your organization and others that support the problem statement? Is this information current? (See the earlier section "Finding pertinent information" for more about research.)

- ✔ Are you seeking funds for a problem that can be solved in one year (the length of most grant awards)?

In a foundation or corporate funding request, your problem statement should be one typed, single-spaced page (private sector funders typically request single-spaced formatting). In a government grant or cooperative request, the problem statement can be anywhere from two to five typed, single-spaced or double-spaced pages.

Beyond simply answering the questions in the previous list, you can capture a grant reader's attention by telling her how the monies can make a difference. Grant readers want to see large population impact numbers that show how far you can stretch their grant dollars, thus making a difference for many, not just a few. You don't want to write in depth about the program design until you're in the actual program section, but including general comments on how the funding will be used is okay in the needs section. (See Chapter 15 for more about program design.)

Write each paragraph in your needs section so that it builds on the paragraph before it. It's important to make your ideas connect and flow because each new paragraph is a step toward the final paragraph that asks for funding support to solve the problem. Each new paragraph adds excitement and urgency. If these steps sound like those used to write a bestselling story, you're right on target. You write your winning grant proposal the same way you do a bestseller!

In my problem statement, I love to use words and phrases that carry a lot of weight, such as *abandoned, alone, isolated, disconnected, helpless, victims of prey, unsuspecting, confused, taken for granted, throwaways,* and *disrespected.* These sample words can be used when there are far too many elderly individuals left to fend for themselves. Are you getting the picture of need? This type of writing works well in government or private sector grant narratives.

You can also crank up the empathy and your chances for funding by using extreme adjectives such as *inadequate, outdated, miniscule, underserved,* and *worthless.* (For more hints on using impactive words, flip to Chapter 11.)

Don't hide key words or phrases in ordinary-type text. Elevate your grant writing by using bold type and italics to make a word or phrase stand out. Personally, I like to call attention to important text with bold black or red font. Stimulating the reader by playing with the look of the text often results in a speedy funding decision. Bold adjectives and dire phrases; keep the style changes minimal, yet effective in making your point.

Knowing when you've written enough of the right stuff

Sometimes the hardest part about writing your problem statement is knowing when you're done. After you've written five to ten grant applications, you develop an intuition as to when it's time to wrap up a section and move on to the next one. But in the beginning, it's difficult to decide whether you've written enough to convince a grant reader that you truly have a need that can only be solved with grant funding.

Generally, when you can answer yes to the following questions, you're ready to move to the next section in your grant application:

- ✔ Did you use recent research by others on the issue?

- ✔ Did you present recent findings of your own surveys and constituent feedback?

- ✔ Did you include relevant statistical indicators?

- ✔ Did you give the grant reader enough information to understand the problem? (Assume that he or she has no prior knowledge of the problem.)

- ✔ Did you use descriptive words to give the grant reader a virtual visual introduction to your organization's operating environment? (See Chapter 11 for more on words that work.)

- ✔ Did you stay focused and write only about the organization's need — staying clear of the solution until the next narrative section?

- ✔ Did you use words that have the ability to create compassion and urgency in the grant reader's mind and heart?

You know you've written a convincing and compelling needs statement when you get out your hanky to dab away a few tears after rereading your masterpiece!

If you have a summary of a needs survey or letters from organizations documenting that the demands for your services are greater than your resources to deliver the services, attach these documents to your application. Always reference such attachments in the narrative so grant readers can refer to them and get their full effect while reading the needs statement. These support documents allow a grant reader to verify the actual need for grant funding. (See Chapter 18 for information on how to organize your attachments.)

Beside all the previous advice, I have another general rule that may help you decide when to wrap up your needs section: When you can't think of anything more to write or say to the grant reader, stop! Running out of thoughts means that you're done with this section and that it's time to move on to the next section of the grant application. If you continue to write more than needed, you may repeat information already written or regress (start begging beyond belief for money).

In the following sections, I provide excerpts from an ongoing example. You can tell that the example problem statement is complete because it includes information that touches on each of the following main topics:

> ✔ Background info on the applicant and the problem

> ✔ The population that the applicant serves

> ✔ The environment in which the applicant works

> ✔ The severity of the problem

Laying out details of the applicant and the problem

The funding agency wants to know about the applicant and the background of the problem. Consider the following example excerpt to see how it's done:

> *The Neighborhood Self Help Group is located in South Peoria. It was founded in 2007 by Cecilia Pasternak, a long-time resident and community activist. Cecilia believes that **anyone can reach their goals for a safe and revitalized neighborhood** if they work as teams or partners to make change — one step at a time.*

> *Our agency is located in a target area which presents myriad challenges: **high substance abuse among youth; high suicide rate; poor peer relationships; behavior/discipline problems; low self-esteem; lack of positive role models; dysfunctional home environments; lack of positive leisure activities; economic deprivation; and unsafe school/ neighborhood environments.***

> *In 2007, a focus group was created for community feedback. The focus group process involved 85 community residents who represented the eight zip codes in the targeted area. Over a three-month period, in five meetings, residents identified specific concerns, needs, services, and programs they desired to improve their lives and economic status.*

> *The results of the focus group showed that the major concerns among South Peoria residents are the same challenges that our Group had already pre-identified in the second paragraph of this narrative section. While this is confirming, **it's still alarming!***

Telling the funder about the people being served

The funder wants to know about the populations that the grant applicant serves and how the services are rendered. Here's an example showing how you might convey this information:

> *The neighborhood residents served are predominantly Hispanic (75 percent) and low income (99 percent). Many do not speak English as a first language and must use their children (who have learned English in school) to interpret for them at community meetings, at school, and in grocery stores. The Neighborhood Self Help Group provides food boxes, utility payment cut-off advocacy, transportation to medical appointments, and housing rehabilitation (air conditioning, furnace, and plumbing repairs).*

Describing the environment in which the applicant functions

The funder needs to know about the environment in which the organization operates, such as a neighborhood location. This paragraph should present the number of people served and who they are. It should also address any service limitations. The following excerpt shows how to describe this information:

The Neighborhood Self Help Group is located in South Peoria — an area long abandoned by two-parent working class families and local businesses. The median income for single-parent households (90% of the residents do not have a spouse) is $12,750. The average household has multiple families struggling to meet their monthly "near downtown" rent which averages 70 percent of their household income. Among this population, 10 percent are elderly and reside in low-income qualifying public housing apartments. The entire area is blighted and depressing. Our Group serves 100 percent of the neighborhood's residents (4,350) through one or more monthly "helping" programs.

Relating how dire the problem really is

The funder should see evidence that the applicant has a thorough understanding of the problem, accomplished by documenting the continuing saga of the organization. It's important to pile on the gloom, doom, drama, and trauma in this paragraph because you need to successfully convey the need for grant monies. You must convey that monies are scarce and times are hard! Check out this example:

South Peoria has been long abandoned by residential and commercial developers. The tax base has declined to an all time low due to the deteriorating single and multiple family structures — many were built before 1950. Most days, residents start lining up at our side door as early as 6 a.m.; our neighborhood food pantry and counseling center does not open until 9 a.m. The volunteers are overwhelmed with the myriad needs of those who seek our services. Our limited paid professional staff of three often work 12 hours a day seeing clients even though our offices officially close at 5 p.m. On Saturdays, which was once a day that we were closed, emergency food supplements and diapers are distributed. It's a never ending struggle to keep up with the demands of those who depend on us for their daily survival.

Our Board of Directors is made of members of the neighborhood. It's truly a stakeholder's Board. However, they lack the education and savvy to participate effectively in the Board meetings; most importantly, they have no skills in fundraising including grant seeking and grant writing. Our budget is stretched so tight now that there are absolutely no extra funds to hire a fundraiser or grant writer. We feel like we're at the end of a long and dark road — there is no light at the end of the days that are full of hundreds of work demands.

Integrating Graphics into Your Problem Statement

Reading nothing but sentences can get dull. Luckily, graphics offer visual relief from chunks of text. Charts, tables, and maps make the grant reader linger longer on a page. And the longer someone reflects on your particular problem, the better your chances are for receiving funding.

Here are some suggestions that can help you to avoid overwhelming the grant or cooperative agreement reader:

- ✔ Limit your graphics to one per page in the problem or needs statement section of the grant proposal.
- ✔ Don't overdo it with colors in your graphics.

In this section, it's important to present the problems in a way that doesn't bore the grant reader. Presenting demographic after demographic in narrative format can confuse or tire the reader. Introducing a table, chart, or other type of graphic breaks up the text and creates an easy-to-read pictorial-type insert. I like to use comparison tables and bar graphs to wow my grant readers.

Adding comparison tables and other graphics

Tables and other graphics are a great way to drive home a point about the target population. Plus it gives the reader a break from straight text.

Figure 14-1 shows a graph that's particularly effective because it tells the reader how the risk indicators in the grant applicant's targeted area compare to state-level risk indicators. This is referred to as a comparison table. It shows how your target population area compares to a similar area or to the state's statistics for the same indicators. In my example, county high risk indicators clearly surpass the state's indicators — a plus for validating your critical need for grant funding.

Use more than one type of graphic if you have a lot of demographics on your target population. Try a mixture of bar graphs, pie charts, and tables. Figure 14-2 demonstrates the increased visual impact of an ordinary pie chart when you use variegated color effects. Using multiple graphics allows the reader to see the extent of the problem from a glance — not a read through.

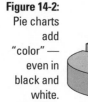

Figure 14-1:
Use a comparison table to compare target populations.

Missouri County HIV/AIDS Indicators (2005–2008) for Targeted Populations – Baseline Data

Indicator	3-Year Total	County Rate	State Rate	Significant Difference
AIDS case rate per 100,000	343	26.8	8.5	Yes
HIV case rate per 100,000	330	25.5	8.2	Yes
AIDS mortality rate per 100,000	97	19.1	2.4	Yes
AIDS mortality rate age-adjusted	97	18.9	2.3	Yes
HIV exposed newborns rate per 1,000 tested	42	22.7	0.9	Yes

Figure 14-2:
Pie charts add "color" — even in black and white.

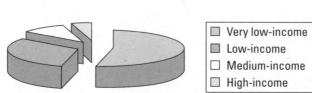

Target Population

- Very low-income
- Low-income
- Medium-income
- High-income

I like pie charts because they take the grant or cooperative agreement reader from linear reading (text lines and rows of table-contained information) to a circular view — a minor visual change aimed to win the reader's approval of the problem or needs statement section of your funding request.

When you create a pie chart, consider including only the most relevant information. Too many categories could make your pie slices indistinguishable. I prefer to limit my pie charts to no more than six slices or divisions of information.

Including relevant maps

When pulling together a needs statement, I especially like to include maps of the proposed service area. Maps tell the grant or cooperative agreement reader where your services will be targeted or how far the problem area spans. Maps are easy to find on the Internet and are almost always in color. You can use a map as a graphic insert, as in Figure 14-3, or as a watermark that would appear in the background of your text. If you use a map as a graphic insert, keep it contained to one-half page or less.

REMEMBER

If you use a map created by someone else, you need to cite the source of the map by entering a footnote at the bottom of the page that your map appears on.

Look for maps that show the service area related to your problem or need. For instance, if the service area is statewide, use a state map; if the service area is regional, use a regional map.

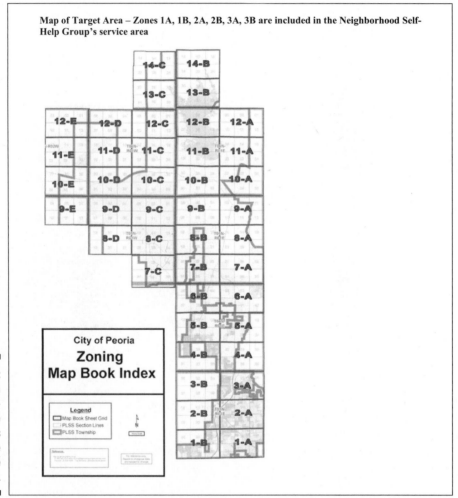

Figure 14-3:
A manage-able size introduces your service area to the funder.

Making visualization work

The previous sections point out the types of graphics you might use in your problem statement, but this section contains some tips on how to successfully use those graphics. Consider the following:

✔ Reserve tables for large amounts of information.

✔ Use bar and pie charts when you want to communicate age ranges by groups, income by groups, and numerical breakdowns of target population indicators.

✔ When you use statistics, always cite the source. You can insert a credit line directly below each graphic, or you can insert footnotes. In some funding documents in which the formatting guidelines bar the use of footnotes, you can create endnotes or a reference page.

Failing to cite the sources of statistics can cause your request to lose peer review points or to be denied funding support.

I was schooled in using the American Psychological Association (APA) reference citation format. This style requires you to insert a superscript number at the end of the citation and then type the source in the document's footer. If the funding agency doesn't have specific instructions on reference citations, you can find all sorts of examples of APA format and others in writing stylebooks, online, or at the library.

✔ When the funder limits the number of pages you have to develop your narrative, you must improvise when it comes to sneaking in much-needed graphics. Try wrapping text around a graphic or typing text over a watermark graphic.

✔ Stay away from using clip art in your needs statement unless that's all you have. Clip art doesn't create an authentic picture of any dire situation, so it will likely make little impact on reviewers. However, sometimes, I use clip art of a broken link to emphasize services gaps or organizational weaknesses.

Conveying Your Knowledge of the Need for RFP Service Delivery Points

When you respond to an RFP (Request For Proposal), you must demonstrate in-depth knowledge of the need for contracted services. And remember that when it comes to writing a problem or needs statement, RFPs differ from grant or cooperative agreement funding proposals.

Contract bid-letting agencies have already researched the problem or need. They're releasing an RFP to address the problem, and in the RFP guidelines, they include research information on the problem or need. These agencies then go on to tell the bidder (also called the *offeror*) which needs are agency priorities and what to specifically address in the program design or scope of services section (jump to Chapter 15 for more information). So, essentially, much of the background work is already done for you.

Be on the lookout for any type of language in the RFP document that asks for "understanding of the need or problem." Here's an example:

> *The City of Peoria has collected vast information on its southern most neighborhoods. However, all bidders are expected to provide their own **detailed knowledge of the demographics of this RFP target area in order to further support the need for neighborhood capacity building — the focus of this RFP.***

To craft a winning reply to this type of request, do the following:

- ✔ Tell the reader what your company does (for example, maybe you plan to propose board of director and volunteer training in the area of capacity building for all nonprofits located in or serving South Peoria residents).

- ✔ Give the reader demographics on your proposed service population.

- ✔ Boldface and italicize words that relate to large quantities and that draw attention to dire circumstances.

- ✔ Use headings and subheadings that reflect the RFP guidelines' instructions for areas to respond to when writing the Understanding of the Needs subsection in your scope of services narrative.

The following is an example of how to write an Understanding of the Needs response in the RFP's scope of services section. To properly format this response, the section title should be centered, and each subsection should be underlined and placed flush left.

Scope of Services To Be Provided

Understanding of the Need

The targeted region of the RFP, South Peoria, is well known to the bidder. For the past 20 years, our training corporation has been training underrepresented residents to become community advocates. Prior to our previously delivered contracted services under the Neighborhood Service Center funding program, there were no Neighborhood Block Clubs or Crime Watches. In addition, the housing abandonment rate was 80 percent. With training and ongoing resources through our dozen or more service delivery contracts, those demographics have changed: 12 Neighborhood Block Clubs were formed and are now meeting regularly and are highly functional; 200 residents now volunteer for seven nights weekly of neighborhood crime watching; and there has been a reduction in the housing abandonment rate from 80 percent to 40 percent. If any one bidder has an understanding of the need for continuing capacity building services in South Peoria, it's us, the Corporation for Housing Support and Neighborhood Revitalization.

Chapter 15

Laying Out the Plan of Action: Program Design and Accountability

*W*ith this chapter, you're revving up for the big event — *the program design.* The grant writing process can make you feel like you're climbing a mountain. But by this point in the game, you've reached the top and you're ready for the high adrenaline, high oxygen level type of thinking and writing. You're ready to write about your vision — about the positive changes you could bring about if only you had some money!

The program design section is the one where you get to tell the funding or bid-letting agency what you're going to do when you're awarded the grant or contract for the proposed services or programs. Your key to success is being optimistic when writing this section. The following are the main ingredients:

1. **A purpose statement:** A one-sentence, direct explanation of why you're seeking funds.

2. **Goals:** Where your program or constituency aims to be when the grant funds are used up.

3. **Outcome objectives:** Measurable benchmarks or specific steps that lead up to the accomplishment of your goals.

4. **An implementation plan with timelines:** A plan listing the implementation tasks that are required to meet and exceed your measurable objectives and when they'll be implemented.

5. **A Logic Model:** Lays out (using table formatting) a graphic road map with inputs, strategies, outputs, and outcomes.

6. **Evaluation:** Shows how you will track the progress of the project's objectives, what data collection tools you'll use to gather information about the project, and who will conduct the evaluation. This section screams accountability!

   In some grant applications, evaluation plans may be asked for separately, in a section following the program design or even in an attachment. However, many government funders, along with foundation and corporate grantmakers, are realizing the importance of having you, the grant applicant, integrate your evaluation plan into the program design.

The entire program design must give the grant reviewer a detailed explanation of the *big picture*. In other words, you must lay out each section as if you were placing the pieces into a large puzzle. The large puzzle is your program design, and the pieces are each of the previously listed elements.

Stating What You Want: Specifying Your Purpose

As the first part of your program design narrative, the *purpose statement* tells the grant reader why you're asking for grant monies. You have two types of purpose statements to choose from: *direct* and *indirect*.

A *direct purpose statement* includes the amount of the requested grant award. Remember that even when you mention a dollar amount, the purpose statement should not exceed one sentence. Get to the point and tell the grant reader the purpose of the grant request and the amount of funds needed. Use the following example as a guide for writing your own direct purpose statement.

> *The Mark Welby Corporation is seeking a contractual arrangement with Ashton County in the award amount of $350,000 to deliver home-based home health care services to 4,000 elderly residents who meet the county's Area Agency on Aging's service eligibility requirements.*

An *indirect purpose statement* simply tells the reader the purpose of the grant request — a program or project in need of funding. The example that follows shows you how an indirect purpose statement should sound.

The purpose of this request is to seek grant funding to establish an endow-ment fund for our nonprofit organization — one that perpetuates sustain-ability for the myriad programs and services provided to the residents of Arlington, Virginia.

I prefer to use a direct purpose statement in foundation and corporate funding requests because it more efficiently gets to the point for the reader who will make the final decisions on whether to fund you and on the amount of funding you will receive. However, I use the indirect purpose statement for govern-ment grant proposals and cooperative agreements because government grant peer reviewers don't make those same final decisions. An agency staff person with authority over the grantmaking initiative is in charge of that. Therefore, no actual amount of monies requested should appear in the purpose state-ment of government funding requests.

Crafting Goals and Objectives

The next ingredients in your program design narrative are goals and objec-tives. Your program's goals address the big-picture success of your program, and the objectives are the ways you plan to reach those goals. Always pro-vide objectives for each goal and each year for which you're requesting funds for an activity. The objectives are benchmarks of what you want to happen during the funding time frame. The benchmarks must be measurable. Funding agencies view measurable steps as signs of accountability — showing how their money will make an impact on the problem.

I don't have a magic number for goals and objectives. However, I can't stress enough that your organization's goals are based on the vision of where you want the program or target population to be when the grant or contract period is over.

When I'm writing a government grant request, I develop my goals using the funder's goals for the funding initiative. I then create measurable objectives to track all the funding initiative's intended outcomes. Everything you need to cue you on how many goals and how many objectives to write is right there in the grant application guidelines. However, when I'm writing a proposal to a foundation or corporation, I have nothing to cue me on what the funder wants to see or fund in terms of funder goals and objectives. In those cases, I keep it light and usually write a minimum of three goals and a maximum of six. And each goal always has one to three measurable outcome objectives.

If the funding decision maker can't look at your goals and objectives and figure out from them what your entire program is about, you've failed to write clearly stated goals.

If you're new to grant or contract bid writing, you may sometimes mistake goals for objectives, or vice versa. To keep these two terms straight, think of *goal* first and remember that it is, according to *Webster's New World College Dictionary,* the "end that one strives to attain." The key word to keep in mind is *end.* A goal is where you are when you're done. Grant application and contract bid document narratives must have goals to show the funder or bid-letting agency that you have a vision for solving the problem.

Okay, so what about an *objective?* An objective is simply a major milestone or checkpoint on your route to reaching a goal. It's a place where you can say (and report to a funder, if necessary), "We've come this far, and we have this far remaining before we reach the goal." Objectives have to be attainable, and they must serve to keep goals realistic.

Writing great goals

When you're in the process of writing your goals, be sure to write clear, concise, one-sentence statements. The goals can apply to where you picture your organization or your target population at the end of the grant period. Goals should be action-oriented and full of verbs (see Chapter 11 for more on choosing impactful words). But don't include any measurements or timelines in the goal statements; those items are saved for your objectives, which I cover later in this chapter.

To be sure you've written effective and well-constructed goal statements, ask yourself the following questions:

- ✔ Did I use one sentence?
- ✔ Is the sentence clear and concise?
- ✔ Does the grant reader know who the target population is?
- ✔ Did I deliberately *not* include measurements and timelines?

The following are examples of some effective goal statements. These statements, used successfully in a Department of Homeland Security grant application, should give you an idea of how to express your own goals:

> *Goal 1: The Mesa Fire Department will design a new Fire Safety Program to meet the public education needs of Latino families with preschool-age children.*

> *Goal 2: The Mesa Fire Department will promote and publicize the "Familias Viajando A Seguridad" Program in the local media and will ask for corporate sponsorships in order to assure that fire safety public education is both long-term and self-sustaining in the community.*

Goal 3: The Mesa Fire Department will continue to target children who are six years and younger — a United States Fire Administration high-risk group — in its public education campaign efforts.

Goal 4: The "Familias Viajando A Seguridad" Program will not only benefit the entire City of Mesa but also will be made available to over three dozen direct aid and mutual aid fire departments in Maricopa County, Arizona.

Goal 5: The "Familias Viajando A Seguridad" Program will signal to the Latino community that injuries to children are preventable and that children are our most important human assets by saturating targeted families with over a dozen take-home injury prevention reminders and installation-ready smoke detectors.

Goal 6: Low-income Latino families will benefit from the four child safety seat distributions planned by the Mesa Fire Department.

Providing out of this world objectives

Successful grant writing requires you to understand the three types of objectives — *process objectives, outcome objectives,* and *impact objectives* — and know when to use them. Putting them to good use can rack up peer review or procurement agency points (see Chapters 9 and 10 for more on the review process). They can also help you win big bucks for your program. *Note:* Objectives can also be referred to as *milestones* or *benchmarks*.

Always provide objectives for each goal and each year for which you're requesting funds for an activity.

Objectives can be measured at a certain point in time, whether you're tracking grade point average increases in youth or the number of parents who participate in a parent-training program. Taking a look at your progress is called *data collection and analysis.* Determining how much progress you've made is called *evaluating.* Later in this chapter, I tell you about the tasks involved in the evaluation process.

Some program designs have more than one objective for each goal. If this is the case with your design, make sure you number and alphabetize the objectives (for example, 1a, 1b, 1c, and so on) to eliminate confusion for the reviewer.

Creating SMART outcome objectives

How do you recognize an *outcome objective?* It's an objective that shows that the project has accomplished the activities it planned to achieve. Always create outcome objectives for your programs or projects. They're the most common type of objectives that funders ask for in their grant application guidelines.

When writing your own outcome objectives, use phrases such as *to increase* or *to decrease*. These phrases imply some sort of measurable change. For example, you can write about an increase of 50 percent in the number of organizations receiving project services by the end of Year 1.

The easiest way to write outcome objectives is to think "SMART." SMART is a quick and easy acronym to keep you on track. Here's what the acronym stands for: specific, measurable, attainable, realistic, and time bound. You can use the following SMART formula for writing outstanding outcome objectives:

- ✔ **S:** Is the objective specific, rather than abstract?

- ✔ **M:** Is the objective measurable? Can it be tracked easily with valid measurement tools, such as surveys, pre- and post-needs assessments, and more?

- ✔ **A:** Is the objective attainable? Can my organization really pull off the objective?

- ✔ **R:** Is the objective realistic? Can the measurement actually be attained for the target population in the given time frame?

- ✔ **T:** Is the objective time bound? Can my organization accomplish all the required tasks to achieve the objective in the given time frame?

The following SMART outcome objectives were written for the six goals in the Mesa Fire Department example earlier in this chapter:

1. By the end of Year 1, increase child injury prevention knowledge among Latinos by 25 percent or more.

2. By the end of Year 1, expand school-based fire safety public education activities by 25 percent or more.

3. By the end of Year 1, increase the "Familias Viajando A Seguridad" Program sites by 100 percent in the second six months of the FEMA funding year.

4. By the end of Year 1, introduce the bilingual injury prevention curriculum to at least 40 percent or more of Maricopa County's three-dozen plus communities.

5. By the end of Year 1, reduce all unintentional injuries among preschool-age Latino children in Mesa by 25 percent or more.

6. By the end of Year 1, reduce unintentional injuries related to improper or no seat belt usage among preschool-age Latino children by 50 percent or more.

Producing process objectives

Process objectives are the activities needed to reach your goals and meet or exceed your measurable outcome (or SMART) objectives. The best way to present your process objectives is in a table format. Make sure to follow the funder's or bid-letting agency's guidelines when setting up your timeline segments. I like to use quarters; however, some funders ask for monthly timelines for all activities.

For effective process objectives, write about the actual, chronological activities that need to occur from the time you receive grant or contract funding until the monies have been spent. List the process objectives, or main activities, in a timeline chart (which I explain in the later section "Preparing a Timeline Chart That Spans the Grant Funding Period"). Figure 15-1 (shown later in the chapter) is an example of how I would write the process objectives for the Mesa Fire Department example that I introduce earlier in the chapter.

Don't write in measurable terms when discussing your process objectives. For example, don't use *increase* or *decrease*. These terms are reserved for SMART objectives. Instead, write in quantifiable terms, such as "40 teachers will be trained to help firefighters deliver seat belt safety curriculum" or "14 new classes will be introduced to the seat belt safety curriculum in the first quarter."

Identifying impact objectives

Impact objectives demonstrate the achievement of the goal of the project or program. They show the reader how you will determine that there has been an impact or change in the participants' knowledge. For example, you can write about changes in the target population's values or beliefs.

If you come across a grant application in which the funding agency asks you to write about *benefits to participants,* respond by using impact objectives. Benefits to participants are really presumptions of how your participants will change because of the grant-funded program's intervention.

Impact objectives are easy to identify. They include monumental changes in the way your target population behaves. This behavior change can include anything from changes in attitude to changes in value or judgment. Unlike process objectives, there are no common words to cue your writing. The funder is looking for signs of significant change — change brought on by the interventions that the funder made possible.

Here are some examples of effective impact objectives:

Impact Objective 1: *Brings public attention to the number of unintentional injuries among the high-risk, limited English-speaking target group: young Latino children.*

Impact Objective 2: *Creates awareness among parents, caregivers, and extended Latino families of the causes of fires and other unintentional injuries and shows how to prevent them.*

Impact Objective 3: *Introduces a fire safety public education program to a segment of the county that has never been included in any municipality's fire prevention campaigns.*

Impact Objective 4: *Brings countywide attention to the need for fire prevention and unintentional injury prevention weaknesses and gaps and encourages contribution of financial support to the Mesa Fire Department in order to sustain the "Familias Viajando A Seguridad" Program after FEMA Federal Fire Act grant funds are expended.*

Preparing a Timeline Chart That Spans the Grant Funding Period

A *timeline* tells the grant reader when activities (also referred to as process objectives) will begin and end during the grant's funding period (which is usually a 12-month period). When you develop a project timeline, keep in mind that the grant reader wants to see answers to the following questions:

✔ What are the key tasks or activities that will be carried out to implement the program successfully?

✔ Did the grant applicant include all tasks, from the day funding is announced or awarded to the last day of the project's funding time frame?

✔ Can each task realistically begin and end in the proposed time frame?

✔ Are evaluation activities included in the timeline chart?

✔ Who is responsible for seeing that each activity is implemented and completed?

You can use your word-processing software to create a simple timeline table. Just be sure not to overdo it with color; stick with one or two shading selections (gray or a light color so the reader can still read the text in the table's cells). Because there are no absolutes on the number of disruptions and malfunctions in implementing a grant-funded program, I prefer to set up my activity start and stop dates in quarterly increments. However, if you have total control over the activities, you can use monthly increments to show when they start and stop or begin and end.

See Figure 15-1 for an example of an activity timeline. It clearly shows what the program plans to accomplish, when it plans to accomplish it, and who is responsible for seeing the activities (process objectives) through the completion phase.

For programs that request funding for multiple years, extra timelines need to be included in the grant application or contract bid showing each year's activities and the quarterly time frames for each activity.

Implementation Activities (also called Process Objectives)	Year 1				Personnel/Agency Responsible
	1st Qtr.	2nd Qtr.	3rd Qtr.	4th Qtr.	
Request City Council approval via a resolution to accept grant award monies.	⚫				Fire Department Administrator
Hire seat belt education specialist to design Fire Safety Program for targeted children and their families.	⚫				Fire Department Administrator
Design public media campaign to promote program.	⚫				Fire Department Public Information Officer
Meet with targeted schools and develop schedule for seat belt safety education.	⚫				Fire Safety Education Coordinator
Implement weekly curricula in targeted schools and classrooms throughout the City of Mesa.		⚫	⚫	⚫	Fire Safety Education Staff
Implement monitoring and evaluation methodologies to test knowledge retention and family applied learning actions for seat belt safety.		⚫	⚫	⚫	Fire Safety Education Staff Regional Seat Belt Safety Advisory Council
Modify or refine initial curriculum to correct message delivery deficiencies.		⚫	⚫		Fire Safety Education Staff
Identify other Maricopa County communities with high seat belt safety-related fatalities for elementary school-age children and meet with Fire Chiefs to plan and implement school-based seat belt safety education.			⚫		Fire Department Administrator and Fire Safety Education Staff
Continue to monitor education impact findings, unintentional injury reduction rates, and other indicators to demonstrate program success to stakeholders.			⚫	⚫	Fire Safety Education Staff Regional Seat Belt Safety Advisory Council
Prepare formal monitoring findings and evaluation reports for stakeholders (including funding agency)			⚫	⚫	Fire Department Administrator
Issue end of program press releases.				⚫	Public Information Officer
Prepare final closeout reports for funding agency.				⚫	Fire Department Administrator and City Grants Manager

Figure 15-1:
An example of a timeline of activities.

Building a Program Design Road Map with the Logic Model

The Logic Model is a graphic blueprint of the key elements of a proposed program. The Logic Model looks at inputs, activities, outputs, outcomes, and impacts.

If you live and work in the world of grants, it's difficult to avoid the Logic Model. It seems like just about every type of funder wants you to include a Logic Model in the program design or action plan section of your grant application or contract bid narrative.

Here's my tutorial on what the columns of your Logic Model graphic should contain:

- ✔ **Inputs:** These are the human, financial, and physical resources dedicated to your grant-funded program. These resources include money, staff and staff time, volunteers and volunteer time, facilities, equipment, supplies, and community partners. (See Chapter 16 for information on personnel and organization resources.)

- ✔ **Strategies:** These are what your program uses to organize the inputs. Using effective strategies helps the program to fulfill its mission.

- ✔ **Outputs:** These are the direct results of your program's implementation activities. They're actually written as indicators of productivity. Outputs usually start with the phrase "number of" and reflect how you will quantitatively track your program activities. You can pull output language from your objectives narrative (found earlier in your program design) and from your evaluation narrative as well.

- ✔ **Outcomes:** These are the benchmarks or measurements for your target population during and after program activities. For the outcomes, you can simply reuse your SMART objectives (see the earlier section "Creating SMART outcome objectives"). Some funders want to see short-term outcomes (3 to 6 month SMART objective measurements) and others want to see intermediate outcomes (6 to 12 month SMART objective measurements).

- ✔ **Long-Term Impact:** Funders want to know what long-term outcomes or impact (changes in systems and processes after the funding is expended) you anticipate for your target population.

Figure 15-2 shows the basic structure for the Logic Model. It's only one example of how funders might instruct you to prepare your Logic Model form.

Figure 15-2:
The Logic
Model
depicts
your orga-
nization's
planned
work and
intended
results for
a given
project.

INPUTS	STRATEGIES	OUTPUTS	LONG-TERM OUTCOMES	LONG-TERM IMPACT
Resources dedicated to or consumed by the program	What the program uses to organize the inputs to fulfill its mission	The direct quantitative product of program activities	Benchmarks for participants during and after program activities	Changes in systems and processes after the funding is expended
For example: -Money -Staff and staff time -Volunteers and volunteer time -Facilities -Equipment and supplies -Transportation -Partner agency cash or in-kind committments	For example: -Provide… -Educate… -Counsel… -Create… -Conduct…	For example: -Number of classes taught -Number of sessions conducted -Number of educational materials distributed -Number of hours of service delivered -Number of participants served	For example: -New knowledge -Increased skills -Changed attitudes or values -Modified behavior -Improved condition -Altered status	For example: -New approaches -New services -Stronger partnership working agreements

If you have a multiple-year program, you need to have multiple-year Logic Models. Each year's model should show a set of inputs, activities, outputs, outcomes, and impacts on its own subset of typed pages.

The Logic Model isn't a process you can pick up overnight. But reviewing the online materials at the W. K. Kellogg Web site (www.wkkf.org) can help with the learning curve. I suggest that you print out the site's Logic Model Development Guide and use it as a desktop reference.

Integrating the Evaluation into the Program Design

The most important part of grant writing is the initial step of deciding what grants to pursue. But evaluating your project after it has been funded is a close second. The *evaluation plan* in the program design section of the grant narrative explains to the potential funder how you plan to evaluate the success of your project.

The evaluation plan includes

✔ A review of your program's objectives and how you'll know whether they've been met

✔ The type of information you plan to collect to use in the evaluation

✔ How often the information will be collected

> ✔ Who will collect the information
>
> ✔ Who will analyze the information and report the results

To introduce you to the evaluation process, I explain evaluation terms and the types of evaluations your organization can perform in the following sections. I also show you how to put together an evaluation plan for your program design section and how to write a dissemination plan.

The W. K. Kellogg Foundation has published a handbook describing how to actually go about conducting an evaluation. You can view or download the handbook on the Foundation's Web site (www.wkkf.org).

Getting a grip on evaluation terms

Before you can write an evaluation plan, you need to have a basic understanding of the terms that are commonly used. So, the terms in this section are ones that you should be familiar with and should use when writing your evaluation plan for the program design.

Data is the information about your project that's gathered using measurement tools. You collect data in order to find out whether you're achieving the objectives that you describe in the project design section of your grant narrative.

Data analysis occurs when you examine the information that you collect with the measurement tools. What you're looking for is whether the data produces information that's relevant to determining the progress of your project. If it isn't, you need to go back and design new measurement tools.

Think about where the problem may lie: Maybe your survey didn't ask the right questions, or perhaps it was administered in a setting that wasn't conducive to getting true responses. (Did your teacher ever hand out a questionnaire at the end of the year to see how you liked his class — and then walk up and down the aisles while you filled it out to see what you wrote? *That's* a setting not conducive to getting a true response.) To ensure that you get true responses, leave the room after you distribute measurement tools to participants. And don't mess with the findings on your project. You're hoping to discover the truth, which is what will help you redesign the objectives and develop new ways to conduct a more effective program.

Evaluation standards are acceptable ways to measure various components of your project. The American National Standards Institute approved the following four nationally used standards in 1994. The entire evaluation process should incorporate these standards if the findings are to be accepted as valid by the funders and others in your field.

✔ **Accuracy standards** are how you plan to show that your evaluation will reveal and convey technically adequate or sufficient information about your project.

✔ **Feasibility standards** are how you plan to ensure that your evaluation procedures will be realistic, prudent, diplomatic, and frugal.

✔ **Propriety standards** are how you plan to show that your evaluation will be conducted legally, ethically, and with due regard for the welfare of those involved in the evaluation as well as those affected by its results.

✔ **Utility standards** are how you plan to evaluate the information needs of the project's participants or end-users.

The **evaluator** or **evaluation team** is the individual or group of persons you select to determine whether your project succeeded or failed in meeting its goals.

You shouldn't evaluate your own project. It's okay for you to be a part of the evaluation team if you decide to conduct an internal evaluation (see the later section "Choosing to conduct an internal evaluation"). However, refrain from coaching or coercing other team members (your co-workers, board members, volunteers, community members, or project participants). Everyone on the evaluation team needs to be able to talk openly about his or her perceptions of the data findings. Focus on being impartial.

Even if your project has failed miserably (for example, your objectives said that 90 percent of the participants would be placed in gainful employment but only 10 percent were successfully placed), you and your stakeholders, including the funders, need to know what went wrong and how the outcome could be reversed. Sometimes in this *failed* scenario, your funding source will actually give you a second grant to fix the problem, which equates to another chance to succeed. But you'll only get the second chance if your evaluation team is objective and accurate.

A **formative evaluation** occurs when you sit down with the project's stake-holders (community members, participants, and staff) and develop a list of questions that the funders may ask about your project when determining whether its monies were well placed and used. Looking at several aspects of the project design — goals, objectives, and activities — stakeholders generate questions about how the project can become more effective or efficient. The formative process continues from the time you receive grant funding to the completion of the grant time frame. In light of this ongoing process, you should set a frequency for when the data will be collected to answer the questions you have posed.

Every funder has its own internal evaluation process for grant-funded programs. So no templates are available to cue you on how a funder will evaluate your project. Of course, all types of funders look at how your organization progressed on reaching all the outcome objectives. Foundation and corporate funders specifically look at the impact objectives and look for proof that an impact occurred. From their viewpoints, benefits to participants take precedence over nitpicking the monetary expenditures. Government funders, on the other hand, look at how well you achieved your outcome objectives, and they nitpick over monetary expenditures — after all, you did implement your program or project with public monies!

Some funders give you due dates for evaluation and financial reports. Others leave the reporting frequency up to the grant applicant or grantee. If this is the case, I recommend, at a minimum, quarterly reporting to all your funders. When you report quarterly, you find flaws or weaknesses in your program's implementation strategies quickly and have time to correct them — well within the funding period.

Always have progress reports or *raw data* (information collected but not compiled into summary form or typed in a formal report) on hand for funder queries or visits.

If you can't make improvements to your project, a formative evaluation may not be the right approach to measure the success of your project; instead, focus on using a *summative evaluation* (see the definition to this term later in the section).

An **internal evaluation** occurs when you decide not to hire an outsider to conduct your evaluation and instead choose to gather stakeholders to assess the effectiveness of your program (see the later section "Choosing to conduct an internal evaluation").

Measurement tools, also known as **evaluation tools,** are what you use to collect the data or information that shows whether your project has met its objectives. Measurement tools can include surveys, pre- and post-questionnaires or tests, and oral interviews.

Objectives are measurable, progressive steps taken to achieve a project's goals. (I cover goals and objectives earlier in this chapter.)

Qualitative describes the approach you take when you want to understand the impact of your project on the target population (the end recipients of the grant-funded services or activities). A qualitative approach means that you develop questions and collect data to measure the success of a project or program that you implemented with grant funds. Your findings must focus on looking closely at your program from an operational standpoint and determining its overall impact on the target population.

Quantitative describes the approach you take to measure your project's effects using a *design* or *experimental group* (the target population receiving the grant-funded interventions or the individuals you're testing the intervention on) and a *comparison* or *control group* (a second group of participants not receiving intervention, but who have similar needs and share common demographics with your target population).

For example, say that you receive a grant award to implement a teen pregnancy prevention program. The teens in your program (the design or experimental group) are placed in a classroom where they're given pregnancy prevention strategies, from tactics to combat peer pressure to taking home an interactive doll in order to experience the responsibilities of teen parenting. To determine whether your intervention is making an impact, you also monitor the attitudes and behaviors of a second group of teens (the comparison or control group). The second group gets no pregnancy prevention curriculum, receives no take-home dolls, and isn't isolated from their peers — they're in the general school setting. Your quantitative evaluation would track outcome objectives for both groups to show that the intervention you proposed and won a grant award for is working.

I like to combine both qualitative and quantitative approaches in order to examine data from a multidimensional viewpoint.

The **stakeholders** in your project are those individuals or entities that stand to lose something if your project falls short of its objectives and stand to gain if the project achieves its proposed objectives.

The **summative evaluation** (also called an **outcome evaluation**) occurs near or at the end of the period for which you were funded. This type of evaluation should answer the following questions (in a narrative format):

- ✔ What did you accomplish?
- ✔ How many participants were impacted and in what ways?
- ✔ What overall difference did your project make?
- ✔ Is this project worth funding again?

A **third-party evaluator** is an individual or company outside your program that designs and conducts your project's evaluation. (See "Selecting an outside evaluator" later in this chapter for more information.) Remember to include an expense line in your project's budget to compensate the third-party evaluator for its services. The standard amount to set aside for evaluation is 15 percent of your total project budget. (See Chapter 17 for more about budgets.)

Choosing to conduct an internal evaluation

When you plan to conduct an *internal evaluation* — meaning that you aren't hiring an outsider to assist with or conduct the evaluation of your project — the best option is to propose a *stakeholder's evaluation* in the evaluation plan of your program design. In a stakeholder's evaluation, you don't need to select the evaluators until you know your project is funded. Once funded, you can identify select stakeholders from your target population, board of directors, and community partners to sit on the stakeholders' evaluation team.

The easiest way to identify your project's stakeholders is to ask yourself the following question: Who has a vested interest in our project and will be impacted by the project's success? The outcome of the project definitely matters to your board of directors, if you have one, as well as to the staff assigned to work on the project. However, it matters most to the project's target population, which is why you should seriously consider inviting some of them onto the evaluation team.

A clue as to when you may need to propose a stakeholder's evaluation can be found in the grant application's budget instructions. Here's what I mean: If the budget instructions for the grant or cooperative agreement don't include a specific line item for evaluation or contracted services, and if your program implementation costs will require all the available grant funding (maximum project award range), I suggest that you consider a stakeholder's evaluation. It's less costly and keeps the entire evaluation process local and manageable.

For example, suppose your organization proposes to implement a recycling program in your community. Each and every citizen who attends your public meeting and provides his or her input on the need for a recycling program is a candidate for the evaluation team. The owner of a local business who counts on reducing her trash pickups by recycling much of her waste may be a good candidate. In fact, anyone who works for the project is a potential candidate. Be creative and bring together people who have different perspectives. I always try to include a younger person, such as a college student, on my evaluation teams. It doesn't matter how many people you have on your stakeholder's evaluation team as long as each side of the project is well represented.

Do you have board members who have wanted to work in a more hands-on way with your organization? Placing them on the evaluation team is an ideal way to divert their energy from (possibly) micromanaging your executive director or staff. They can really help shape the outcome of your grant-funded program — a program that could very well be the most important part of your organization.

When it comes to an internal evaluation team, you're not looking for group-think. You want independent-minded people who can bring objective ideas to the table, giving you a credible evaluation process for your funded project.

Selecting an outside evaluator

If you decide to bring in an outsider to conduct your evaluation, that person is referred to as a *third-party evaluator* in the grant narrative. To find a qualified evaluator, look in your community first and ask other organizations that provide programs similar to yours which evaluator they've used. Their evaluator may have been a university research department, a college faculty member, or a retired government employee with expertise in the project area. However, be aware that you may have to look outside your home area for an evaluator.

A clue to when you may need an outside evaluation can be found in the grant application's budget instructions. If the budget instructions discuss evaluation costs and ask you to provide information on third-party evaluators, I recommend you plan to bring in an outside evaluator. Even though outside evaluators are costly (some need up to 15 percent of your total project budget to conduct the evaluation), the right outside evaluator can bring credibility and visibility to your project, which in turn attracts continued funding.

What to look for in an external evaluator

You must choose an individual or organization that has experience in developing evaluation plans, creating monitoring guidelines that track the progress of a project's objectives, and conducting both simple and complex evaluations in the project's focus area.

What to ask a prospective evaluator

During your telephone conversation or meeting with the prospective evaluator, work through a list of prepared questions and write down the evaluator's answers. You may have to decide from among several possible evaluators, and having the answers on paper will help you review and make your decision.

Start off with the following questions:

- ✔ What methodology will you use to understand the day-to-day operations of my project?
- ✔ How much time will the work take, and what is the cost?
- ✔ How many on-site days can you provide in order to meet with project personnel and talk to representatives from the target population?

> ✔ Are you willing to give me a written description of your services and the projected cost of service if my organization can't afford your services for the duration of the project?
>
> ✔ Are you willing to meet with my board of directors to provide progress reports on the evaluation?
>
> ✔ At what points will you give me written evaluation reports?

Brainstorm with your staff to come up with even more questions. Selecting an evaluator is an important part of your project, and falling short in writing this part of the narrative can result in being denied funding.

After you select an evaluator, see whether that organization or person can help you write the evaluation plan for the grant narrative. Of course, you will have to pay a fee for the evaluator's time, but the money is well spent if you're going after a multi-million-dollar, multiyear grant with heavy competition. (If fewer than ten grants will be awarded nationwide in a major grant competition, that's what I call *heavy*.) After all, a funder wants to be assured that the evaluator will bring to light information that will significantly contribute to a national database for programs funded under its particular grant competition.

The evaluation process and resulting information must be approached from a scientific standpoint. So, find a qualified evaluator and get a check cut for the pregrant submission expertise provided. Make sure you write this same evaluator into your budget to bring that person or group back for the full evaluation process when you have a funding award. (See Chapter 17 for more on how to incorporate the cost for postgrant award evaluation into your project budget.)

Writing an outstanding evaluation plan

After you decide whether to conduct an internal stakeholder or external third-party evaluation, the next step is to start writing or incorporating your evaluation plan into the program design section of the grant application narrative. The evaluation narrative goes at the end of the program design narrative. The funder's formatting guidelines usually determine the length of each narrative section in the grant proposal. The program design is usually the largest section, so write succinctly but include sufficient details for the funder to see you have a comprehensive evaluation plan.

Your evaluation plan narrative must always be written to meet and exceed the funding agency's guidelines. A comprehensive evaluation plan includes narrative on how the program will be evaluated (qualitatively, quantitatively, or both). It also tells the funder what type of data will be collected; who will be collecting, analyzing, and interpreting the data; and the frequency for the data collection process. Don't forget to add detail about each target population subgroup that will be included in the evaluation process and tell how information or data will be collected from them (by way of survey, questionnaire, visual observation, and more).

Most importantly, make sure that all data to be collected is connected to determining the progress of your measurable outcome objectives, which are presented earlier in the project design section. And remember that your evaluation plan must be specific to your program goals and objectives.

Examples of evaluation plans abound on the Internet. For starters, visit the Web site for the W. K. Kellogg Foundation: www.wkkf.org.

The evaluation plan also needs to include information about how the grant applicant will share its evaluation findings with other organizations interested in replicating a successful model program. This sharing process is called *dissemination.* The dissemination plan, which is usually a paragraph or two, is written at the end of the evaluation plan.

Worried about giving away too many secrets? Well, don't be. When you receive a grant award, the funders expect you to share your findings with other organizations and associations. With government grants, everything you do — information and program activities — is subject to public access. Foundation and corporate funders want to maximize their investments — this means you're obligated to disseminate your evaluation findings. Practically all funders ask for your dissemination plans in their grant application guidelines.

When you write your dissemination narrative, include information on what will be shared and how it will be shared. List conferences, forums, Web-site postings, and printed documents mailed out (and to whom they'll be mailed).

When you're writing your grant applications or contract bid documents, you should always, *always* follow the guidelines provided for preparing your narrative sections. In foundation funding requests, the dissemination plan can be short and to the point, like my preceding example. However, in government funding requests, you may be instructed to write multiple pages on the dissemination process. Carefully reading and following the funding agency's guidelines can be the difference between a funded project and a rejected one.

Chapter 16

Presenting Your Staff and Resources

*A*fter you've written a compelling needs statement (see Chapter 14) and designed the road map for the goals and SMART objectives you'll achieve when the grant or contract funding is awarded (see Chapter 15), it's time to demonstrate that you have the right people for the project.

In this chapter, I show you how to write about existing and incoming staff in a way that convinces funders that you have the savvy to manage their monies once they're awarded. I also show you how to put together winning project management profiles, organizational resources, and a fair approach to selecting project personnel.

The personnel, resources, and equity section of the grant application narrative (also called the key personnel, adequacy of resources, and equal employment opportunity statement, respectively) can range from one page to several pages. Developing narrative language that meets the requirements laid out in the funding source's grant application guidelines is important. Otherwise, your application may be rejected and not considered for the grant funding.

Introducing Your Project Personnel

Just for fun, pretend for a moment that I'm your grant reader. I've already read the key opening sections to your application narrative, and now I'm *almost* convinced that your organization is worthy of my funding agency's investment monies. At this point, I just need to be taken to the finish line. In other words, before I can make a confident decision, I need to know who's in charge of your organization and the proposed project. From a funder's perspective, I want written validation that the grant monies will be managed by competent administrators.

Grant-, cooperative-agreement-, or contract-funded personnel is gathered in one of two ways: by reassigning an existing staff person to the grant-funded project or by hiring someone after the project is funded. When you're writing about to-be-hired personnel, you won't know the specific qualifications of each individual, but you should know and be able to write about the minimum job specifications of those who will carry certain responsibilities.

No matter how you gather project personnel, making good choices can help you win a big grant award. And when you have qualified personnel on your project, your personnel narrative is a lot easier to write.

As a regular grant peer reviewer, I can tell you that even if the rest of your grant narrative is perfect, you can easily lose up to ten points if your project personnel aren't up to snuff. As you probably know, ten points is a fatal loss. (See Chapters 9 and 10 for more about the point system and review criteria.) On a point scale of 100, projects scoring in the high 90s are recommended for grant awards. Ninety-point projects just won't cut it.

Dealing with existing staff and new hires

Before you start writing about staffing, resources, and equity in hiring, sit down with existing staff members or your human resources director and go over the project narrative that you've already written. Look at your Implementation Plan to see what personnel you've committed to carry out the proposed activities. (Refer to Chapter 15 for more on the Implementation Plan.) Highlight the job titles and any other information that gives you a clue as to how many staff members you need to implement the grant funded project. After you've chosen your staff, you can begin writing your personnel narrative.

Choosing your staff

When compiling information for the project's personnel profile section, be sure to do the following:

> ✔ **Identify a project administrator.** The *project administrator* is the individual who provides management oversight. This person should be able to allocate up to five hours per week of his or her work time to making sure the project meets its grant-funded conditions. The project administrator (along with the project director) usually attends meetings with the project's community partners. (Chapter 13 covers establishing partnerships with other organizations in your community.)

✔ **Identify the personnel needed to carry out the project on a day-to-day basis.** This usually means selecting a *project director.* The person is responsible for the program's implementation. This individual reports directly to the project administrator. Identify a project director who has relevant and extensive experience in the same area as the project.

✔ **Identify all remaining personnel who will be paid from the project's grant-funded budget.** Work with your financial or business manager to review the project design and determine 100 percent of the staffing that's needed to implement the project, if funded. (Flip to Chapter 15 for details on project design and implementation.) List all other personnel who will be hired for or assigned to the project in the adequacy of resources section of the funding request.

There are no set personnel positions. Each project differs when it comes to the personnel needed to carry out activities.

When you're in the process of choosing personnel, it isn't the time to do a favor for your out-of-work, unqualified buddy! Not only does he have the potential to drag your project down, but he also drags down your funding request because decision-making readers shudder when they see unqualified personnel on a project that they're considering funding.

Writing your personnel narrative

The grant cooperative agreement or contract bid reader (the person employed by the funding source to review, rate, and make recommendations for funding or not funding your request) looks for the key personnel narrative to answer the following questions:

✔ What are the project administrator's qualifications?

✔ What are the project director's qualifications?

✔ Which project personnel will carry out the day-to-day activities?

✔ Do the personnel members have extensive experience in the project's focus area?

✔ What percentage of the personnel's time will be charged to the project?

✔ Is the time allocated for each person sufficient to carry out the activities described in the plan of operation or program design?

✔ Will the personnel's time be paid for with grant monies or through in-kind contributions?

✔ What is the personnel *line of accountability* (in other words, who do they report to)?

Keep in mind that you absolutely must follow the funding agency's guidelines when it comes to writing about your project personnel. Your actual key personnel narrative could look entirely different than my example.

The basic profile

For a basic personnel profile, write about what makes each person qualified for his or her proposed position. Give information on relevant work background, awards, acknowledgments, and special recognitions. Follow this with educational information. End with a final sentence to blow the readers away — impress them with one more fact that qualifies the individual for the proposed position. If individuals filling some or all of the budgeted positions have yet to be hired, write a short description of their desired qualifications.

Unless the funding agency has page limitations for this section of the funding request, write one paragraph for each budgeted personnel position. (Refer to the later section "The profile with page limitations" to determine what to do when you have to watch how much you write.) This recommendation remains the same whether personnel costs will be charged to the grant, cooperative agreement, or contract or whether they'll be covered by your own organization's in-kind or cash match. (See Chapter 17 for budget definitions and explanations.)

In the following example, I present the narrative language on the proposed director. Notice that I use boldface to highlight the individual's name, position, and expertise. Also, note that I use future tense. I want to plant the idea that this funding "will" be awarded and the proposed staffing-related tasks "will" occur.

Key Personnel

Project Director (1.0 FTE grant funded) Dr. LaTasha Cosby will be the Director for the Awesome Academics Project. She has worked for the Orange County School District since 2000. *During her tenure, Dr. Cosby has created six afterschool academic programs for middle schools in the District. She has 34 years of experience as a public educator, District administrator, and private sector consultant. Most recently, Dr. Cosby was recognized by the Governor's office for her outstanding contributions to public education. She holds degrees from Florida International University, University of Miami, and Texas State University. Dr. Cosby will report directly to the District's External Programs and Partnerships Director. She has the vision and professional savvy to take this proposed project from ordinary to extraordinary!*

Sometimes the expertise is in the team as a whole. In this example, Dr. Cosby has all the necessary qualities to fulfill her position. What's more common, however, is that one person is qualified for his or her position, but the surrounding team complements that person's knowledge, skills, and talents. In those instances, you may have to be a little "creatively" honest when profiling your key personnel. (If you aren't familiar with FTE, take a look at the next section where I explain it.)

The profile with page limitations

If your funding request has page limitations and you can't write at least one full paragraph on all project staff members, you can include a brief list of key personnel, including volunteers, in the grant application narrative. Also, if the funder's guidelines allow attachments, feel free to attach to the narrative more detailed information on your key personnel.

The following is an example of how to develop a list of key personnel. Note that I include the job title and the time assigned to the project for each person in terms of Full Time Equivalent (FTE), which equals 40 hours per week (8 hours daily times 5 days a week). So, if an individual is only assigned to the project at 0.5 FTE, this means they'll be working 20 hours per week; 0.25 FTE is 10 hours per week.

> *In-School Liaison (0.5 FTE in-kind contribution from the Orange County School District): The District has agreed to designate a middle school teacher at one of the six targeted middle schools to act as the In-School Liaison. This individual will coordinate the recruitment and enrollment of eligible middle school students into the Awesome Academics Project. This position will rotate between the six middle schools to meet with counselors and teachers and explain the purpose of the Project. Once enrollment targets have been met, the In-School Liaison will work to synchronize the in-school homework assignments with the afterschool academic support Individual Education Plans (IEPs). This position will report to the Orange County School District's External Programs and Partnerships Director and the Awesome Academics Project Director.*

> *Afterschool Tutors (30 tutors at 0.6 FTE grant funded): Five tutors will be assigned to each of the six middle schools in the District. They will work from 3 p.m. to 6 p.m. Monday through Thursday. These individuals, yet to be identified, will help students with each day's homework assignments and mentor them from an older youth perspective on how to succeed at academics. The tutors selected will be honor students from Joe Jackson High School — the feeder school for the six middle schools targeted in this proposal.*

> *Volunteer Parent Advisory Council (12 persons at 0.1 FTE in-kind each): The Awesome Academics Project will create a volunteer council to oversee the afterschool project from a stakeholder's viewpoint. The council will be composed of 12 volunteer parents who will meet monthly at rotating middle school sites. The Council will report to the Project Director. All Project staff will attend the monthly meetings.*

The profile for personnel that won't be paid by grant funds

When you can provide personnel at no cost to the grant, you look *great* in the eyes of the grant reader. And when you look great, you score more points. For example, you may include the project director's salary in the grant proposal budget, but the project administrator's time will be in-kind or not charged to the grant proposal budget. This shows the funder that you're focusing on the best use of grant funds and you want to put the money toward providing services to the target population.

The grant, cooperative-agreement, or contract-bid reader is looking for answers to some hard and fast questions that are critical to the success of your project. Even if you aren't asking for grant funds to cover personnel, you should still include a brief paragraph on the key personnel and include the résumé of the project director in the application's attachments.

When you have a volunteer board or council, write a paragraph about their individual FTEs and how often they will meet. This shows funders that you have non-monetary resources that are also stakeholders. In other words, they have a vested interested in seeing your project succeed!

Including the principal investigator

In federal grant applications for scientific or research requests, you're asked to provide a biographical sketch for the principal investigator. The *principal investigator* is similar to the project director (see the earlier section "Choosing your staff"). However, the principal investigator usually holds a doctorate degree in the project's specialty field.

The form for a biographical sketch can change from agency to agency. Here are the most common information fields found on the form:

- ✔ **Name:** Type in the first, middle, and last name of your principal investigator.

- ✔ **Position Title:** Type in the project-assigned position title.

- ✔ **Education/Training:** List the colleges attended and locations, beginning with the baccalaureate degree. Fill in the degree column, the year earned or awarded, and the field of study for each institution of higher education attended.

- ✔ **Positions and Honors:** List, in chronological order, previous work or job positions, ending with the present position. List any honors, including present membership on any federal government public advisory committees.

✔ **Selected peer-reviewed publications (in chronological order):** List any publications in which work has been published and read or reviewed by professional peers.

✔ **Research Support:** List all ongoing or completed (past three years) research projects (both federal and non-federal supported).

You should find a place at the bottom of the biographical sketch form for a page number. Government grant and cooperative agreement applications and contract bid documents are often formatted for you to insert a page number. When you see the cue at the bottom of a form page, read and reread the funding guidelines to see whether your narrative and all accompanying forms must be paginated (numbered) in sequential order, from beginning to end.

Composing the management plan

The *management plan* tells the grant reviewer (that's the funding decision maker, in case you forgot!) who's accountable to whom. It clearly shows where the buck stops when questions arise from the funder. You can integrate the management plan into the key personnel descriptions (as I did in the personnel list earlier in this chapter), or you can develop a separate graphic, like the one in Figure 16-1.

I like to show the management plan in black and white — no color graphics except a lightly shaded title row. The funder wants to see the position name, FTE allocation, line of accountability (who reports to whom), and how the position will be funded (grant budget, cash match from funding applicant, or in-kind contribution). I prefer to list the project personnel in order of ranking, beginning with the highest administrative position and ending with volunteers, if any.

The Awesome Academics Project Management Plan

Position	FTE	Reports To	Funded By
Project Director (1)	1.0		Grant
Lead Coordinator (1)	1.0	Orange County School District's External Programs and Partnerships Director and the Project Director	Grant
In-School Liaison (1)	0.5	Project Director	In-Kind from the Orange County School District
Afterschool Tutors (30)	0.6 Each	Project Director	Grant
Parent Advisory Council Members (12)	0.1 Each	Project Director	In-kind contribution

Figure 16-1: An example management plan table.

In the figure, the number in parentheses behind each position title indicates the number of individuals hired for each title position. For example, the Council will have 12 volunteer (parent) members.

When the funder's management plan guidelines call for something that's not applicable or necessary to your project, write a response to indicate why that particular something will not be attached or discussed further in your application. For example, because they're volunteers, the Parent Advisory Council Members don't cost the funder or the applicant agency any monies. Rather than leave them off the management plan, I include them. Why? Because in the world of grantmaking, volunteers are as valuable as paid staff; they're stakeholders who provide wisdom and feedback to benefit the grant-funded project's overall outcomes. Funders look for volunteer involvement first at the pre-grant-proposal planning stage and again in the grant proposal's management plan. In the example from Table 16-1, the volunteers' time is an in-kind contribution.

The management plan should also include a *statement of fiscal agency responsibility*. This concise, one-paragraph written statement by the chief financial officer (CFO) of the applicant organization attests to the fact that the agency will accept the responsibility of accepting the grant award, managing the grant award, and preparing and submitting financial and evaluation reports. Basically, it's just one more affirmation to the funder of the grant applicant's internal accountability. The statement of fiscal agency responsibility is presented depending on the type of request it is:

- **For foundation and corporate funding requests:** Written on the grant applicant agency's letterhead, signed by the CFO, and attached to the application
- **For government grant and cooperative agreement requests and in contract bid documents:** Included at the end of the management plan

Make sure to include the following accountability information in your statement of fiscal agency responsibility:

- Legal name and corporate structures
- The year in which your organization was founded and whether it has any special recognitions
- Whether your organization will be the fiscal agent (If not, provide information on the fiscal agent and tell the funder why you're using another organization to act as your fiscal agent.)
- Who will monitor your fiscal activities
- A generic statement about your finances being managed prudently and cost-effectively (This statement sounds good, and it works to convince funders that you have a solid financial grip on handling all incoming revenues.)

✔ Who conducts your financial audits and the frequency of those audits

✔ The amounts and sources of funds you've received from grants, cooperative agreements, loans, and contract awards

The following example shows you what a good statement of fiscal agency responsibility sounds like:

> *The Awesome Academics Project is a nonprofit organization created by the Orange County Educational Foundation. The Foundation is the philanthropic and grant seeking arm of the Orange County School District. The Foundation has its own separate IRS nonprofit approval and operates with a separate Board of Directors. The Foundation's finances are managed prudently and cost-effectively. All financials are audited annually by the District's CPAs and Financial Directors. Created in 1990, the Foundation has raised over $10 million in contributions to benefit in-school and out-of-school programs at the Orange County School District.*

Keep in mind that if you're writing to foundations and corporations, the funders don't usually ask for a separate narrative section on the management plan. You include it instead in the section for key personnel. However, state and federal funders usually ask for a qualification of key personnel section and a management plan. In this situation, these sections are to be written separately and labeled clearly.

Always include a project organizational chart in the management plan — room permitting. A chart amplifies your key personnel narrative section and gives the grant peer reviewer a visual break from reading line after line of typed text. If the grant application's guidelines limit the number of pages that you can write in the narrative, the organizational chart may have to be your entire management plan section, with no other narrative. If this is the case, make sure to include FTEs (Full Time Equivalents, which are explained earlier in this chapter) for any salaried project personnel.

Identifying Resources Available to the Project

In government grants, cooperative agreements, and contract bids, you have to address something that's usually called *adequacy of resources*. (You may be asked to address this issue in only the budget section — see Chapter 17 for budget-related details.) With the adequacy of resources section, the funder looks at your organization's available resources — resources needed to implement a successfully funded project — and decides whether the resources are sufficient to support the project.

A graphic table is a great way to profile your resources for the funder. Figure 16-2 gives you an example of how to graph your adequacy of resources information. When you use a table instead of narrative, you can show everything in one graphic. I like to use a three-column table with the following headers:

- ✔ **Resource:** Record all the resources (monetary and in-kind) that will be available to help you implement a successfully funded project. I list the partner agencies and what they will be contributing to the funded project.

- ✔ **Cash Committed:** Type in the actual cash committed to the funded project.

- ✔ **In-Kind Value:** Type in the value of the in-kind donations from each partner. (You can find detailed explanations for in-kind donations in Chapter 17.)

Figure 16-2:
Government grants and contract bids require you to include information on your project's adequacy of resources.

Resource	Cash Committed	In-Kind Value
Orange County School District: Facilities at six middle schools, maintenance, utilities, and transportation.	$325,000	
The Afterschool Evaluation Initiative: monitoring and evaluating the impact of afterschool programs in inner city middle schools.	$250,000	
Awesome Academics Project Parent Advisory Council: 3 hours monthly x 12 months x 12 individuals @ $19.51 per hour.*		$8,428**
Total resources to support funding request	**$575,000**	**$8,428**

*independentsector.org – 2007 research on the Value of a Volunteer
**rounded off to nearest dollar

If you choose to write a resources narrative instead of create a table, keep your narrative to one detailed paragraph.

When you use volunteers as resources, be sure to use the most current official research on the value of a volunteer. This hourly value amount changes every two years. There is a national value and a state-by-state value. The Independent Sector's Web site (www.independentsector.org) has an updated table for the national hourly value and for each state's hourly value.

Showing Equity in Your Personnel and Participant Selection

Equity is created when you manage a program in such a way that no one is excluded. All the individuals hired with grant funds and all the members of the target population (those people the grant funds will help) must be given equal access to program opportunities — to be participants (target population) and to be hired without discrimination (your project staff).

You show equity by opening your project to all who apply, providing they meet objective eligibility criteria. For example, exclusively serving a target population of senior citizens who all belong to your church in a daily hot lunch program isn't discrimination. However, if a senior citizen who is not a member of your church walks into your facility and you refuse services, you are discriminating and not showing equity. Funders want assurances that you won't violate federal or state antidiscrimination laws.

Federal and state funders mandate a grant application section on equity. Foundations and corporations usually don't have anything on equity in their guidelines, but it doesn't hurt to include a paragraph on the subject to show your awareness of the issue.

When evaluating the statement of equity, the grant reader asks the following key questions:

- Does the grant applicant propose to assign or hire project personnel who reflect the demographics of the community and target population to be served under the grant funding?

- Does the grant applicant embrace a sense of fairness to all human beings?

Here are a few quick and easy tips for writing the equity section without stress:

- **Ask human resources for help.** Some grant application guidelines require that your equity statement actually cite the federal and state legislation that your organization adheres to in its hiring practices. The acts that you need to cite can be obtained from your human resources department.

- **Address equitable access for everyone.** The equity statement should include personnel (including the selection of volunteers for the project) and project participants.

✔ **Be straightforward and make a statement.** Writing that discrimination will not be tolerated is important. Cite the federal and state antidiscrimination laws to which your organization will adhere.

The following example received high peer review points (see Chapters 9 and 10 for more on the peer review). Notice how the example addresses the makeup of program personnel and how the personnel will be recruited as well as makes a statement regarding discrimination and fair employment practices.

> *The Awesome Academics Project will use both existing District staff and newly hired individuals for the grant funded program. Recruitment for staff will target all local and regional media. In order to identify qualified staff whose demographics reflect the target population, the staff search will be extended to nonprofit and for-profit entities located in the middle school neighborhoods. Every effort will be made to appoint and/or hire staff that reflects the multicultural mix and demographics of the targeted neighborhoods.*

> *It is the policy of the Orange County School District not to engage in discrimination or harassment against any person because of race, color, religion, sex, national origin, ancestry, age, marital status, disability, sexual orientation, unfavorable discharge from the military, or status as a disabled veteran or a veteran of the Vietnam era and to comply with all federal and state nondiscrimination, equal opportunity, and affirmative action laws, orders, and regulations.*

Chapter 17

Connecting the Budget to the Plan of Action

*I*f you're like me, when you finally finish the narrative components of your grant application, you'd like to think you're finished. Unfortunately you aren't! Instead, at this point in the grant writing process, it's time to connect the cost for grant-funded project implementation to the real-time expenses that you want your grant award to cover (whether it be in part or in total).

Your budget is linked directly to your project's objectives. And in order to achieve the objectives, a series of implementation activities or process objectives must occur (see Chapter 15). The line items in your budget are the costs of what it will take to carry out the activities that lead to your objectives.

This chapter walks you through the budget preparation process for grant applications and contract bids. It also tells you what the funder's and bid-letting agency's expectations are when it comes to your budget section.

Examining the Basic Budget Terms and Sections

Most of the terms associated with the budget section of grant applications, cooperative agreements, and contract bids are everyday terms — no big deal. But just knowing the terms isn't enough; thoroughly understanding the section that's behind each one changes you from the "I'm not so sure" grant writer to the "I know how to do this" grant writer or consultant who's ready to tackle the down side of the grant writing mountain. As you start the final climb down, don't forget your enthusiasm and don't forget to breathe!

Allocation and budget summary

Allocation is the dollar amount you assign to each line item, and *budget summary* is the skeletal outline of how the project's total cost is allocated to line items. When a funder asks for a budget summary, it only wants to see a graphic table (created by you) or a completed short form (provided by the funder) with your main budget line item categories and the total amounts for each category. Funders usually don't want to see narrative detail within a budget summary.

For example, if you're requesting funding only for a staff position, the two columns in the graphic table would be *Line Item* (left-hand column) and *Cost* (right-hand column). The first line item is *Personnel,* and the second line item is *Fringe Benefits.* These two line items are flush left in the left-hand column. The total project budget, also flush left in the last row of the left-hand column, is the sum of *Personnel* and *Fringe Benefits.*

Budget detail narrative

Funders require a detailed explanation of how you plan to spend their monies if they choose to fund your project. So they typically request your *budget detail narrative.* The budget detail narrative section isn't the place to spring surprises on the funder. Anything that shows up here should have already been discussed in the project plan of action section of the application (see Chapter 15 for the lowdown on the plan of action). Read the funder's guidelines and explanations for what should be included in each line item explanation.

You'll see FTE (Full Time Equivalent) used throughout the funder's budget instructions and on budget forms. FTE is based on a full-time work schedule of 35 to 40 hours per week. Each organization or company has its own meaning for who's considered a full-time employee. For the following budget detail narrative example, I use 40 hours per week for a full-time employee. A 1.0 FTE is 40 hours per week; a 0.75 FTE is 30 hours per week; a 0.5 FTE is 20 hours per week, and a 0.25 FTE is 10 hours per week.

The organization I write about in the following budget detail narrative example (and that I use throughout this section) is a nonprofit performing arts organization that has been in existence for more than ten years. The organization needs additional funding to provide a Mobile Arts Outreach Project to day care centers and assisted living facilities. In my example, I include full-time and part-time personnel, and I use a standard and widely accepted percent for calculating fringe benefits.

Because fringe benefits vary from organization to organization and from state to state, you need to check with your human resources department to find out your organization's fringe benefit calculation. This is always a double-digit percent that's multiplied by the total salaries for the grant-funded and in-kind personnel.

Personnel Budget Detail Narrative

In-Kind: One 0.25 FTE Executive Director will be assigned to the grant management duties and project oversight tasks. The Executive Director's full-time salary is $80,000 annually. 0.25 FTE equals $20,000.

Requested: One 1.0 FTE Mobile Arts Outreach Coordinator will be hired at $45,000 per year. The individual selected will be responsible for the management, execution, and coordination of all outreach administration and implementation tasks.

Total Personnel Costs: $65,000

Requested: $45,000

In-Kind: $20,000

Fringe Benefits Budget Detail Narrative

Fringe Benefits are calculated at 28 percent of total salaries; fringe benefits include medical, dental, vision, short-term disability, worker's compensation insurance, unemployment insurance, and employer's FICA match for each salaried position.

Total Fringe Benefits: $18,200 (28% × $65,000)

Requested: $12,600

In-Kind: $5,600

As far as the order of your budget documents goes, the budget detail narrative section usually follows the budget summary. Before you start working on the budget detail narrative, however, it's important to research the funding source's preference for developing this section of your grant application. Some funders only want the budget summary, but others require the summary and detail narrative.

Personnel

The personnel portion of the budget summary and budget detail narrative is where you indicate the costs of project staff and fringe benefits that will be paid from the grant funds and the project staff that will be paid by the grant applicant (but not out of the grant funds). This section also includes the value of volunteer hours. If your organization plans to assign existing staff to the grant-funded project but not draw the staff salaries from the grant monies, you need to create an in-kind column to show the funder how you plan to support the costs of the project's personnel.

Funding for your project's personnel either will be requested from the funding agency or will come as an in-kind contribution from your organization (the grant applicant).

In-kind resources refer to administrative services, access to materials and supplies, use of equipment and facilities, printing support services, and other resources that will be made available to the grant-funded project and its personnel at no cost to the funding agency. (I discuss in-kind items in more detail later in this chapter.)

Requested contributions refer to the funds you need to obtain from outside your organization — from the funding agency.

I want to emphasize that in-kind contributions of the grant applicant should not be commingled with or included in the "Requested" line item of the budget summary and in the budget detail narrative. Your in-kind items should appear in a separate column. See Figure 17-1 for an example.

Figure 17-1:
A table used to separate requested and in-kind contributions in the personnel section of the budget.

Mobile Arts Outreach Project Budget Summary for Personnel and Fringe Benefit Expenses

Line Item	Requested	In-Kind	Total Line Item Expenses
Salaries	$45,000	$20,000	$65,000
Fringe Benefits	$12,600	$5,600	$18,200
Totals	**$57,600**	**$25,600**	**$83,200**

Travel

If you plan to reimburse project personnel for local travel, traditionally referred to as *mileage reimbursement,* include this expense in the travel line item of the budget summary and in the budget detail narrative. Also, if you plan to send project personnel to out-of-town training or conferences during the course of the project, you need to ask for out-of-town travel expenses.

Your travel explanation in the budget detail narrative needs to include the number of trips planned and the number of persons for each trip as well as the conference name, location, purpose, and cost. Don't forget to include the cost of transportation to the events, lodging, meals, and ground travel.

When reviewing the budget-related portions of the grant and cooperative agreement guidelines and contract bidding guidelines, you're likely to come across the term *per diem*. Per diem in this context means the daily allowance that your organization gives employees to spend on meals and incidentals during their travel. Federal grant applications may have per diem limits, such as $54 per day.

Keep in mind that setting a per diem amount could backfire when you or another employee travels to an area with a higher cost of living than the norm, such as Alaska, the East Coast, or the West Coast. Before you finalize your budget line items, contact the funding agency to see if you can use higher per diem amounts for higher cost locales.

If you want to set a per diem for your project but aren't sure what a reasonable number may be, you can check the federal per diem rates for your state at the General Services Administration Web site: www.gsa.gov.

When you're planning to request money for travel expenses, don't forget that you have to have both a travel budget detail narrative and a budget summary. I explain both in the following sections.

Travel budget detail narrative

The following is an example of a portion of the travel budget detail narrative from the Mobile Arts Outreach Project's grant application. (I introduce this project earlier in the chapter.) Notice that the purpose of the travel is clearly explained for the funder. The funds requested are clearly not for "luxurious" travel amenities.

> ***Travel:*** *Grant funding will enable our performing arts organization to pay the daily travel-related expenses necessary to take the donated recreational vehicle on the road to community destinations (day care centers and assisted living facilities in Rain County). Travel-related expenses for the Mobile Arts Outreach Project are calculated at $600 per month × 12 months for a total of $7,200 annually.*

> ***Regional Arts Conference:*** *The Mobile Arts Outreach Project Coordinator will attend one regional arts conference sponsored by the Wyoming Arts Council. This year's conference, scheduled for August 28-30, is in Jackson Hole. Mileage reimbursement at $.485 per mile (federally approved rates for Wyoming) × 400 miles (round trip) is $194. Hotel expenses are $200 per night for two nights totaling $400. Total cost for Regional Arts Conference: $756.*

Total Travel Expenses: $7,956

Requested: $7,956

In-Kind: $0

Travel budget summary

When you're writing a grant application that requires matching funds (see the later section "Digging Up Matching Funds"), always show four separate columns in your budget summary table and explain the source of matching funds in your budget detail narrative. Follow these guidelines for the summary table:

- ✔ The first column is for the specific item information.

- ✔ The second column is for the amount of grant or contract funds requested.

- ✔ The third column is for the amount of funds you have to match the requested funds (also referred to as *in-kind contributions*). Only use the third column when you have matching funds.

- ✔ The fourth column is for the total of the two monies: grant + in-kind or other matching funds.

Figure 17-2 shows you an example of how to graphically present this type of budget information.

Be conservative, yet accurate, in calculating travel expenses. No funder wants to see its money pay for junkets or extended vacations. Looking for conferences in exotic places raises a red flag that could get your proposal tossed out during the review stages. (See "Crunching the Numbers Ethically" later in this chapter for more info about the right dollar amounts to include.)

Figure 17-2: Make sure to include four separate columns of information in a table of travel expenses.

Mobile Arts Outreach Project Budget Summary for Travel Expenses

Line Item	Requested	In-Kind	Total Line Item Expenses
Travel	$7,956	$0	$7,956
Totals	**$7,956**	**$0**	**$7,956**

Equipment

The equipment line item of the budget summary and budget detail narrative is where you ask for grant monies to purchase a major piece of equipment, such as a computer or copy machine. Usually this equipment costs $250 or more and has a *useful life* (the length of time the equipment is expected to be in service) of two years or longer.

Government funds may be used to purchase equipment when current equipment either doesn't exist or is unable to perform the necessary tasks required by the grant. Equipment purchased with government grant funds must be used 100 percent of the time for the grant-funded project.

Do your homework before requesting grant monies to cover capital (big-ticket) equipment. Sometimes, you're better off asking a local office supply company to donate a big-ticket piece of equipment rather than bogging down the grant budget by adding it to your line items. Also, think about leasing capital equipment. Funders who don't allow you to use grant funds to purchase equipment may allow you to lease it instead. At the end of the lease, you have the option to purchase the equipment. Of course, you also need the funds to do so. Luckily, a lot of vendors have end-of-lease buyouts for $1.

Equipment budget detail narrative

Here's an example of the equipment budget detail narrative for the Mobile Arts Outreach Project:

> **Equipment ($2,000):** *The Mobile Arts Outreach Project will purchase mobile backdrops, lighting, and other audio/video equipment to conduct first-class performances at community venues.*
>
> **Total Equipment Expenses:** $2,000
>
> **Requested:** $2,000
>
> **In-Kind:** $0

Equipment budget summary

Figure 17-3 shows you how to graphically represent your equipment expenses using an equipment budget summary. The table contains information from the Mobile Arts Outreach Project.

Mobile Arts Outreach Project Budget Summary for Equipment Expenses

Line Item	Requested	In-Kind	Total Line Item Expenses
Equipment	$2,000	$0	$2,000
Totals	**$2,000**	**$0**	**$2,000**

Supplies

The materials and supplies needed for the daily implementation of the project go on the supplies line of the budget summary and in the budget detail narrative. Examples include office supplies, program supplies, and training supplies.

Supplies budget detail narrative

The following is an example of the supplies budget detail narrative for the Mobile Arts Outreach Project:

> **Supplies ($3,000):** *Grant funds will purchase small types of musical instruments, costume masks, and other types of noise makers for use by audience members at each venue (day care centers and assisted living facilities). These props will enable audiences of all ages to participate in the performing arts program, which is intended to be interactive — drawing out the very young and the very old. Instruments purchased will include: chimes, kazoos, marimbas, wooden spoons, and other starter instruments.*

> **Total Equipment Expenses:** *$3,000*

> **Requested:** *$3,000*

> **In-Kind:** *$0*

Supplies budget summary

Figure 17-4 shows a budget summary for the Mobile Arts Outreach Project. It shows the funds needed from the grantor or funding agency, in-kind (organization is not committing in-kind for this specific line item), and the total line item for supplies.

Mobile Arts Outreach Project Budget Summary for Supplies Expenses

Figure 17-4:
A supplies
budget
summary.

Line Item	Requested	In-Kind	Total Line Item Expenses
Supplies	$3,000	$0	$3,000
Totals	**$3,000**	**$0**	**$3,000**

Contractual

The contractual line of the budget summary and budget detail narrative is where you list the money needed to hire anyone for the project who isn't a member of the staff (whose expenses are listed under the personnel section of the budget — covered earlier in this chapter). For example, you may plan to hire an accounting firm to handle the fiscal reporting side of the grant's management, an evaluation specialist to work on that portion of the application, or a trainer to work with your staff, clients, or board members.

In some smaller nonprofit organizations, personnel hired with grant funds are considered contracted services because the term of employment is dependent on continued grant funding. The pro side of categorizing personnel as contractual is that it eliminates having departing project personnel file for unemployment compensation. The con side is that some really qualified and available individuals may want more of a commitment and may not remain with your project for the duration of the grant period. Also, the constant changing of personnel can be a problem when it comes to the evaluation process. (Chapter 15 covers evaluation responsibilities.)

Contractual budget detail narrative

The following is an example of the contractual budget detail narrative for the Mobile Arts Outreach Project:

> **Contractual ($15,000):** *This line item includes two independent contractors who are critical to our organization's mission and fulfillment of the terms of this proposed grant-funded project. First, at a cost of $10,000, we will contract with a social marketing consultant to help launch the new Mobile Arts Outreach Project. This contractor will perform the following scope of services: project management and relations skills; fostering relations with potential performance venues; preparing all print and broadcast media press releases and public service announcements, and helping to development long-lasting goodwill throughout Rain County for the Mobile Arts Outreach Project. Lastly, at a cost of $5,000, we will contract with a Certified Public Accountant to manage all financial reporting for the grant award and to prepare an annual audit statement for this project and for the organization as a whole.*

Total Contractual Expenses: $15,000

Requested: $15,000

In-Kind: $0

Contractual budget summary

To see a contractual budget summary for the Mobile Arts Outreach Project, check out Figure 17-5.

Mobile Arts Outreach Project Budget Summary for Contractual Expenses

Line Item	Requested	In-Kind	Total Line Item Expenses
Contractual	$15,000	$0	$15,000
Totals	**$15,000**	**$0**	**$15,000**

Construction

When you write a grant that's exclusively seeking funds for construction (also known as *building funds*), you don't need to bother with a budget summary and a budget detail narrative. Just insert the bid. The bid is the written document submitted to you by the construction company that lists all the costs involved in the project. Shortcuts are nice!

Other

You may need to include this section in your budget summary and in the budget detail narrative if you have items that don't fit into any of the other categories. List items by major type and show, in the budget detail narrative, how you arrived at the total sum requested. The following is a list of the types of items I list in the *other* category:

- Janitorial services
- Rent
- Utilities
- Reproduction (printing)
- Security services
- Stipends or honorariums for speakers or special project participants
- Telephone
- Vehicles

Seeing the value of volunteers

For decades, volunteers have rolled up their sleeves and stepped in to serve their communities. Volunteers are most often used where staffing shortages or gaps occur due to funding shortfalls. Nonprofits and for-profits that use volunteers in their organizations treat those volunteers as personnel; they have scheduled hours, they sign in and out of shifts, and they have job descriptions on file in personnel or human resources departments. Volunteers don't receive paychecks or contracted services fees for their volunteer work commitment; however, they're considered workforce or workplace contributors.

The Independent Sector (www.independent sector.org) brought the omission of the monetary value of volunteers' contributions to the attention of the philanthropic community. For over a decade, the Independent Sector has given volunteer work time an hourly cash value.

For the Mobile Arts Outreach Project examples in the following sections, I also add the value of volunteers (from visitor guides to housekeeping and clerical support) and the donated recreational vehicle as line items in the budget.

All types of funders familiar with the nonprofit sector recognize the "Value of Volunteer Time" reports issued frequently by the Independent Sector (www.independentsector.org), which works to promote a just and inclusive society of active citizens and healthy communities. Reports show the national estimated dollar value of volunteer time, a figure that shows the amount of money that organizations save by using volunteers. The Independent Sector Web site also lists dollar values of volunteer hours by state.

For federal and out-of-state foundation and corporate requests, use the national hourly rate to calculate the total value of volunteer hours. The national hourly rate is the number of volunteers on your project multiplied by their average hours each, annually. For state funding agencies as well as foundations and corporations in your state, use the hourly amount listed for your state to calculate the value of your project's volunteers.

Other budget detail narrative

Here's an example of the *other* budget detail narrative for the Mobile Arts Outreach Project:

Other ($100,000): This amount has two contributory components. The first is a donated two-year-old state-of-the-art recreational vehicle. The motor home was given to our performing arts organization by a former Board of Director's President who envisioned a mobile arts outreach project that would travel throughout Rain County. The fair market value of the motor home is $60,980. The second contribution is our dedicated volunteers. These individuals help our seasoned performing professionals get ready for performances and work as stage hands, both in-house at our mountainside theater and at community outreach venues. There are five long-time volunteers who contribute at average of 10 hours weekly for 40 weeks annually. The total value of their contribution is calculated at $19.51 per hour for a total value of $39,020.

Total Other Expenses: $100,000

Requested: $0

In-Kind: $100,000

Other budget summary

Figure 17-6 shows the budget summary for the Mobile Arts Outreach Project's expenses that are included in the *other* category. In this example, the organization requesting the funds is not asking the funder for any monies. However, the organization does show that they have $100,000 in in-kind contributions for the *Other* line item category.

Figure 17-6:
A budget summary detailing miscellaneous expenses.

Mobile Arts Outreach Project Budget Summary for Other Expenses

Line Item	Requested	In-Kind	Total Line Item Expenses
Other	$0	$100,000	$100,000
Totals	**$0**	**$100,000**	**$100,000**

Direct costs or line item totals

Direct costs are expenses for services and products that you need for the project and that are not otherwise available at your organization. These services and products include personnel, travel, equipment, supplies, contractual services, and anything included in the *other* category.

Direct costs and the category's corresponding line item are used only in those government grants or contracts where you actually see direct costs and indirect costs in the application guidelines and on the preprinted budget forms.

Indirect costs

Indirect costs — often called *overhead* — cover services and products that are essential for your overall organization and are consumed in some small degree by the project. Some indirect costs include things such as the telephone bill, rent payments, maintenance costs, and insurance premiums. ***Remember:*** Like direct costs, the indirect cost line is one of those terms reserved for government grant applications and contract bids.

Indirect costs are usually calculated as a percentage of total direct costs. They can range from as little as 5 percent for a charter school to as much as 66 percent for a major university. Your agency may already have an approved indirect cost rate from a state or federal agency. If you have an approved rate, that information is probably on file in the business manager's office. If your agency's business manager doesn't have that information, contact the U.S. Office of Management and Budget or your state's Fiscal Agency.

I've actually written federal grant applications with 50 percent indirect cost rates built in. This means that if the application is funded and the direct costs total $1 million, another $500,000 will be tacked on for indirect costs. (Those are your taxes at work!)

If you apply for a government grant and your organization has an indirect cost rate of 20 percent, you can choose not to ask for the entire 20 percent from the funding agency. Instead, because you want to look good and capable of managing a grant, you can ask for 10 percent from the funding agency and make up the other 10 percent as an in-kind contribution. (See the later section "Digging Up Matching Funds" for more.)

The following is an example of an indirect costs narrative. Note that the $7,056 requested for indirect costs covers project-related expenses for vehicle maintenance and repairs, utilities, office space for the project staff, and printing.

> *Our performing arts organization has been approved for an indirect cost rate of 10 percent by the U.S. Office of Management and Budget. This approval was granted in 2004 when we applied for and received our first National Endowment for the Arts capacity building grant. Indirect charges are calculated for the total government funds requested ($85,556) minus the contractual funds requested ($15,000), which equals $70,556 multiplied by 10 percent, or $7,056.*

> • ***Total Direct Costs (Federal Request): $85,556***

> • ***Total Indirect Costs: $7,056***

- *Total Federal Request: $92,612*
- *Matching Funds: $125,600*
- *Total Project Budget: $218,212*

When you tally up the total amount of federal funds requested, you add the total direct costs to the total indirect costs. Then you calculate in your matching funds, which results in the total project budget.

Entire budget summary

Figure 17-7 shows you how the entire budget summary for the Mobile Arts Outreach Project example looks when it's pulled together.

<u>Mobile Arts Outreach Budget Summary</u>

Figure 17-7:
The Mobile
Arts
Outreach
Project's
entire
budget
summary.

Line Item	Requested	In-Kind	Total Line Item Expenses
Salaries	$45,000	$20,000	$65,000
Fringe Benefits	$12,600	$5,600	$18,200
Travel	$7,956	$0	$7,956
Equipment	$2,000	$0	$2,000
Supplies	$3,000	$0	$3,000
Contractual	$15,000	$0	$15,000
Other	$0	$100,000	$100,000
Total Direct Costs	**$85,556**	**$125,600**	**$211,156**
Total Indirect Costs	**$7,056**	**$0**	**$7,056**
Total Project Budget	**$92,612**	**$125,600**	**$218,212**

Digging Up Matching Funds

Eventually, every grant or contract bid writer faces the challenge of finding the matching funds required to meet the conditions of a funder's guidelines. Push your fears aside and rev your engine because finding matching funds is about to become a lot easier. First of all, read the grant application instructions regarding matching funds. Ask yourself how this funder defines matching funds. Can the match be an *in-kind contribution,* also referred to as *soft cash,* or are you required to identify actual cash (called a *hard match*) for the match?

In my travels across the country, I'm amazed at the feedback I get about how difficult it is for grant applicants to come up with required match amounts in order to qualify for some state and federal grants. I've put together the following information to assist you in finding those much sought-after matching funds.

In-kind (soft matching funds)

The in-kind part of the budget summary and budget detail narrative is where you list the value of human and material resources that your organization will make available to the grant-funded project (meaning that you aren't asking the funder for all the resources needed to implement the project).

When a grant application requires matching funds, every dollar requested from the funding source must be matched with a specified percent of your own monies. The funder's guidelines tell you whether the match is 10, 20, 50, or 100 percent of the grant request.

The following are potential sources of soft matching funds or in-kind contributions:

- **Construction:** Eligible construction is any aspect of infrastructure work that will be donated by trade professionals or volunteers.

- **Contractual:** Eligible sources are contracted consultants who will lend their expertise and time to the project, once funded, but whose expenses may not be requested from the funder.

- **Equipment:** Eligible equipment must be existing or to be purchased; coverage of costs can't be requested from the funder.

- **Fringe benefits:** Fringe benefits for administrative, clerical, contracted, and facilities personnel. Eligible fringe benefits are prorated based on the actual amount of time to be contributed to funder-supported activities.

- **Indirect charges:** Eligible indirect charges can be a line item request in the grant budget; however, if you're struggling to identify matching funds, use indirect charges as a matching contribution to be absorbed by your project. Indirect charges range from 5 percent to 66 percent of the budget subtotal and are allowable only in federal grant applications.

- **Miscellaneous:** Other eligible sources include utilities and telephone expenses that are related to implementing the project but aren't allowable line items in the funding request; printing, copying, postage, and evaluation expenses not included in contractual or supplies; and any other costs to be incurred by your project that haven't been requested from the funder.

- **Personnel:** Personnel who will provide direct or indirect services for the grant-funded activities but who won't be charged to the project's budget expenditures as a line item request to the funder. So, on a pro-rated basis, administrative, clerical, contracted, and facilities personnel (including custodial staff) positions can all be used as soft match line items.

✔ **Supplies:** Eligible supplies must be newly purchased or be on hand from existing inventory; coverage of costs can't be requested from the funder.

✔ **Travel expenses:** Eligible travel must be grant-related for key or ancillary personnel, and coverage of the expenses can't be requested from the funder.

Cash match (hard matching funds)

Inventory your cash on hand and work with your finance person or business manager to determine how much of the cash on hand can be used as cash match for the project, if funded. Here are a couple scenarios of how a cash match can be pulled together:

✔ **You hire a full-time staff person for special projects.** The money you use to hire this person comes from your general operating budget (explained later in this section). At a later date, when you're writing a funding request, you decide to reassign the full-time special projects staff person to a full-time position on the project for which you're requesting funding. This person's salary is already covered by your operating funds. So, when you include the special projects staff person in the personnel section's total in the budget summary and in the budget detail narrative, you can earmark this person's salary and fringe benefits as matching (cash) funds.

✔ **You decide to pay for all target population training supplies out of your existing operating budget (general operating expenses).** The cost for the training supplies is $10,000 — the amount of your cash match or matching funds for the supplies line item in your budget summary and budget detail narrative.

When you're trying to find available money for a hard cash match, some places you should look to first are

✔ A specialized allocation (when your chief financial officer transfers cash from the general operating funds account into a specially allocated account to be used for hard cash matching funds)

✔ Other state or federal grant funds

✔ Private sector grants for portions of the project

✔ Your general operating funds (unrestricted monies to pay the day-to-day operating expenses of your organization)

Be sure to check with the funding agency to which you're applying to make sure that these types of matching funds are allowed.

Crunching the Numbers Ethically

Completing a project budget can be an individual effort or a team effort. Either way you go about it, however, developing thorough and accurate project budgets to present to funders or bid-letting agencies involves more than just putting numbers down in a line and adding them together. Many factors affect how much you ask for in grant funding.

When a grant's awarded, it's awarded in good faith and based on both your budget request and the funding source's grantmaking capacity. So, your first goal in developing the budget section of your application narrative should be fine-tuning your budget request to reflect the actual costs of your program needs. Your second goal is getting your program funded in full, of course!

Compiling accurate cost figures

Aren't sure what kind of budget numbers to put down? Can't figure out how much you'll have to pay a program director? Don't know how much you'll have to spend on a copy machine? I've got an easy solution: Use your telephone. Call the United Way in your area, for example, to determine their salary ranges for program directors, program coordinators, clerical support, accounting clerks, and other staff positions. Call vendors for specification sheets on equipment. It's amazing how quickly you can find answers by asking people in the know!

The Internet has a wealth of information on nonprofit organizations, including salary surveys. Run a quick Internet search, using your favorite search engine, for nonprofit salary surveys.

Network with other organizations in your community to locate purchasing cooperatives. With these co-ops, multiple agencies get together to place orders for like items in bulk, thus receiving a bulk purchase discount. All the members of the cooperative benefit by reducing their overall operating costs. Take notes and create a cooperative purchasing information file so you know who to call or e-mail for future cost-sharing opportunities.

Funders call applicants to get more information on a line item. So be prepared!

Including all possible program income

If you anticipate having any program income at all, you must list a projected amount at the end of your budget summary table and subtract it from the total project costs, which results in a lesser amount needed in grant funds. Examples of possible program income are:

✔ **Interest:** For instance, you may earn interest on an endowment fund that you're allowed to use annually to assist with program costs.

✔ **Membership fees:** For example, a museum might have members who pay an annual fee for discounted entry passes.

✔ **Special events revenue:** For example, you may be planning to hold a fundraising auction to collect additional monies for field trips, equipment, or other items or activities in the project's design.

✔ **Ticket sales for planned events:** For instance, you may work within a performing arts organization that puts on three plays at the local community theater, and patrons purchase tickets to see your troupe perform.

✔ **Tuition:** For example, you may receive payment or reimbursement from a state agency for training welfare-to-work participants, and your grant request is for monies to counsel and provide intensive follow-up coaching to new job entrants from the welfare-to-work pool.

Not reporting your income is unethical. Just think about the dozens, hundreds, or thousands of proposals a foundation or corporate giving entity receives daily, weekly, and monthly. Ninety percent of the time, the funding source must send out letters to grant seekers regretfully stating that there are simply not enough funds available to fund all the requests received. If you choose to omit the fact that you expect program income and greedily ask for the whole ball of wax, you're taking thousands of dollars out of the funder's annual grantmaking budget. Your excess could have funded another grant, perhaps for a struggling start-up agency with no other resources. From an ethical standpoint, asking for grant funds means taking a private oath never to ask for more than you actually need.

Avoiding leftover funds

Asking for too much isn't looked upon favorably by any funding source. In fact, giving leftover money back at the end of the grant period is a straight road to grant suicide — meaning you may not be able to go back to that funder, ever! No funder wants money back. Why? They have already worked the grant award or allocation into their annual giving budgets. Returned money is a hassle, from accounting to reallocation, if the funder has a specific amount of grant funds that it has committed to awarding annually.

To top it off, giving grant award money back may send the following signals to funders:

✔ Your organization (the grant applicant) didn't submit an accurate budget request — you overshot some of the line items and now you have more money than you know what to do with!

✔ You aren't creative enough to find a way to use the leftover monies in your project to better serve the target population.

✔ You failed to carry out all the proposed activities and had leftover monies.

No matter how *you* view the fact that you have leftover monies, the funder doesn't see it as a positive thing. Meet with your board of directors or project advisory council to brainstorm how the monies can be spent, legally, on project-related needs.

Don't pat yourself on the back when you have money leftover at the end of a project. Wherever it was that you cut corners or scrimped, your end beneficiaries (target population) didn't receive the high-quality program that you originally proposed to your funders. You look cheap, inefficient, and unreliable as a candidate for additional funding from that particular funder.

Projecting Multiyear Costs

When you're planning to construct a building or purchase specific items of equipment, engineers or vendors can usually give you bids that are very close to the actual cost of the construction or equipment you'll need if you win the grant and make the expenditure. However, when you're seeking funding for personnel or line items with prices that fluctuate, take care to account for inflation when preparing your budget. In a multiyear request, your line items should increase by at least 5 percent annually. Here's how to create an award-winning multiyear budget summary table:

✔ **Column 1:** Type your line item categories (listed at the beginning of this chapter).

✔ **Column 2:** Type your Year 1 in-kind contributions by category.

✔ **Column 3:** Type your Year 1 cash contributions by category.

✔ **Column 4:** Type your Year 1 amounts, by category, requested from the funder.

✔ **Column 5:** Type your Year 2 in-kind contributions by category.

✔ **Column 6:** Type your Year 2 cash contributions by category.

✔ **Column 7:** Type your Year 2 amounts, by category, requested from the funder.

Continue this sequence for all remaining years in your multiyear budget support request. Only run your total at the bottom of each column, vertically. Don't run horizontal totals (at the end of rows); it's too confusing for the funder to nail down the actual costs and requests for any specific year.

Using a Fiscal Sponsor When You're a New Kid on the Nonprofit Block

A *fiscal sponsor* is an organization that has 501 (c)(3) nonprofit status awarded by the Internal Revenue Service. Usually, a fiscal sponsor is a veteran agency with a long and successful track record in winning and managing grants.

The role of fiscal sponsors is to act as umbrella organizations for newer nonprofit organizations that have little or no experience in winning and managing grant awards. Your new organization is the grant applicant, and the established agency is the fiscal sponsor. It acts as the fiduciary agent for your grant monies. In other words, it's responsible for depositing the monies in a separate account and for creating procedures for your organization to access the grant monies.

Why would you use a fiscal sponsor instead of applying directly for grant funds yourself? Because some foundations and corporate givers don't award grant monies to nonprofit organizations that haven't completed the IRS advanced ruling period. Government agencies don't have advanced ruling period–related requirements.

Sometimes a fiscal sponsor wants you to include expenses for accounting services or grant management in the *other* section of your budget summary and in the budget detail narrative. This practice is acceptable to funding sources. Just make sure to select a fiscal sponsor with whom you're on good terms and have open lines of communication. Otherwise, your grant monies could be slow in trickling down.

If your fiscal sponsor indicates that it will provide the fiscal management services at no cost, mention this at the end of your budget detail narrative. Also present the fact upfront, in the Building Grant Applicant Credibility section of the narrative (see Chapter 13 for more details). The following is an example introduction of an organization that plans to use a fiscal sponsor:

> *The Mercury Outback Riders Club will use the Community Foundation of Fairfax County as its grant applicant. While our organization is a recognized nonprofit organization in the Commonwealth of Virginia, we have not filed for IRS 501 (c)(3) nonprofit status. Our Board of Directors is planning to apply for this status later this year. In the meantime, the Board has approved working with the Community Foundation of Fairfax County who has agreed to act as our fiscal agent.*

When selecting a fiscal sponsor, do the following:

✔ Always find a well-established nonprofit organization that has a successful financial management track record.

✔ Ask your local banker to make a recommendation for a suitable fiscal sponsor.

✔ Look for community-based foundations that are set up to act as umbrella management structures for new and struggling nonprofit organizations.

Creating a written agreement is a good way to prevent any misunderstandings between you and your fiscal sponsor regarding how the money will be used and accessed.

When it comes to your relationship with your fiscal sponsor, keep the following points in mind:

✔ The fiscal sponsor is responsible if your organization mismanages the money.

✔ The fiscal sponsor is responsible if the fiscal sponsor mismanages the money.

✔ If an audit for financial expenditures is in order, the funding source can audit the fiscal sponsor, and the fiscal sponsor can audit your organization.

Following Special Rules for a For-Profit Financial Proposal

If your business is seeking contract awards, the budget line items still need to be presented in a detailed narrative format accompanied by either a budget summary table that you create or a form designed by the bid-letting agency. The budget line items for nonprofits are the same as the budget line items for for-profits (businesses). However, in addition to the guidelines I provide earlier in this chapter, I offer these recommendations to help you when you're preparing the financial or cost section of your contract bid:

✔ Ask the bid-letting agency whether you can include your costs for services or products in the body of the bid response document narrative or whether you have to prepare a separate financial or cost proposal.

✔ Ask the bid-letting agency whether the financial or cost proposal must be submitted under separate cover (in a different envelope).

✔ Ask the bid-letting agency whether you can add your administrative overhead costs and a profit margin to the final total costs for the delivery of your services or products. *Overhead costs* are the costs to do business — the expenses that aren't connected to any specific line item but would be considered indirect costs (which are explained earlier in this chapter). A *profit margin* is the money you want to make after all the expenses have been paid.

Part V
Reaching the Finish Line

The 5th Wave   By Rich Tennant

"I'm guessing, but I suspect our funding came through."

In this part . . .

*B*efore you can cross the finish line (and cross it first, of course), you have to properly finalize your funding request package. There are also a ton of follow-up tasks you must take care of. In fact, there are so many tasks that you'll want to create a checklist to make sure you don't forget one of these critical follow-up steps.

When everything has been researched and written, you probably expect results or feedback from the funding source. So, in this part, you get to read about how to celebrate your success — or how to take the right actions on a rejection notice. Finally, I round out this part by explaining how to write a winning corporate letter request.

Chapter 18

Wrapping Up Your Funding Package

In This Chapter

▶ Creating checklists for absolute assurance

▶ Proofreading your work to avoid mistakes

▶ Organizing your attachments

▶ Polishing your final application package

▶ Using the Internet to send your application

*W*hen you're nearly at the bottom of the tall grant writing mountain, there are just a few finishing touches that you can't afford to over-look. At this point, it's time for you to wrap up your funding package (another name for the finished document you're about to submit). Why are these fin-ishing touches so important? Because if you fail to adhere to the funder's packaging guidelines, you could lose technical review points (see Chapters 9 and 10 for more on the peer review). And if you lose points, your grant appli-cation or contract bid could be eliminated before it starts the race for a com-petitive monetary award.

Yes, I want you to feverishly read every chapter in this book and take my advice to heart and to pen or keyboard. However, if you read only a handful of chapters, this should be one of them. This chapter gives you the final com-petitive advantage to winning grant and contract awards; it tells you the final steps you must take before submitting your grant application or contract bid for funding consideration.

Checking All Requirements

If you can't find a funder-provided checklist or suggested table of contents listing when you first start reading your grant application or contract bid instructions, make your own. Based on what you read in the funder's instructions, type your own list showing the order of the application. In other words, what's the first document the funder needs to read when opening your funding package? After you figure out the first, most important document, go on to list the next and the next until you have a completed listing for the forms, narrative sections, and attachments. (Be sure to also hash out the recommended length for each section or for the entire narrative.) Creating your own checklist gives you peace of mind and will cue you as to when the funding package is complete and ready for submission to the funder.

Some funding agencies help you out by including a checklist in the grant application guidelines to guide you as you put your grant application package together. Use this checklist to mark off each section of the grant application that the funder expects to find when your envelope is opened by funding agency staff. Some funders even ask you to include the checklist in the funding application package. Read carefully for instructions on where to place the checklist in the final application package.

Cover materials

The cover materials are the first things grant reviewers see when they pick up your application, so make sure that each part listed here is finished, well done, and in its proper place. (See Chapter 12 for more details about these items.)

- ❏ A **cover letter** typed on the organization's letterhead and signed by the president of the board or the executive director.

- ❏ All **prenarrative forms** in place, with empty information fields filled in with the requested information.

- ❏ The **abstract or executive summary,** which should be limited to 250 words or less and should appear on a separate page. This section is merely a brief overview of the application's contents.

The executive summary is the same as the abstract, only with a different title. The executive summary is used in federal grant applications, and some regional grantmaking forums have designed applications that call for an executive summary. Private sector funders (foundations and corporations) usually ask for abstracts. Your abstract should be placed before the grant proposal narrative.

- ❏ The **table of contents,** which is required by most federal and state grant applications.

Introduction to your organization

The organization and history section of your grant application narrative introduces the funding agency to the grant applicant. This is a formal "this is who we are" type of written introduction. Double-check what you've written in this section; make sure you've addressed the following information points:

- ❑ History of the organization
- ❑ Major accomplishments relevant to the proposed grant-funded project
- ❑ Current programs and activities relevant to the proposed grant-funded project
- ❑ Target population demographics that mirror the types of populations the funder wants to support in its current funding cycle
- ❑ Collaborations with local, regional, and statewide nonprofit and for-profit partners

In your introduction, did you refer the reader to any attachments? If so, keep a running list of attached documents so you can double-check that they're in place before sending the application out.

Flip to Chapter 13 for more about building your organization's credibility as a grant applicant in the introduction.

Problem or needs statement

Make sure that your problem or needs statement touches on the following topics:

- ❑ The problem that's in critical need of grant funding
- ❑ How the problem was identified
- ❑ How the problem looks from national-, regional-, and local-level perspectives
- ❑ The current national research that proves the existence of the problem
- ❑ The gloom, doom, drama, and trauma that justify the need for grant funds

If you refer the reader to any attachments, list them for double-checking later.

Take another look at the first two narrative sections in your funding request. If you didn't include at least one or two graphics, go back and look for key pieces of information that can be presented in table or chart form; even a map of your location will help give the grant reviewer's eyes a visual break!

Check out Chapter 14 for the scoop on conveying a hopeless situation for your problem statement.

Program design or plan of operation

The program design or plan of action is the real meat of your grant application (see Chapter 15 for details). That's why it's so important to make sure you've hit all the right points. Be sure that your program design contains the following:

❏ One concise statement expressing the purpose of the program

❏ Goals that shadow the funder's specific funding goals

❏ SMART outcome objectives written in quantifiable terms

❏ Process objectives in "activity talking" terms

❏ Impact objectives expressed in terms of their benefits to end recipients

❏ The Logic Model graphic, which helps the grant reader connect the dots between goals and objectives

❏ The time frame for starting and ending all proposed grant-funded activities

❏ Integration of the evaluation plan into the overall program design or plan of operation

❏ A dissemination plan

Did you refer the reader to any attachments or appendices? If so, remember to add them to your running list so you can check them later.

Evaluation and dissemination

If the funder requires you to submit a separate evaluation section with your application, make sure yours addresses the following information points:

❏ The methods your organization will use to evaluate the progress of your objectives

❏ How you plan to share your findings with others

In some Common Grant Application formats, the evaluation belongs in the attachments section, not in the grant narrative.

If you refer the reader to any attachments, add them to your attachments checklist for double-checking later.

See Chapter 15 for more about the evaluation process, which is a part of the plan of action.

Key personnel, resources, and your equity statement

In this portion of your application, make sure you provide details on the following elements of your program:

❏ Key personnel, including each person's qualifications and the amount of time he or she will allocate to the project

❏ Resources that your organization and its partners bring to the program

❏ A demonstration of equity (fairness/equal opportunity for all) in hiring staff and recruiting program participants

In most Common Grant Application formats, key personnel information belongs in the attachments, not the grant narrative. If you referred to any attachments, don't forget to add them to the attachment checklist.

Flip to Chapter 16 for more on how to present your resources and show fairness.

Budget summary and detail

The budget portion of your application is where you must be as accurate as possible. After all, money's a pretty serious thing — especially to the funder that's handing it over! Be sure that you

❏ Double-check your budget summary totals.

❏ Write a detailed narrative to support the budget summary's line item amounts.

As you've done for the other sections of your application, note your references to any attachments so you can ensure that the attachments are in place.

For further information on connecting the information in your budget to the plan of action, refer to Chapter 17.

Finalizing a Contract Bid with Care

Earlier sections in this chapter guide grant writers in pulling together the final documents for a funding request application. Be sure to go back and review those sections because as a for-profit business going after contract bids, you can expect to see some of the same sections in Request For Proposal (RFP) guidelines.

When you're preparing a contract bid, the RFP guidelines tell you exactly what elements you're required to submit. If the bid-letting agency requested information about your company's experience, check to verify that you've included the following:

❏ Your company's legally incorporated name as well as its Doing Business As (DBA) name

❏ The name of the person(s) who founded your company and the year it was founded

❏ The state of its incorporation

❏ The number of years your company has been providing services or products similar to the contracted services or products you're proposing to deliver to the bid-letting agency

❏ Your concise and focused mission statement

❏ The company's areas of expertise

❏ The track record for winning and managing contract awards

❏ Collaborations with other agencies

❏ The background on your contract-specific services or products, including the number of individuals served or number of products sold

❏ Insider information on the extent of the problem or the supply and demand issues that the bid-letting agency is seeking to solve with a contracted services award

❏ Recent research citations to validate the problem statements and/or national trends supporting the problem or product-related data

❏ All points required in the scope of services section (using the same headings and subheadings as those found in the bid document)

❏ How you will monitor the progress of your benchmarks (measurable outcome objectives) and who will be responsible for these activities

❏ The name and qualifications of the principal investigator or project director

❏ The type of bid specifications required to meet the bid-letting agency's cost proposal requirements

As you wrap up your contract bid, take a moment to do the following:

❏ Check the bid document's instructions for how to package your financial or cost proposal

❏ Recheck all calculations

Be sure to check out the contract-specific info I provide in Chapters 13 through 17.

The Eyes Have It: Preventing Fatal Mistakes

I don't know about you, but I can never spot my own mistakes — not when I started writing grant applications and not now! After putting so much time and energy into your application or bid proposal, your eyes may be too strained to spot fatal writing or formatting errors. Unfortunately, the individuals who will be reviewing and evaluating your materials (program officers and peer reviewers) are trained, like hawks, to find your mistakes. And guess what happens when they find one? Your application is at high risk of not being funded. That's why it's important to recruit a fresh pair of eyes when it comes to making sure your writing, formatting, and adherence to the funder's guidelines are spot on.

To get the most from your final edit, you have three options:

✔ Finish your funding proposal early (one to two days before it's due) and lay it aside for 24 hours before rereading.

✔ Have a colleague proof and edit all your work. Be sure to pick someone who doesn't feel intimidated or shy about marking up your mistakes.

✔ Secure the services of a proofreader or editor.

For the last two options, you may need to allow a little more than one or two days. You want to know ahead of time what you're going to do. That way you can line up the resources you choose to work with, and then build the needed time into your deadline schedule.

After allowing a few dozen *near fatal* mistakes to slip by, I decided to pay someone else to run their fresh eyes over my bloopers and blunders. I'm proud to say that I've used a professional editing company for over 18 years.

Whether you choose to proofread your application yourself or hire someone to do it for you, always run the spell-check feature on your word-processing program. It takes only a few minutes, but fixing spelling errors early in the proofreading game saves you time later on, when you may be working to fix more prominent errors.

If you decide to proofread your own grant application or bid proposal, here's a list of the types of bloopers and blunders to look for and correct:

- ✔ Nonmeasurable objectives (Watch out, because failing to write SMART objectives is the most common reason proposals aren't funded.)

- ✔ Narrative section headings and subheadings that aren't the same as the funder's review criteria headings

- ✔ Unpaginated pages in the narrative

- ✔ No sequential pagination from the cover form to the last attached or appended item when the funder has requested total document pagination

- ✔ Different font types and sizes when the funder instructs you to use only one particular font type and size

- ✔ Incorrect spacing between sentences when the funder indicates single- or double-spacing only

- ✔ Orphan lines, headings, or subheadings left hanging alone at the bottom of a page

- ✔ Blatant spelling errors or transposing of words (For example, using *there* instead of *their, hour* instead of *our,* and so forth.) Use a hard-copy dictionary and a thesaurus or your word processing spelling and grammar check options to ensure that you've selected the correct word.

- ✔ Omitting a heading or subheading response because you believe it doesn't apply to your organization or failing to type "Not Applicable" under the heading or subheading or in the information field box

- ✔ Grammatical, punctuation, and sentence structure errors

Check out Chapter 10 for more about the importance of formatting your application properly.

Different funders and bid-letting agencies have different rules. You can win the grant or contract seeking game if you read and adhere to each funder's specific formatting rules.

Putting Your Attachments in Order

The attachments to your grant narrative go in a specific order. For most government grant applications, the attachments are compiled in the order that you refer to them in the narrative. So, read through the narrative from beginning to end and put your attachments in that order. Also in the narrative, you should have numbered each attachment when you referenced it — for example, *attachment 1, attachment 2,* and so on. Make sure you type the attachment number on each attachment. I like to type this in the upper right-hand corner of the attachment.

Organizational structure/administration

A funding agency may request lengthier information on your organization's structure and administration processes. If you don't have sufficient space in your grant application or contract bid narrative, you can refer the grant reader to the attachments.

In your attachments, you should include a brief description of how your organization works, including responses to the following questions. (See Chapter 16 for the personnel information that can be expanded on in the attachments.)

- ✔ **What are the responsibilities of the board, staff, volunteers, and (if a membership organization) the members?** Write a brief paragraph giving the reader a one- or two-sentence description of each group's responsibilities. Sometimes for a new, nonprofit organization, I insert a copy of the bylaws to fulfill this attachment requirement.

- ✔ **How are these groups (the board, the staff, and so on) representative of the communities with which you work?** What are the general demographics of the organization? For this attachment requirement, I usually provide a board roster that includes each board member's name, address, occupation, gender, ethnicity, and term on the board. I also attach a list of key staff members and give gender and ethnicity information for each individual.

- ✔ **Who will be involved in carrying out the plans outlined in this request?** Include a brief paragraph summarizing the qualifications of key individuals involved. For this attachment requirement, I put in one-page résumés for each key staff person.

- ✔ **How will the project be organized?** Include an organizational chart showing the decision-making structure. Make sure the chart is up-to-date and includes a box for volunteers (if your organization uses any). Titles are more important than names, especially given that the staff could change over the duration of the grant's funding period.

Finances

The attachments in the finance section should cover or include

- ✔ The organization's current annual operating budget.
- ✔ The current project budget.
- ✔ A list of other funding sources for this request. Include the name of each funder, the amount requested, the date you sent the grant proposal, and the status of your request (whether funds have been received, committed, or are projected/pending). I like to use a four-column table to present this information in an easy-to-read format. See Figure 18-1 for an example.
- ✔ The financial statement for the most recent complete year (expenses, revenue, and balance sheet). Use the audited version, if available. If your organization has one of those 20-pound financial reports, pull out the comments and breakout budgets for each department and just attach the overall organization expenses and revenue along with the balance sheet.
- ✔ A copy of your IRS 501 (c)(3) letter. If you don't have 501 (c)(3) status, check with the funder to see whether it's willing to fund through your fiscal sponsor. You may need to submit additional information and add information on your fiscal sponsor to the portion of your grant narrative that introduces your organization. Another possibility is that the funder may be willing to exercise expenditure responsibility.

Flip to Chapter 17 for details on the budget information that goes directly into grant applications.

Figure 18-1:
A table neatly lists other funding sources, amounts, dates sent, and request statuses.

Funding Sources Receiving This Request:

Potential Funder	Amount Requested	Date Request Sent	Status
Ronald McDonald Children's Charities	$25,000	December 2008	Pending
KaBoom!	$15,000	January 2009	Pending
Mattel Children's Foundation	$25,000	February 2009	Pending
Citigroup	$100,000	February 2009	Rejected

Other supporting material

Other miscellaneous materials may include letters of support or commitment (up to three). It's okay to have some handwritten letters of support from your constituency; handwritten letters have a lot of impact on the reader. And don't correct spelling or grammar errors, which make the letters more authentic.

Additional relevant materials include your most recent annual report (an original, not a photocopy), recent newsletters sent out by your organization, newspaper clippings about your programs, and previous evaluations or reviews (up to three). *Warning:* Newspaper articles are useless if they aren't dated.

Finally, this section is the one where I put supporting documentation that I've referenced throughout the grant application narrative that doesn't fit in any of the other attachment sections.

Dressing Up and Mailing Your Final Application

You can apply some final touches to give your grant application that extra edge. The techniques I cover in the following sections have helped me achieve my own funding success rate of 90 to 95 percent. Sharing these tips with you means that I want you to be successful in getting most, if not all, of your grant requests funded.

Using the right bindings

All government grant application guidelines tell you how to secure and submit your final grant application package (the cover forms, assurances, certifications, budget forms, narrative, and required attachments). Usually, you're instructed not to staple or spiral bind the finished document. Practically all government funding agencies need numerous copies for the peer review process, and it's easier to make copies of a document that hasn't been stapled together or bound. Even if an agency's grant guidelines tell you to send one original and two copies, the funder will still make additional copies for the review process.

Anything other than a simple clip looks (and is) wasteful. Unless instructed otherwise, stick with what's unobtrusive and effective. Also, don't create fancy graphic-filled covers; no one asks for them and no one looks at them!

Mailing the right way

For cover letters and cover forms, you can use your word-processing software's mail merge feature to set up the following merge fields for your funder information: *contact person, title, funder, address1, address2, city, state, zip,* and *amount req.* (Use your software manual to walk through mail merge steps.) You can insert the appropriate information into each data field, which then allows you to mail merge into your cover form or cover letter, print out a master funding source list for tracking purposes, and print mailing labels.

If you aren't mail-merge savvy, I strongly recommend that you get up to speed. To do so, check the software manual of your word-processing program or consult the *For Dummies* book that covers your program.

As you know, if the funding source sets a deadline, your application must reach the funding source by that time. Government grant guidelines dictate that the application must be postmarked or uploaded by a certain date and time. Personally, I don't work 25 to 100 hours on a government grant application and then leave the application to regular mail. I prefer a guarantee stronger than a mere postage stamp, so I use an express courier service. I always get the application to the courier two weekdays before the date by which the package must be postmarked. For foundation and corporate grants, I use regular mail when I can be sure I'm not going to miss a due date.

Using an express mail service may cost a little more, but it ensures that your application will make it to its destination and enter the review process. By the way, government agencies make no exceptions for late grant applications. Even a natural disaster isn't a valid excuse. If the grant application is due on a specific date, you better have it uploaded and checked in by Application Control Center by that date. All the pleading, whining, and cajoling in the world, including calls to the funder from your congressional representatives, won't make a difference.

Submitting Your Information Electronically

Well, I've certainly been like an old dog learning new tricks over the past few years. I've managed to learn how to register with Grants.gov (see Chapters 4 and 5 for full details on this public funding epicenter). I've also figured out how to download application guidelines and forms, upload completed narratives and attachments, and fill in PDF forms. Today, e-grants are the only way to submit your funding request to many corporations and foundations and to most government agencies, especially the federal government.

The Grants.gov Web site is the gateway for federal e-grants. In this section, I guide you through this Web site, one of the most comprehensive e-grants systems. Getting a handle on the ins and outs here prepare you for the much easier online application processes used by corporations and foundations.

The Grants.gov Web site allows you to do the following:

1. **Find and download a grant or cooperative agreement application package.** To download an application package, enter the CFDA number and/or Funding Opportunity Number (found at the top of a Grants.gov alert bulletin), and then click the "Download Package" button. (See Chapters 4 and 5 for how to subscribe to the Grants.gov system and read a grant opportunity announcement.)

2. **Complete your grant or cooperative agreement application package.** After you download the application package, you can complete it offline (meaning you're not connected to the Internet). This gives you the ability to route the application package to others in your organization as an e-mail attachment, much as you would with any shared document.

   Four sets of instructions are available to assist you when completing an application package:

   - **Agency instructions:** These are agency-specific application package instructions and must be downloaded separately from the application package.

   - **Application package cover sheet instructions:** These are additional instructions providing information on how to complete application package forms. These instructions are located on the cover sheet of the application package.

   - **Application package instructions:** These are located at the bottom of the application package and provide information about filling out the application.

   - **Field-level instructions:** These instructions are available by selecting the field-level help button, and they provide specific information about each field on the application.

Treat your application as you would any important document. Remember to save it to your computer often because changes are NOT automatically saved. When you complete the application package, be sure to save the application prior to submitting it. Also, the application package can't be submitted until all required fields have been completed.

3. **Submit the application package.** The Submit button on the application package cover page becomes active after you download the application package, complete all required forms, attach all required documents, and save your application package. Click on the Submit button after you do all these things and you're ready to send your completed application to Grants.gov.

   Review the provided application summary to confirm that your application will be submitted to the program you wish to apply for. If you aren't already connected to the Internet, you're directed to do so. Log on to Grants.gov using the username and password that you registered with in the Get Started step. When you log in, your application package is automatically uploaded to Grants.gov, and a confirmation screen appears when the upload is complete. Note that a Grants.gov tracking number is provided to you; record this number so you can refer to it should you need to contact customer support.

4. **Track your application status.** This section of the site lets federal grant applicants log onto Grants.gov to determine whether they've registered successfully with Grants.gov, to check the status of their grant application submissions, and to manage their applicant profiles.

If you try the electronic grant submission process and fall in love with online grant writing, then I have the Web site for you. Log on to www.cybergrants. com and get ready to pop open the bubbly and celebrate. This Web site is for grant seekers (nonprofits wanting money) and grantmakers (foundations and corporations giving away money). To familiarize yourself with CyberGrants' online application process, click on the Online Demonstrations link. Here you'll be asked to register so that CyberGrants can process your request for a demonstration. After you register, you'll receive prompting (via e-mail) on how to access the online demonstration Web page.

If you decide to use CyberGrants for some of your grant seeking, you need to register with the site. Make sure to have your organization's Tax Identification Number on hand. Practically every funder requires it, whether you're submitting an online grant application or a regular hard copy application.

Chapter 19

Managing Follow-Up Tasks

- -

In This Chapter

▶ Keeping your hard copies tidy

▶ Providing follow-up information to your partners

▶ Keeping track of your request after it's submitted

- -

*A*fter you've submitted your grant request, you're on solid ground. Are you ready to mosey away and never look back? I hope not! You can't start relaxing just yet. It's time for the filing, clean up, and follow-up tasks. From organizing your stacks of project information to keeping track of where your project went, tying up loose ends is a must for any well-organized grant writer. This chapter shows you how to deal with all the housekeeping issues related to seeking grants and contract bids.

Housekeeping 101: Making and Organizing Your Paper Copies

I'd like to tell you that you don't need any paper copies of your hard work. Unfortunately I can't! Why? Computer hard drives, external backup systems, and even thumb drives can become damaged and non-functional. What happens when all your electronic safety systems fizzle? You panic and lose copies of everything that's near and dear to your heart. So, in this brief, but important warning, I want to emphasize the need to maintain hard copy (paper trail) files.

After you start making hard copies of everything, you may feel overrun by paper. That means you need to organize the paper copies of your grant applications, funding sources, and project information so you have a running start on finding grant-related information in the days, weeks, and months after you mail your application to the funders.

To get a jump on organizing your grant-related paperwork and materials, follow these tips:

- Buy a box of file folders and a few dozen hanging file folders, and then create a hanging file labeled with the project name and the month and year the application was mailed. This hanging file will be the collection place for the file folders outlined in this list — giving you easy access to all project-related information.

- Put the completed grant application and the application's guidelines from the funder in a file folder labeled *Application.*

- Put the background research, meeting notes, and other project-related information in a separate folder labeled *Background Information.*

- Make a file folder titled *Funder Communications.* This folder contains any communications you receive from the funding source.

- Purchase some cardboard file boxes (the ones with tops) and store all of your project-related files in their own box. Make sure to mark the box with the name of the project, the date submitted, and the date for anticipated funding. Store these out of sight but within quick reach in case the funder calls with questions.

After the funding request or contract bid has been mailed, time passes quickly. You may start to wonder when the funding agency or contract bid-letting agency will be making a decision. Go back to your hanging file and review all the funder's or bid-letting agency's guidelines and instructions to find the time frame for interagency review and information on when funding decisions are announced.

Making writing and tracking easier with grants-management software

A grants-management software program allows you to keep track of the entire grant application process, including preplanning steps, partner information, funder information, due dates for fiscal reports and evaluation reports, and grant closeout. Commercial software programs are available to capture any segment of the grant seeking process — or all of it.

Here are a couple of places to look for grants-management software reviews and advertisements:

- Tech Soup: www.techsoup.org
- Foundation News: www.foundation news.org

I continue to use this hard-copy tracking process (hanging files and folders) because I write several applications or contract bids a month for more than one client. And I like to see my projects and their statuses in a more traditional form — folders and files. However, you may decide that the hard-copy tracking approach is too cumbersome. In that case, you can purchase grants-management tracking software that organizes information about the funder, due date, decision date, and outcome of your funding request. See the nearby sidebar "Making writing and tracking easier with grants-management software" for more details.

Debriefing and Sharing with Your Lead Partners

Before you were able to write your grant request, you convened your staff, volunteers, community partners, and other interested parties to help your organization develop the plan of action (covered in Chapter 15) and provide the information for the needs statement (see Chapter 14).

After your grant request has been turned in, it's time for you to bring the stakeholders in your grant's process back together for a debriefing. (If you need more information, Chapter 9 covers your work with stakeholders and how they should be involved in the planning phase of grant proposals.)

Follow these debriefing steps:

1. **Bring each group of stakeholders in to review their efforts with regard to how the information gathered from them in the grant planning meetings was included in the final grant application.**

2. **Give each person or agency a complete copy of the final grant request.**

3. **Answer questions and propose some what-if questions to find out whether the stakeholders understand their roles and responsibilities if and when the grant application is funded.**

   Consider asking the following questions, in addition to others appropriate for your project: What if we're funded for less than we ask for? What if we're not funded at all? What if the needs of our constituents change before we're funded?

4. **Provide a general overview of the time frame in which the funder makes its decision.**

Even though you may have worked as a group when putting together the narrative information, people present at the debriefing meeting may not have been present at the meeting for the document's final draft review. Some feelings may be hurt when a writing contributor sees massive changes in the final document. Remind those who appear to be upset by this type of situation of the ultimate goal — to get funded and help a segment of the community.

Don't just share copies of the final grant request; also give your partners a list of the funding sources and their contact information. Someone on your team may know a foundation trustee or a corporate giving officer personally. And sometimes a simple telephone call or an e-mail to a connected friend can make the difference between getting funded and not getting funded.

You should share other critical information with your partners, too. Such information includes

- ✔ A list of the funders
- ✔ Timelines for funder decisions
- ✔ A master list of partners with contact information
- ✔ Other projects or programs your organization is planning (this info opens the door for future partnering opportunities)

What can partners do for you as a result of the sharing process? They can commit seed monies to begin program implementation on a small scale. Partners who know your needs can unexpectedly make donations of needed equipment, program space, or other items and services. Partners can also give you leads on other funding sources for the project.

Tracking Your Request When It Reaches the Funder

Your grant application has been submitted. You know the funder has received it, but you don't know whether it's still snug in its envelope or laid out on someone's desk for review and decision making. This section gives you the postsubmission protocol of when to call, who to call, and when to just chill out and wait for the mail. The rules are different based on the type of funding source you send your application to for consideration, so this section looks at each type individually.

Managing the follow-up process with government grant requests

As soon as you mail your grant application off to a state funding agency or upload it via Grants.gov to a federal funding agency, start the tracking process. You have specific rules to follow because the money you're requesting comes from public funds. Now's the time to use those great political contacts you've made in your state's capital and in Washington, D.C.

Here are some political do's and don'ts to keep in mind:

- ✔ **Do** send a complete copy of the grant application to your elected officials.

- ✔ **Do** send directly to the funding agency head (state or federal) any letters of support from elected officials that were written too late to submit with your grant application.

- ✔ **Do** call your senators' or representatives' local and Washington offices to remind them that you need their assistance in tracking the grant application.

- ✔ **Do** ask your elected officials to keep you posted on future grant opportunities (no matter what your funding status is). Get in the information loop for state and federal monies.

- ✔ **Do** ask your elected officials to look for "discretionary" grant award opportunities near the end of the state or federal fiscal year (the state fiscal year usually ends June 30 and the federal September 30). At this time, leftover monies are quickly dispensed before they have to be returned to the state legislature or to Congress.

- ✔ **Don't** scream at or threaten elected officials. You really need their influence to help you get your grant funded — if not this time, the next time it's submitted for funding consideration.

- ✔ **Don't** overlook elected officials when you convene the debriefing meeting (covered in the section "Debriefing and Sharing with Your Lead Partners").

- ✔ **Don't** count on always getting your grant funded just because you ask your elected officials to get involved in the tracking process.

You're funded!

At the state level, you receive a funding award letter when your project is selected for funding. Monies are transferred electronically into your organization's bank account. Some monies are awarded and transferred in advance; other monies are released on a reimbursement basis.

At the federal level, you receive a telephone call from one of your elected officials in Washington. He or she notifies you of your funding award and issues the official press release to your local newspaper. Shortly after that, you receive a call or an e-mail from the Office of Management and Budget, known as the OMB. The OMB calls to negotiate the grant award, and yes, that means it may not offer you the full amount you requested. If you agree to a lesser amount, you need to rewrite your goals, objectives, and timelines to match the reduced funding. (Chapter 15 gives details on goals, objectives, and timelines.)

Here's my logic: If you're going to receive fewer grant monies, your promised program design (goals, objectives, and timelines) shouldn't remain at the same level where you expected full funding. Reduce your promises by serving fewer members of the target population. Decrease your SMART objectives to take the heat off of having to hit 80 percent or higher. Do less with less — that's the rule!

You're not funded!

At both the state and federal levels, you receive a rejection letter when your project is denied funding. No call, no advance warning. Just a cold, very disappointing rejection letter or e-mail.

If you're not funded, request a copy of the grant reviewers' comments using the language of the Freedom of Information Act. Contact your elected officials for assistance in getting a face-to-face meeting with funding agency personnel. And check out Chapter 20 for more on what to do after losing your grant request.

You can find information about the Freedom of Information Act as well as a sample letter requesting documents at this Web site: www.tncrimlaw.com/foia_indx.html.

Understanding the follow-up process for foundation and corporate grant requests

Some foundation and corporate funders use their Web sites to post information on procedures for grant proposal awards and declines. If you can't locate the funder's guidelines, it's okay to call the funder for more information on your funding application's status. However, wait at least six to nine months after your submission date to make this call.

These funders want you to be involved in the process that eventually leads to either your success or your failure. Communicating with funders is the key to getting your project or program funded, if not the first time, the second time!

You can expect foundation and corporate funders to notify you that

- ✔ The status of your request is pending
- ✔ Your request has been rejected for funding
- ✔ Your request has been awarded funding

Round one: Determining whether your request is under review

The most desirable and immediate communication from a funder tells you that your funding request has been received and is under review. You're likely to receive this communication by e-mail or postcard. For example, you might receive something that sounds like this:

> *We recently received your request for funding. Our Board of Trustees meets four times per year. Our next meeting for your area is scheduled for June. If we need additional information, someone from our office will contact you via e-mail or telephone. Once we have had the opportunity to fully review your proposal, you will be advised of the Board's decision. Sincerely. . .*

A response such as this means you're still in the running for the money. Don't call this funder!

The least desired immediate communication from a funder tells you that your grant application was received and that the funder isn't considering it for a grant or other type of funding award. This communication could also be sent via e-mail or postcard. Here's an example:

> *Your recently submitted grant proposal was reviewed by our program staff and then forwarded to our Board of Directors. The Board met on August 4 and reviewed over 50 grant proposals seeking Foundation funding. Regretfully, your grant proposal was not selected by the Board for funding consideration. There was nothing wrong or weak in your proposal; there simply was not enough money to fund every "great" funding request. Sincerely. . .*

Sometimes, a rejection letter such as the previous one comes with a further stipulation that you not submit another grant request for at least one year. Most rejection letters are sent to you within 90 days of the funder's receipt of your grant request.

Round two: Finding out whether you're funded

After your first positive communication from the funder indicating that your request is under review, expect a letter within several months (some come in 90 days; other funders can take up to 18 months) that tells you the outcome of the funder's review. The most desired letter from a funder includes information on the amount of your funding award and how to begin the process of transferring funds. Consider this example:

> *The Board of Directors for the Michael J. Fox Foundation for Parkinson's Research met on August 4 to review your grant proposal. I'm pleased to notify you that the Foundation is awarding $150,000 for your Stem Cell Research Project. We ask that the money be spent exclusively to ensure that the goals and objectives of your project will be achieved. The grant will be paid to you in one payment, and processing will begin as soon as the grant agreement is signed and returned to us. On behalf of the Foundation, I wish you every success. Sincerely. . .*

Some foundation and corporate funders, as well as state and federal funders, require that *grant agreements* (contracts signed by the grantee and the grantor, indicating that you'll spend the money as promised in your funding request) be in place before the check is put in the mail. This is standard procedure. However, always have your legal department or attorney examine the language before you sign on the dotted line. Failing to sign a grant agreement means no grant. Call the funder if you have questions.

The least desired letter, however, is a rejection letter stating that you won't be awarded any funding. The previous section shows an example of a typical rejection letter. Read on to find out how to proceed once you've been rejected.

Round three: Following up after a rejection

When your project is denied funding by a foundation or corporate funder, your options for what to do next are similar to your options when dealing with a state or federal funding agency (see "You're not funded!" earlier in this chapter).

First call each funder to determine why your grant proposal was rejected. Then ask for face-to-face meetings with all funders located within driving distance. It doesn't matter whether you submitted your grant proposal to a corporate giving office, a local foundation, or a state agency.

How can you correct narrative weaknesses based on the feedback from a standard form rejection letter, or worse yet, a standard form rejection e-mail or postcard? When you consider the time spent researching and writing your grant proposal, you owe it to yourself to find out why you failed. I used to advise grant writers not to contact the funders because they're too busy. But times have changed; the grant writer's efforts aren't to be dismissed lightly when a funder issues a rejection letter.

If funders are located too far away to schedule face-to-face meetings, call and ask for the best time to discuss the weaknesses in your funding request with a program officer. Tell whomever you speak with that you spent dozens of hours researching the funder, looking at previous grantees, and reviewing the funder's grant application guidelines. Go on to say that you're perplexed as to why your grant proposal was not selected for funding. Be humble, hurt, and open for suggestions. Okay, grovel!

At no time should you become argumentative with a foundation or corporate funder about your grant proposal's rejection. After all, you may want to submit another grant proposal to the funder in the future.

Discovering the contract bid follow-up process

When you fill out and submit a contract bidding document (an RFP, or Request For Proposal), you don't receive any notification from the bid-letting agency that your bid was received. You also don't receive any information about the agency's internal review process or decision-making time frame. The only communication you can expect to receive is notification if your company makes it to the final stages of contract bid acceptance. If this is the case, you receive written notice that's likely to be followed by a telephone call to set up a meeting time.

If your company is one of the finalists in the contract bidding process, you're asked to attend, in person, a *Best and Final Offer meeting*. This invitation means your company's bid is very close to receiving a contract award. The bid-letting agency notifies you of the meeting in writing and poses questions about your bidding document's narrative or costs. Usually you're asked to provide greater detail on some of the sections in your bid narrative, such as the scope of service or cost proposal.

When you're ready to resubmit the updated narrative, the bid-letting agency meets with you, face to face in the Best and Final Offer meeting. This is your company's opportunity to present its best and final offer to the bid-letting agency. The agency contact will tell you whether they want this new and improved document before the meeting or whether you should bring it with you to the meeting.

Only a few contract bidding finalists are asked to sit down in a Best and Final Offer meeting. In order to beat your competition, give the bid-letting agency 100 percent of the additional information needed in writing (page numbers no longer count!). Add new graphics and update your demographics, if needed. Dress up as you would for a job interview. In all reality, you're going for a pre-contract-award interview, so show the agency you mean business!

The waiting is the hardest part

How much patience do you need to have when you're waiting for communication from a funding source? It depends on the funding source:

✔ **Federal:** Expect to wait three to six months from the date you mailed the request. The length of time between the time you mailed or electronically submitted the grant application and the time the decision is made varies from agency to agency.

✔ **State:** Expect to wait up to six months from the date the request was mailed or submitted electronically. State agencies have rather quick turnarounds on decision making.

✔ **Foundation:** Expect to wait up to 12 months from the date the request was mailed or submitted electronically.

✔ **Corporate:** Expect to wait up to six months from the date the request was mailed or submitted electronically. Of all funding sources, corporate funders are the most likely to fail to notify you when your grant request is rejected. Eighty percent of the time, communication from a corporate funder means you have a check in the mail.

Chapter 20

Celebrating or Commiserating: Do It the Right Way

*A*fter you know the status of your grant with a funding source, you need to attend to some tasks in order to wrap up loose ends. All too often, the grant writer drops the ball after finding out that a request for funding has been rejected. The inclination is to retreat, nurse some wounds, and wait until next year. And when grant writers find out that their requests have been funded, they tend to want to celebrate and bask in the light of success. But in both situations, there's more to it than that. Whether you get the bear or the bear gets you, you still have work to do. This chapter guides you through the actions you should take — win or lose.

The Check's in the Mail (or Bank): Dealing with the Post-Award Process

When the word finally reaches you that your grant proposal has been selected for funding, celebrate! But then get ready to hunker down and begin the post-award process. During this process, you must follow some steps, which are shown in the following list. These steps secure your role as the grant or contract recipient. (Don't worry if some terms throw you for a loop; I provide definitions in the section "Translating post-award lingo.")

1. **Notify all your administrators, including the chief financial officer (CFO), of the award.**

2. **Add the item "Accept grant or contract funds" to the agenda of your board of directors' next meeting.**

3. **Prepare an overview of the grant request or contract bidding document for board review prior to the meeting.**

    In the overview, include the purpose, objectives, timelines for program implementation, project budget, and a copy of the official award letter from the funding source.

4. **Prepare a brief oral presentation to give to the board and draft resolution language.**

    The resolution will be to accept the grant or contract award.

5. **If grant agreements or contract forms need to be signed, have these documents ready for the board.**

6. **Prepare a press release (providing the funder doesn't want anonymity) for board approval.**

    Contract awards are public knowledge, so you don't need permission from the bid-letting agency to issue a press release.

7. **Create or purchase a certificate of appreciation for foundation and corporate funders, and get it signed by your board officers.**

    This step isn't necessary if you're dealing with government agencies or bid-letting agencies.

8. **Meet with the CFO to discuss fiscal accountability, including creating a clear or single audit trail.**

Translating post-award lingo

In case you aren't familiar with some of the terms used in the preceding steps, this section gives you some shortcut definitions for terms you hear when your organization has been notified of a grant award or successful contract bid.

The *chief financial officer* (CFO) is the person who makes the financial decisions for your organization. In smaller organizations, the CFO may be a bookkeeper working in concert with an executive director. In larger organizations, entire departments may handle the finances, including fiscal reporting.

Any agency with a board of directors or trustees or any government agency with a decision-making body (such as a city council, town board, or county board of supervisors) needs a *resolution* to apply for and accept grant funds after an official letter has been received announcing a forthcoming award. Even if the funding source includes a check with the award announcement letter (foundations and corporations occasionally do so), you need a formal resolution before you deposit the check.

The resolution should include the name of the grantee (agency receiving the grant funds), the name of the funding agency, the amount of the funding awarded, and the intended use of the funding. Here's an example:

> *The Louisville Children's Museum, operated by the City of Louisville, hereby resolves to accept $200,000 from the National Endowment for the Humanities for the Cultural Capacity Building Project. These funds shall be used exclusively for this project. Any unexpended grant monies will be reported and returned to the grantor as required by federal legislation.*
>
> *Approved unanimously by the Louisville Children's Museum Board of Directors on 1/4/2009 and by the City of Louisville City Council on 1/4/2009.*
>
> *Signed by Mary Moffett, CFO, Louisville Children's Museum, and by Bill Climber, City Clerk, City of Louisville*

Send the *original* resolution to the funding source; the funder needs to see the original signature. Keep a copy for your own files.

Fiscal accountability is the obligation to ensure that the funds granted are used correctly. Fiscal accountability lies with the organization or company responsible for the management of grant or contract funds. In most cases, this is the grant applicant or contract offeror. In some instances, it's the fiscal sponsor. (Chapter 17 explores what it means to be a fiscal sponsor for a non-profit organization.)

A *clear or single audit trail* is an arrangement that allows any auditor, whether internal or from the funding source, to track the grant monies from the *money in* stage to the *money out* stage without finding that grant funds have been commingled with any other organizational funds.

Any grant funds received should be deposited into a separate account and tracked individually by using accounting practices that enable tracking by date, by expenditure, and by line item allocation against the approved project budget (the budget approved by the funding source).

Referring to post-award guidelines for help

In federal grants, the Office of Management and Budget (OMB) works cooperatively with funding agencies to establish government-wide grants-management policies and guidelines. These guidelines are published in circulars and common rules. At the federal level, these documents are first introduced in the *Catalog of Federal Domestic Assistance* (CFDA). New circulars and common rules are published in the Federal Register.

On the federal OMB Web site, `www.whitehouse.gov/OMB/grants/index.html`, you can find out more about the OMB and explore the circulars. (Chapter 4 introduces the CFDA and Federal Register.)

Table 20-1 lists the different federal grants-management OMB circulars. The circular numbers are the keys to locating the document on the OMB Web site.

Table 20-1	Office of Management and Budget Circulars	
Circular Number	*Category*	*Applicable Agencies*
A-16	Coordination of Geographic Information	State and local governments
A-21	Cost Principles	Education institutions
A-87	Cost Principles	State and local governments
A-97	Specialized and Technical Services	State and local governments
A-102	Administrative Requirements	State and local governments
A-110	Administrative Requirements	Institutions of higher education, hospitals, and other nonprofit organizations
A-122	Cost Principles	Nonprofit organizations
A-133	Audit Requirements	State and local governments and nonprofit organizations

At the state funding level, the funding agency provides you with the funding stipulations, including the regulations for accessing, spending, reporting, and closing out grant funds.

Foundation and corporate funders give you their funding stipulations and/ or regulations, if any, when the funds are awarded. Other than asking you to sign a *grant agreement* (a contract indicating that you'll use the awarded funds as promised in your grant application), most private-sector funders don't have a ton of regulations.

Getting More Than You Asked For From Funders

Suppose you've applied for grants with ten funding sources. One of the ten funding sources funds you in full. The money has been deposited, and your project is up and running. But more mail comes in, and guess what? Your project has received four more grants, totaling an amount equal to the full funding request. You must have written one fabulous narrative!

If your project is overfunded, here's what to do:

- ✔ Immediately contact each funder and explain your predicament.
- ✔ Ask the funder's permission to keep the funds and expand your project's design.
- ✔ Ask the funder's permission to carry grant monies over into another fiscal year.

The worst-case scenario is that all funding sources except for the first funder ask you to return the additional funding. The best-case scenario is that you're allowed to keep the funding and create a bigger and better project or program.

The best way to avoid the predicament of having too much money is to write a letter to each outstanding funding source (sources who haven't communicated with you on their decisions to fund your grant requests) immediately after you know that you've reached full funding with the first funder or first group of funders. Be honest and quick. It's the right and ethical thing to do — even though having too much money *sounds* like a good thing. (Chapter 17 talks more about the ethical approach to grant seeking.)

Being Protected by the Freedom of Information Act

If your grant application was rejected by a state or federal funding agency, you're entitled to review the grant reviewer's comments under the Freedom of Information Act (FOIA). Unfortunately, if you're rejected by a foundation or corporate giving entity, you probably won't receive any reviewer's comments, and you can't use the FOIA as your trump card to get them. (Chapter 19 covers the type of communication you can expect from a foundation or corporation when you aren't funded.)

If you receive a rejection notice from a state or federal funding agency, you need to write a letter requesting the peer reviewers' comments (there are usually three peer reviewers per one federal grant application). When you use the FOIA, you receive the federal peer reviewers' actual written comments and scores (the points they bestowed on each narrative section in your grant application). For more information on the federal peer review process, turn to Chapter 10.

In order to invoke the FOIA, your letter should include the following information, at a minimum, to assist the funding agency in locating your requested documents:

- ✔ The name of the federal funding agency from which you're seeking the information must be in the address of the letter.

- ✔ The application identification code (at the federal level, the Application Control Center assigns an identifying number to your incoming grant application) must be included. You receive this number after uploading your grant application via the Grants.gov e-grant system online.

On the envelope and at the top of your FOIA letter, write "Freedom of Information Act Request." Keep a copy of your request; you may need it in the event of an appeal or if your original request isn't answered. Federal agencies are required to answer your request for information within ten working days of receipt. If you don't receive a reply by the end of that time frame (be sure to allow for mailing time), you may write a follow-up letter or call the agency to ask about the delay. Other government agencies have their own set time frames for replies. Calling and asking before writing your letter is the best way to find out how long you should wait for a reply.

Oh No! Picking Up the Pieces and Starting Over

Failed efforts in the grant writing field are upsetting, but remember that they don't signal the end of your grant writing career. After all, just because a grant proposal isn't funded doesn't mean that it doesn't have some salvageable parts. It's time to look at why it failed, and then plan the fix-up!

Transforming failed federal or state grant applications

When you receive a rejection from a federal or state funder, order the peer review comments you're due thanks to the Freedom of Information Act (see the previous section). Use the comments to find out what your peers found wrong with the narrative sections of the grant application. Fix the weaknesses, and if parts of your sections were confusing or incomplete, rewrite them. If others helped you put the application narrative together, now's the time to reconvene the grant writing team.

If you're stuck holding a failed grant request, why are you doing all this work? Here's why:

✔ To get the grant ready for resubmission to the same federal or state grant competition when it cycles again, which is usually once per federal or state fiscal year

✔ To make sure you have a great working document for cutting, pasting, and reworking into state, foundation, and corporate grant application formats

However, face the facts. You went to the feds or the state government because you needed mega monies for your project. No other single funding source can fill the gap that would have been filled with a federal or state grant award. So, if you requested $400,000 from the feds or a state agency, you need to scale down your project design and project budget when you take your request to other funding sources; your adjustments should be based on each funding source's limitations, which you uncover through research. Identify any possible government monies (federal and state), and then look for foundation and corporate funding opportunities to augment your government prospects.

In Chapter 4, I tell you how to find state- and federal-level grant opportunities. Chapter 6 covers how to find out about foundation and corporate funding sources.

Reworking failed foundation or corporate funding requests

Never, ever throw a rejected foundation or corporate grant request into your files, walk away, and give up. Instead,

- ✔ Go back and do another funding search to identify a new list of foundation and corporate funders that you can approach with your grant request (see Chapter 6 for more about private-sector funds).

- ✔ Convene your stakeholders' planning team to discuss the failed attempt with the first funder or funders. Sometimes, other people in the community have funding leads to share with you. After all, they want to see your project be funded as much as you do.

- ✔ Beef up your original foundation or corporate proposal to meet the requirements of state or federal funding opportunities. This means writing more narrative and adding more research to support your needs statement. You also need a new project budget based on federal or state funding limitations.

Modifying failed contract bids

When you lose a contract bidding opportunity, call the bid-letting agency and find out:

- ✔ **Who received the contract award:** Find out if the bid-letting agency awarded the contract to one of your competitors or to a new player in your business's service or product area. You may even consider calling the winner of the contract bid to see whether there's an opportunity to subcontract for some of the contracted work or products. If you lose a contract bid award, focus on making the best of a negative situation.

- ✔ **Why your contract bid was rejected:** This feedback helps you in future contract bids. Your bid may have been too high (money is a prominent deciding factor in contract bid awards). Or your bid may have been incomplete. (Failing to fill in all forms and sign on the dotted line a hundred times can result in failing to have your contract bid reviewed.) Take as much as you can from the rejection so you can improve your bid and increase your chances of receiving an award the next time around.

Before you look for and submit any more contract bids — to any agency — stop and fix your weaknesses (in pricing, language, and whatever else needs improvement). Also, note that not all bid-letting agencies will give you feedback. You must be persistent in finding out why you weren't selected for the bid award. It's impossible to ever win a bid if you don't know where you failed!

Sharpening Your Grant Writing Skills by Becoming a Peer Reviewer

How can you reduce the number of grant rejection notices you receive? How can you feel better about the entire grant writing process? You can do all this and more by signing up to become a peer reviewer for the federal government. That's right, you can actually participate in the reading and rating (the duties peer reviewers are paid to do by federal funding agencies) of someone else's grant application.

Most state-level government grant making agencies don't pay peer reviewers' travel-related expenses or pay for time spent at the state capital reading gobs of grant applications. However, federal government agencies have budget line items to compensate peer reviewers.

Peer reviewers read, analyze, and rate grant proposals. Individuals selected for peer review must possess work experience and/or educational credentials in the area of the grant funding. You have to convince the funding agency that you know the field well enough to read a grant application and understand everything the grant applicant has written, from jargon to field-based research models. Also, you should be comfortable with reading a large volume of material in a short period of time (paper copies and electronic files).

To find open peer reviewer positions, type the phrase "call for peer reviewer" into your favorite Internet search engine Your search will produce all announcements containing that phrase. When you locate a position you want to apply for, you need to have an updated résumé (with work experience and education-related achievements) ready to e-mail or enter into an online peer review application or survey.

You can submit your résumé and peer review application to as many federal agencies that you find *call for peer reviewer* announcements for; however, you may find that, for scheduling reasons, you can't participate in or attend all peer review opportunities.

When you're accepted as a peer reviewer on a particular funding competition, you receive an orientation packet with information on the peer review process, review deadlines, and the process for submitting your completed reviews either electronically or via express mail. As a peer reviewer, you're required to submit a clear and thorough analysis of each application you read. You also must include a rating for each. When you've completed your individual peer review of the assigned grant applications, you write individual reviewer work sheets for each proposal and then discuss your findings with other peer reviewers who have read the same set of grant applications.

Based on the availability of federal funding for the peer review process, you may work

- From your home or office.
- During a funding agency–arranged teleconference in which you're able to communicate with your team.
- At a three- to five-day meeting in Washington, D.C. in which you attend a live orientation session and meet face to face with your peer review panel members.

When you reach the panel consensus stage of the peer review process, you're required to come to consensus on the quality of the applications — with alternating panel reviewers preparing final review forms that reflect the group's decision.

Chapter 21

Crafting the Corporate Letter Request

*W*hen your organization is in need of donated goods or services, you don't always have to write a full grant application. There are easier ways of obtaining cash, supplies, materials, equipment, videos, technical assistance, and more. Simply use my world-famous and proven *corporate letter request*. I have received hundreds of e-mails from organizations that have used my well-publicized corporate letter request format. They have overwhelmingly confirmed that the corporate letter request can be used to raise hundreds of thousands of dollars from businesses, small foundations, and individual donors! In this chapter, I walk you through the quick and easy steps of using my corporate letter request format.

Getting a Refresher on What You Can Ask For

By now your enthusiasm is building — perhaps so much so that you've forgotten what exactly your organization needs. Here are some reminders of what the corporate letter request can be used to obtain:

✔ **Equipment:** Copy machines, computers, fax machines, printers, all-in-one machines, assistive devices for hearing- and visually impaired persons, new or used vehicles, appliances, audio visual items, or other new and used capital equipment items.

✔ **Materials:** Training videos, curriculum packages, and project-related materials (such as canvas, easels, and so on).

✔ **Supplies:** Copy paper, printer or copy cartridges, standard office supplies, or special project supplies. These supplies may include ink pens, paper clips, computer software, or other age-specific or target group–specific supplies.

✔ **Professional services:** A trainer for your board of directors, an accountant to prepare your organization's annual audit statement, someone to evaluate your funded project, and more.

A corporate letter request can also result in cash contributions, just as if you'd received an actual grant award, to meet the following financial needs:

✔ Monies to start a building fund

✔ Monies to start an endowment fund

✔ Monies to support general operating expenses

✔ Monies to attend a professional conference or training program

✔ Monies for education scholarships

✔ Monies to support project or program needs not covered by your existing grant award

Knowing Your Funding Target

Writing an effective corporate letter request requires you to do some homework. Be sure to take these steps before putting pen to paper — or, more accurately, before putting your fingers to the keyboard:

✔ **Research the companies that manufacture the items you need.** Try using Hoover's Web site (www.hoovers.com) to find some good leads on corporations that make what you need. Hoover's is a great online resource because, for a monthly subscription fee, you can retrieve an overview of your target company that includes its history; recent news articles; and a list of officers, locations, subsidiaries (look for sites within a 100-mile radius of your project's location), competitors (other names to look up on Hoover's), and financials.

Even if you don't subscribe to the Hoover's service, you can still get free access to its basic corporate information, such as the name of the company, its location, a list of its products or services, limited financial information, and officers' names.

Financial information gives you an idea of the company's ability (and therefore its potential willingness) to make a donation. Look for a healthy profit line in the company's most recent fiscal year.

✔ **Research the corporations that provide technical assistance.** To find such corporations, go to the Foundation Center's home page (www.foundationcenter.org) and click on the Find Funders link at the top of the page. Then click on Corporate Giving Online. You need to subscribe to Corporate Giving Online in order to access the Center's massive searchable database. Subscriptions for individual users are $59.95 monthly. When you start your search for corporate funders, first read the Center's detailed profile. Then click through on the funder's Web site link to read more specifics, such as Community Involvement, Social Responsibility, or Corporate Giving Guidelines. These are the Web pages that lead you to information on the corporation's technical-assistance offerings.

✔ **Get vendor specifications on any needed equipment, materials, or supplies.** For example, if you're seeking to purchase six laptop computers, print out the technical specifications to show potential funders the hard drive memory capacity, software included, and equipment maintenance warranties. Most vendors will have specification sheets with photos and details of the equipment that their company sells.

✔ **Find out the name of the company official to whom you need to write.** For larger corporations, I always write to the CEO. If I'm approaching a small business, I write to the owner. Even if the person you write to doesn't handle the actual request, he or she will pass it down to the administrator who does. Always start at the top!

Make sure to only approach corporations that have headquarters or operating locations in or within 100 miles of your community. Approaching more than one corporation for the same item is okay, because not everyone says yes. (If they do, celebrate and plan bigger and better for next time.) If you wind up with more goods than you need, call the donating corporation and ask whether you can give the extra items to another nonprofit organization.

Before you dig into your writing, make sure that you receive approval from your board of directors to proceed with letter solicitations. To involve the directors even more in the process, give them your list of targeted recipients so they can call anyone they know personally to expedite the requests.

Using the Corporate Letter Format

First and foremost, keep this letter to two pages maximum, not including your attached supporting documentation. Corporations don't have the time to read cumbersome or lengthy requests. In my two decades of grant and request writing, I've found that two pages is a perfect length for the writer and the reader.

Make sure that you use your organization's letterhead and that your letterhead includes your organization's name, address, voicemail and fax numbers, e-mail address, and Web site address. If it doesn't, add this information to the end of your letter.

The following steps explain how to construct your letter and what it should contain:

1. **Record the date.**

   Use the current date if you're mailing the letter immediately; otherwise, postdate your letter to match the actual mailing date. If you stagger the mailing for multiple letters, be sure to change the date on each letter before mailing them.

2. **Write the opening address for the letter's recipient, including his or her name, job title, the company's name, and the complete mailing address.**

   Be sure to use the correct personal title (Ms., Mr., Messrs., or the Honorable). Call or e-mail the targeted recipient to double-check the gender of the contact person, his or her job title, and the company's current mailing address.

3. **Use a professional salutation before the recipient's personal title and surname.**

   I use the word *Dear.* Only use the recipient's first name if you know him or her personally. Because this is a business letter, follow the salutation with a colon, not a comma.

4. **Start your letter with three bulleted introductory sentences.**

   One approach to these initial bullets is opening with accurate, startling facts about your target population or the beneficiaries of the goods or services you're requesting. (See Chapter 14 for info on how to research target populations.) Another approach is to try stirring the memory of the reader and quickly connecting him or her to a past event that he or she experienced personally, or that close family members or friends experienced. Make sure that the memory-jogger starts out sad but ends happily (see my example in Figure 21-1 for this type of corporate letter request opening).

5. **Introduce your nonprofit organization in the first few sentences.**

   You don't have to repeat your organization's name or location because that info is on your letterhead. However, you do need to share your organization's structure (nonprofit, membership association, or private operating foundation) and who you serve. Provide enough detail on your organization to put the recipient at ease about giving to your agency for the first time. Flip to Chapter 13 for suggestions on how to profile your organization for a funder or donor.

6. **State your problem in the next few sentences.**

   Tell the recipient what's wrong at your organization that requires you to seek outside funding support, equipment, supplies, or consulting assistance. Give sufficient information on the problem to answer all the recipient's questions about why assistance is needed. Turn to Chapter 14 for more tips on writing a winning needs or problem statement.

7. **In one sentence, ask for the money (specify the amount), services (list the services), or equipment (give the piece of equipment's name — the one most commonly used by the company) that you need.**

   Tell the recipient why you need the requested item(s). (Note that asking for money is very similar to drafting a purpose statement, so see Chapter 15 for advice on how to write one.)

8. **In one to three sentences, explain the measurable objectives that will be achieved.**

   This is your chance to show the recipient that you plan to take steps to show your organization lived up to its end of the donation. See Chapter 15 for help with crafting futuristic goals and measurable outcome objectives.

9. **In one or two sentences, tell the recipient why you chose his or her company or foundation and point to your knowledge of the recipient's company.**

   Use the Internet to do your homework on the recipient's organization. First, read all the press releases on its Web site. Then, using a search engine, type in the company or foundation name to see what "outside" information surfaces. Look for the positives and share, in writing, your knowledge of any awards or accolades.

10. **Tell the recipient that if his or her company or foundation helps your organization, the contribution will mean much more than the money, goods, services, or equipment donated.**

    Stroke the recipient's ego by explaining how a donation from his or her organization makes you partners in promoting community change.

11. **Close your letter with a sentence that tells the recipient who to contact with further questions and when you need to have the funds, goods, or services in place.**

    Don't forget to provide this deadline for the giver's decision-making. Otherwise, you may receive a response to your request way after you could've actually used the donation.

12. **Say goodbye.**

    I usually use one of these terms: *Sincerely, Hopefully, Awaiting Your Response, Praying for Support* . . . you get the idea. Remember that you want a soft heart (with maybe a few tears) and a quick contribution of some sort!

13. **Space down four lines and type the name and title of the administrator authorized by your board of directors to sign legal documents.**

    Although this letter *isn't* a legal document, it *is* a formal request and should be signed by the individual authorized to sign other types of accountability documents for your organization. Make sure to give your letter, in draft form, to the official signatory for review and approval before showing up at his or her door with a finished letter.

14. **If you're attaching a budget, a catalog page showing the item you want to purchase, or other supporting documents, type the word *Attachment* after the administrator's typed name and signature.**

    I recommend including the following basic attachments to give your letter's recipient an in-depth look at your organization's internal components and nonprofit status:

    - A total project budget

    - Your organization's most recent financial statement

    - A brochure listing your programs and activities

    - Your IRS nonprofit letter

    - A catalog page that features the item you're requesting (if you're requesting an item)

    Whatever you ask for and receive is a tax deduction for the contributor.

15. **At the very end of your letter, add a handwritten postscript *(P.S.)* of no more than three sentences that appeals to the reader's emotions.**

    The handwritten postscript is your last chance to get the recipient to identify with your organization's values. Recipients who can relate to your need because of personal experience will be the first ones to respond favorably to your request. The postscript is important because it takes the recipient from the typed wording in your letter directly to your handwriting. This level of personalization gives your letter the edge over any others the recipient may receive. (If you want to add some winning words to your postscript so as to impart the importance of your request, flip to Chapter 11.)

If you're planning to send letters to multiple recipients, you can create a template using your word-processing software and simply fill in the information fields. Check out Figure 21-1 for a complete example of a corporate letter request.

Second Ward Community Center
6666 N. Dead End Avenue
Cupcake, MI 15151-5555
Voicemail: 111-555-5555
Fax: 111-555-5556
E-mail: swcc@cupcake.ci.mi.gov
Web site: www.secondwardcc.org

September 7, 2009

Ms. Marcia T. Givens
Corporate Giving Officer
Commercial Ground Surface Equipment Corporation
7777 W. Lucky Business Avenue
Wonkaville, NY 17171-7777

Dear Ms. Givens:

- 100% of the 189 children enrolled in our after-school and summer programs live in substandard single- and multiple-family housing with no grass, cracked sidewalks, and mud holes for play areas.

- In the past five years, 60 children in the community were gunshot victims of drive-by shooters aiming at older siblings who are or were gang members.

- The neighborhoods surrounding our community center are crime-infested; there are no safe places for children to gather with their peers and play — no swing sets, no sandboxes, no jungle gyms, nothing!

The Second Ward Community Center is located in Cupcake, Michigan. The Center was founded in 1995 by Sherman Mitchell, a local community artist and longtime advocate for young children. The Center's mission is to *provide a safe and nurturing environment to support the social, educational, and health needs of neighborhood youth.* Over 200 volunteers and four full-time staff assist in the Center's daily programs and activities. In 2009, the Center will continue to offer its award-winning model programs:

- Time Out: An anger management and conflict resolution program to defuse neighborhood youth of all ages. Over 40 youth are currently enrolled in this program; 20 have been remanded to the program by Youth Court.

- Read It!: An after-school and summer reading tutorial program for youth who have failed to make a grade level promotion. Over 120 elementary school-age youth enrolled in the 2008 summer program, and 75 participate in the after-school program.

- Midnight Basketball: A basketball league for older youth, ages 14 to 17, who were prone to hanging out on the street corners and getting into serious trouble. Over 20 youth belong to the Center's Midnight Basketball team.

According to the April 2001 issue of the American Journal of Public Health, children are 400% to 500% more likely to be physically active if they are afforded safe and attractive places to play. Children living in Cupcake's Second Ward are seldom fed nutritional meals; they exist on high levels of starchy and fried foods. They cannot play safely outdoors where they live. The Center, which is surrounded by a 10-foot-tall fence, is the only safe nucleus for organized activities. We are open six days per week from 8 a.m. until after midnight to feed, clothe, educate, and shape the minds and bodies of children who have fallen through multiple social and human services gaps. Outsiders refer to children living in the second ward as *throwaway kids.*

Figure 21-1:
This sample corporate letter request tells how the receiver can help a nonprofit program with a donation.

As the Center's Executive Director, I am writing to you to request ground surface preparation equipment manufactured and distributed by your company. The Center is located adjacent to vacant land that our board of directors would like to transform into a community playground. The equipment requested is needed to prepare the surface of a nearby vacant lot for a community Build It Now playground initiative, in which volunteers from throughout the community arrive early on a Saturday morning and erect an entire handicap-accessible playground in one day.

Your donation of the ground surface preparation equipment will help the Second Ward Community Center realize its goal to provide a safe and nurturing environment for neighborhood youth.

Your donation will enable the Second Ward Community Center to extend recreational activities to the new outdoor area, which in turn will help achieve the objective of increasing its summer recreation program enrollment by 25% or more in 2010 and beyond.

I selected your company over 20 other commercial ground surface equipment manufacturers. My extensive research on quality equipment showed that your 4567 Model has received the John Browning 4000 ISO Award for three years in a row. I am impressed by this model's durability, quality, and minimal maintenance requirements.

If your company is able to help our organization, The Commercial Ground Surface Equipment Corporation will have contributed more than ground surface preparation equipment. Your company will be a major partner in building the developmental assets for nearly 200 youth. From self-esteem to personal responsibility awareness to academic achievement, youth enjoying the playground and your products will be better prepared for surviving and thriving in times of turmoil.

In closing, please do not hesitate to contact me at 111-555-5555 with any questions about this request. The Center needs to have the playground ready for use by June 10, 2010.

With hope for your partnership,

Sister Joanne Goodfellow

Sister Joanne Goodfellow

Attachments (annual report, program brochure, and letter from the City of Cupcake)

P.S. As I was writing this letter to you to request playground surface preparation equipment, a neighborhood parent rushed in to ask me for help. Her 7-year-old daughter was shot in the arm by a local gang looking for an older brother who did not show up for the gang's initiation. The mother had no telephone to call for help. This family does not have a car, either. I was able to call 911 and send a volunteer crisis response team to the house immediately. The Center has so far to go, yet so little to get there with. . . the new playground is critically needed.

When a board member personally knows the recipient of a letter, give the finished letter to that board member and ask him or her to cross out the typed salutation and write in the recipient's first name. For example, in "Dear Dr. Browning:" you can cross out "Dr. Browning" and replace it with "Bev." Doing so shows Bev, the recipient, that someone at the requesting organization knows her personally. When you do this though, make sure the board member is the official signatory so Bev knows who's calling her Bev!

Following Up After You Mail the Letter

After you mail your letter requesting funds, goods, or services, wait 90 calendar days and then call the individual to whom you addressed the letter. Ask the person whether he or she received your request and offer to answer any questions. This important courtesy can speed up the recipient's decision to help your organization.

If a member of your board of directors handwrote the salutation and signed the letter (as suggested in the preceding section), then your board member needs to make the follow-up telephone call because he or she has a personal relationship with the recipient. This action can increase your chances of receiving what you ask for in your corporate letter request because one officer is now talking to another officer or chief administrator.

Always express gratitude for contributions at any level. Have your board write a letter of thanks to the donating foundation or corporation and ask someone at your organization to call the donor to invite representatives of his or her foundation or corporation to public events, grand openings, ribbon cuttings, and more. Essentially, invite the donor to witness, firsthand, the impact of his or her organization's contribution on your group and on your target population. Such actions show the donor that your organization really does want a long-term partnership, not just a donation.

Part VI
The Part of Tens

The 5th Wave   By Rich Tennant

"The money for this grant proposal is probably coming from the Dept. of Agriculture, so make sure to use words like 'yonder,' 'mosey,' 'y'all,' that sort of thing."

In this part . . .

This grand finale part was written based on your many e-mails and telephone calls about what you want to see in this, the Part of Tens. I hope I haven't disappointed you! In these chapters, I show you how to find hard-to-find information and peer review opportunities. By the end of this part, you'll be an Internet detective, and you'll know how to switch hats and read funding requests written by others (which will in turn allow you to apply your new knowledge to win more grant applications!). And don't forget the appendix, which shows a complete example of a grant narrative.

Chapter 22

Ten Tips for Unearthing Hard-to-Find Information

In This Chapter

▶ Searching for citable data

▶ Making use of external resources

When you put together your grant application narrative, you need to be able to incorporate current and relevant demographics (also known as *statistics*) into the section where you convey your organization's hopeless situation. (I cover this section in detail in Chapter 14.) Knowing how to find the Web sites that house the info you so desperately need is the key to organizing your writing and presenting the gloom, doom, drama, and trauma of your organization's particular situation.

Unfortunately, these statistics aren't always easy to find when you need them. That's why in this chapter I'm showing you where you can dig up hard-to-find information — everything from risk indicators for your target population and service area to internal data that's chock-full of outcomes from your organization's previous grant-funded programs and activities.

Not all the tips in this chapter will apply to your type of organization, so pick and choose the most applicable.

Locate the Labor Database

If you're writing about employment trends, unemployment rates, or occupational demand in your narrative, use the Internet to locate your state's Department of Labor Web site. After you've found it, look for reports, publications, and research statistics related to your service areas. If you can't readily locate this information, call your local employment services office and ask whether it has a recent labor market report that you can copy.

Try calling your local *One-Stop Career Center* (state-funded offices to help high-risk individuals obtain training and get jobs). If you don't know the exact name this publicly funded employment and training service provider goes by in your area, visit `servicelocator.org` to find your nearest One-Stop Career Center. This service provider collects historical data on employment trends for a county or a series of adjacent counties (depending on its state-designated service area).

Peruse Public Health Indicators

If you need statistics regarding incidences of death, pregnancy, HIV/AIDS, teen pregnancies, cancer, diabetes, or other diseases, use the Internet to locate the Web sites for your state and county public health departments. Usually both entities make recent public health indicators available for public access. Here are some of the types of reports that are available:

- ✔ Behavioral risk factor surveys
- ✔ Birth defects registries
- ✔ Child fatality reviews
- ✔ Community health profiles
- ✔ Communicable diseases data and epidemiology
- ✔ Cost reporting and discharge data
- ✔ Environmental health reports
- ✔ Infectious disease epidemiology and reports
- ✔ Other public health statistics and reportable disease statistics

Print out five years of data so you can build comparison tables in your grant application narrative. And *always* cite the source of your data.

Gather Education Data

If you're writing a grant application to benefit your school, you need to gather education data on your district and state-level comparison data. Start by using the Internet to locate your state Department of Education's Web site. Search for data on your school district or on an individual school in the district. Also, look for comparable state-level data so you can compare your own statistics with statewide statistics. Look for links to research, reports, or school report cards. The demographic reports on districts and individual schools are typically called *school report cards.* Most of these reports contain

✔ Adequate yearly progress reports (which show students who perform above the average, at the average, and below the average)

✔ Current state and district enrollments

✔ Educational qualifications of all employed teachers

✔ Standardized testing results for mathematics, reading, and writing for each grade level you're writing about in your grant application

If you require stats on the percent of residents who've graduated from high school and those who've dropped out of school, check out the U.S. Census Bureau's Web site (www.census.gov).

Seek Out Updated Census Data

If you're writing about your target population's increasing or decreasing growth trends, the best source is the United States Census Bureau (www.census.gov). I like to use QuickFacts, which is one of the Bureau's data tools. Find it at quickfacts.census.gov/qfd/index.html. Here you can find state, county, and city-level trends for population, housing, income, poverty, and employment. You can easily find the following facts on the Bureau's site:

✔ Population by race and age

✔ Number of foreign-born persons and limited English-language speakers

✔ Number of high school and college graduates

✔ Number of persons with disabilities

✔ Travel time to work

✔ Number of housing units

✔ Homeownership rates

✔ Median value of housing

✔ Per capita income

✔ Poverty rates

✔ Business and geographic quick facts

When you write about your organization's specific service population's demographics, always create a table so you can compare your stats to those for the state. Doing so shows your highs and lows in critical indicator areas.

Track Down the Community Needs Assessment

Lately, most types of funders (private and public sector) are asking for validation of your needs. The most frequently requested type of validation is results from a recent *community needs assessment,* which is a survey that's taken from a representative percentage of a community's general population. It shows a community's risk factors as they relate to education, health, substance abuse, income, housing status, and more. The most recent community needs assessment for your area may be difficult to locate, but you can start by calling your local United Way.

This agency may not be physically located in your town, but even if it's located in another area, it may still include your county and town in its service region. If you aren't sure how to find your local United Way, visit www.live united.org/myuw.

Large nonprofit organizations (such as the Boys and Girls Clubs of America, YMCAs, YWCAs, your county's board of commissioners, or your city council) are additional sources for accessing community needs assessments. If you can't obtain the most recent assessment from these groups, try talking to your public library's reference librarian.

Obtain a Regional Environmental Scan Report

When you need to present a larger picture of the problems in your community or county, it's best to look for a recent *environmental scan report.* This is a thorough and frequently updated document that captures the demographic characteristics of a county or a local community. Environmental scans are done by county boards of commissioners, mayoral offices, large universities with research centers and healthcare providers, and other human and social services agencies. To track down any environmental scan reports that have been done in your area, type "Environmental Scan for [fill in your county's name here] County" into an Internet search engine. If you can't find an environmental scan report this way, call your nearest university or even the United Way to locate a recent one. (For tips on finding your local United Way, see the preceding section.)

Acquire Crime Statistics

When you're writing intervention and prevention applications for high risk youth and adult populations, it's important to incorporate the crime statistics in your community. First, check out your state's Department of Justice or Department of Criminal Justice Web site by looking for the governor's Web page for your state. All state governors have Web sites with complete listings of the state's agencies. Then look for a link to statistics, reports, or county-level data. Or you can browse your State Police or state Department of Public Service's Web site for critically needed and up-to-date statewide crime statistics. For more local info, turn to your local law enforcement agency's Web site or give the agency a call directly.

If you're pressed for time, search online for your regional newspaper's archives. Newspapers often publish the latest crime statistics and cite the source of their data.

Determine Who's Tracking Your Service Statistics and Trends

When you want to write about historical services numbers and show the number of males and females assisted by your organization, you need accurate and reliable data. In some instances, your board of directors requests frequent reports from your executive director on the organization's service statistics and demographic trends (such as average age, income, and education level). Ask around your office to see who has this report or has access to the electronic files containing this type of information. If you're having a difficult time finding this data, consider revising your organization's evaluation data collection tools (presented in Chapter 15) to capture current and future statistics for grant writing purposes.

Retrieve Archived Data for Comparison Studies

If you're trying to show that a problem has worsened, you can use target population comparison studies. These types of studies come in handy because they contrast one year to another year for the same target population. If you're lucky, someone else has already done the study, and so you just need to search the Internet for a current study or an older one (which may be archived in the authoring agency's Web site publications).

Your first stop when searching for this archived data should be your local or regional college or university library. Why? Often graduate students conduct extensive research on population groups and trends and publish their theses or dissertations (which are then available in the library). Another possible source for this info is your local community foundation.

Pin Down Previous Evaluation Reports

Previous evaluation reports created by your organization for past grant applications can be treasure troves of old statistics and program outcomes and outputs, so start scrounging around for them. The best places to begin are with your organization's administrators and your board of directors. If you hit a road block looking for old evaluation reports, try to find old grant applications to see what was supposed to be evaluated and who was responsible for the evaluation process. Often you can glean more information on program outcomes from the evaluating agency (third-party contractor) or the previous staff person who was in charge. If this doesn't work, try looking at computer hard drives throughout the organization for any old evaluation reports or grant application files.

Chapter 23

Ten Ways to Secure Peer Review Opportunities

....

In This Chapter

▶ Tapping into government peer review networks at all levels

▶ Selling yourself to the folks who select peer reviewers

▶ Making connections with the people who make the decisions

....

A *peer reviewer* is an individual selected by a government grantmaking agency to read and score grant applications. Because a peer is someone who's thought of as your equal, you couldn't apply to become a peer reviewer for the Parent Resource Center grant competition, for example, unless you were either a parent educator or a parent with experience in dealing with the K–12 public school system.

Working as a peer reviewer may or may not give you additional income, but it will definitely provide you with an inside peek at the peer review process — knowledge that can only further your own grant writing efforts. After you've assessed your skills, education, and experience, as well as which funding agencies may be interested in your résumé, you'll be ready to check out these ten ways you can go about securing peer review opportunities.

Call Your Congressional Contacts

Your federally elected officials (and their staff) can give you the inside scoop on the federal grantmaking agencies looking for peer reviewers, so pick up your telephone and call your senator's and representative's Washington, D.C.–based staff to inquire about their insider knowledge. You may also want to e-mail your most recent résumé to your federal contacts to remind them of your education, expertise, and experience in fields that likely match grant funding areas.

Get in Touch with Federal Grantmakers

Public servants are available free of charge. Don't feel like you're bothering a federal program officer, or any other agency staff person, when you pick up the phone and call to inquire about how you can apply for and qualify as a peer reviewer for grant applications. One of the best ways to obtain the telephone numbers for federal grantmaking agencies is to look each agency up on www.usa.gov, the U.S. government's official Web portal.

The federal government pays its peer reviewers anywhere from $100 to $300 a day. It also takes care of your air fare, hotel arrangements, and meal reimbursements. Or you might receive a per diem.

Contact State Grantmaking Agencies

Like federal grantmakers (mentioned in the preceding section), state grant program staff are public servants who should be ready and willing to answer your questions about becoming a peer reviewer for state agency grants. Call everyone you can and take notes on who you spoke with, the date of the conversation, and the results of your inquiry. If you hit a dead end, call the governor's office for assistance. Ask if the office has a Web site link to connect with all the state's grantmaking agencies without doing a site by site check.

Most state grantmaking agencies are strapped for cash and probably won't pay you for participating in the peer review process. You'll also have to foot the bill for gasoline, a hotel the night before (if you live a long ways from your state capitol), and your own meals.

Reach Out to Your Municipal Grantmakers

When it comes to pursuing peer review opportunities at city grantmaking agencies, start at the top by contacting the mayor's or county commissioner's office. Find out the names and contact information for departments with public grantmaking staffs. Most municipalities have Community Development Block Grant funds that they regrant. (These funds are publically earmarked for economic development projects that benefit low income populations.)

Some municipalities have neighborhood development programs that award grants to neighborhood block clubs, and others give out cash through their community funds.

Clearly, lots of peer review opportunities are available in local units of municipal government. To stake a claim on one of them, offer to help wade through the masses of incoming grant applications, even if your city has no funds to pay you for your assistance.

Polish Your Résumé with the Right Credentials

Freshen up your résumé by using to your advantage the descriptors found in grantmaking agencies' peer reviewer requests. Here's an example of a typical call for a peer reviewer:

> **Mentoring Program of the Drug Free and Safe Schools Office** — *Areas of Expertise Required: mentoring of children, design, safeguards, and administration of mentoring programs for children.*

To have a better shot at securing this peer review opportunity, you'd want to incorporate the terms listed under "Areas of Expertise Required" when updating your résumé.

E-mail Your Credentials to Key Contacts Monthly

Don't be afraid to contact the folks who select peer reviewers. In fact, you should contact them on a monthly basis, at minimum. Be tenacious, and be sure to have an updated résumé with your professional credentials for all agencies to review and keep.

If at any time, an agency staff person seems irritated at your aggressive approach to be included in the peer review process, back off and try another agency. Wait at least three months before approaching the "tired of hearing from you" agency contact again. After all, you aren't the only expert or layperson seeking to land a peer review gig — especially one that pays you for your time and credentials. (If you need a refresher on where to find peer reviewer decision makers, check out the previous tips in this chapter.)

Enhance Your Credibility as a Thorough Reviewer

Building your credibility as a thorough reviewer step by step just might land you lots of peer review opportunities. If you have keen eyes and can easily spot typographical errors, a great way to build your credibility among grant-making agencies is to notify them in writing when you find glaring errors in their publications and materials. Make sure to fully describe the errors and include your contact information and credentials. Why? You want the agencies to know that you're reading their publications and that you're familiar with grant guidelines or RFP (Request for Proposal) instructions.

Get in the Door with Smaller Grantmakers

Many times small, local funders like community foundations, bank trust departments, and smaller corporations that contribute to community causes don't have specific grant guidelines. The fact that they often receive tons of irregularly formatted grant requests calls to their attention the need for clarity and consistency. Use the yellow pages and your local United Way to identify these smaller players in the grantmaking arena, and then approach them by calling and requesting an exploratory meeting.

When you go to the meeting, have a list of questions like these: How many requests for funding do you receive annually? How large is your grant request review staff? Would you like to have one standard reader-friendly document for all potential grant applicants? How can I help you reduce the incoming request chaos? Do you have an internal team that reviews all incoming grant requests? Do you ever use laypersons to assist with your grant review process? Ask all of these questions, and then find a way to help with and participate in their peer review process.

Attend Technical Assistance Workshops

All types of funding agencies have technical assistance workshops. These workshops provide insider tips on how to research and write a winning grant application. I try to attend up to six of these local and regional workshops each year to get the latest scoop from program officers on what's in and what's out when it comes to applying for grant funding opportunities.

While I'm at the technical assistance workshops, I seek out program staff from the funding agencies and give them my business card and indicate that I'm interested in participating in the peer review process. Knowing a face and a name helps open the door to the peer review process database quicker than a cold e-mail from stranger to stranger.

Network with Decision Makers

Most anyone can get heavy media coverage when hosting a fundraising event, open house, conference, or some other public event related to making money decisions. As a result, your local daily newspaper can be a source of info on the dealings of peer reviewer decision makers. Read it religiously and start planning to attend meetings, conferences, and other community or state-level events that the folks who make the decisions about funding or grant requests attend.

I once attended a wedding reception of someone whom I'd met only briefly and hit decision-maker gold! I was introduced to the governor and several state agency heads, which led to an invitation to sit on a public advisory board for the state's Department of Labor. After I knew how this agency worked and who got funded, I stepped down from the board and applied to be a grant peer reviewer. My offer was accepted, and I reviewed incoming competitive grant applications for nearly three years. I didn't get paid, but I did get lots of insider information on how the department wanted its grants written and what its funding preferences were. A few years later, I had a job where I was required to write grant applications to the Department of Labor. My insider knowledge helped me win millions of dollars in competitive state funding for my organization.

Appendix

A Complete Example of a Grant Application Narrative

• •

*T*his appendix contains the complete text of a grant application narrative that led to an awarding of funds. It's addressed to a public state government funding agency. My intent with this example is to show you how various writing and formatting techniques — wording, spacing, highlighting, and bulleting — can work together in a successful document requesting grant monies.

In this example, I use a lot of boldface type to make the statistics leap off of the page for the agency's grant reader(s), which of course is the decision making person or review team. Footnotes, a magnetizing table, and paragraph borders round out the visual appeal to the decision makers. Remember that visual appeal is an important inclusion in a grant application narrative.

Note that this was also a very short grant application narrative for a government agency. Don't expect to see many guidelines that only require eight pages of single-spaced narrative. In this example, the agency asked for just enough information to make an expedited decision on who will receive this competitive funding.

A.   Background/Need:
1. Description of the need/problem in the target area. According to the Police Department of **Hooterville and Browning County**, in 2006 at least 73 homicides occurred in the county.[1] A November 21, 2006, Public Safety Committee report on the Hooterville Police Department's Uniform Crime Statistics Year-to-Date contained the following alarming facts:

- In 2006, **45%** of homicide **victims (33) were between the ages of 16 and 25 years old.**
- Juvenile males of color who are 14 to 17 years of age make up 0.9 percent of the Browning County population, but **accounted for 21 percent of all robbery arrests** in Hooterville in 2006.
- In 2006, **juveniles accounted for 15.9 percent of all Part I arrests** and **23.5 percent of all Part I violent crime arrests** in Hooterville.
- In 2006, there was a **13.9 percent increase in the number of juveniles arrested** for Part I violent crime offenses.
- In 2006, juveniles were responsible for **25.4 percent of total robbery arrests** compared to 23.5 percent in 2005.
- In 2006, **87.7 percent of all juveniles arrested for robbery had previously been arrested. 81.6 percent of which had between 2 and 12 previous arrests!** Charges included: 26 homicides; 6 kidnappings; 243 robberies; 76 weapons violations; and 93 assaults (32 aggravated).
- In 2006, there were 114 unique juveniles arrested for robbery. These juveniles have amassed **1,255 total charges including their most current robbery arrest.** In 2005, 93 unique juveniles were arrested 111 times for robbery.

Juvenile crime rates are alarmingly high, and they are even more alarming given the average age for first crime (12 years old). The five top reasons for referral to the Area Juvenile Court are traffic violations, theft of property, truancy, assault, and possession/consumption of alcohol (State Council of Juvenile and Family Court Judges, 2005). Everyone involved with high-risk children and teens — from parents and teachers to Area Juvenile Court workers — agrees that these youth are out of control. The county's risk factors for juveniles far exceed the protective factors (family, school, peers, and the community). **Notable risk factors include the following:** children who are delinquent by age 13 have little or no relationship with their father and/or mother; have siblings who have been court-involved; have experienced domestic violence in their home; have a parent with substance abuse issues; and have a parent who has been or is currently incarcerated. Also, delinquents are likely to have mental health issues and suicidal ideations or attempts.

Clearly, delinquency prevention strategies need to progress beyond alternative school settings, suspensions, and harsh parental disciplining. Hooterville/Browning County youth need primary prevention programs that incorporate therapeutic mentoring, anger management, substance abuse prevention, programs to encourage self-respect, and parent education/family management components. The 2003 research conducted by the State Commission on Children and Youth shows that **Browning County was the second highest county in the state for incarcerated juvenile populations** (State Hall of Records, 2002) — *this trend continued in 2006.*

_____
[1] http://www.police.hooterville.org/news/reports/serpas_to_public_safety_committee_061121.ppt#291,22, SIMULTANEOUSLY: 34-month pre-post ADL analysis. Retrieved online April 30, 2007.

2. How the project will address the need/problem. The Mentoring Initiative for Underserved Truant Entrants (**MINUTE**) Program proposed by Dreaming for Youth, Inc. of Hooterville is a continuation of a comprehensive and coordinated system of services that involve collaborations with the Area Juvenile Court system and a local church. MINUTE incorporates U.S. Department of Justice (UDOJ) Office of Juvenile Justice Delinquency Prevention (OJJDP) and U.S. Department of Health and Human Services (HSS) – Substance Abuse and Mental Health Services Administration (SAMHSA) model program components. MINUTE uses screened and trained older youth mentors as positive role models for younger mentees. Therapeutic peer group counseling and discussion sessions address alcohol, tobacco, and other drug (ATOD) prevention, peer pressure resistance, low self-esteem, anger management, failing academics, and truancy. Intensive family counseling supports (including the youth) address positive parenting, family relationships, adolescent pregnancy prevention, and the creation a safe home environment, and these supports also connect families with critically needed human and social service resources. The purpose of MINUTE is to reduce the incidents of delinquent acts among 40 high-risk, predominantly low-income youth (50 percent will be females), ages 12 to 16, who reside in Browning County and are referred to the program by the Area Juvenile Court system.

3. Standard Program Category. The MINUTE Program falls under the **Delinquency Prevention Program Category – Year 2 Continuation Grant Request.**

4. How the project will assist the State Commission on Children and Youth (SCCY) in maintaining compliance with the JJDP Act. MINUTE addresses multiple JJDP mandates leading to delinquency prevention and improvement of the juvenile justice system. The MINUTE Program assists the SCCY in the following ways: MINUTE's integrated service framework is a part of a comprehensive and coordinated community system of services already available to Hooterville/Browning County youth under the grant applicant's state and county intervention and prevention services contracts. MINUTE provides direct delinquency prevention services to targeted youth. At least 50 percent or more of the youth referred to the program are and will continue to be minorities (leading to reduction of incidences of minorities in the juvenile justice system). In addition, the MINUTE Program incorporates best practices from UDOJ OJJDP and/or DHSS – SAMHSA. Dreaming for Youth, Inc. received SCCY funding in 2006.

B. Project Implementation

1. Description of the target population. The target population for SCCY 2007 funding is 40 new high-risk, predominantly low-income youth, ages 12 to 16, who reside in Browning County and are referred to the MINUTE Program by the Area Juvenile Court system. At least 50 percent of youth targeted will be female.

2. Description of the strategy for providing minority responsive programming. Dreaming for Youth, Inc., the grant applicant, was founded by a visionary with decades of professional counseling experience in the state's low-income neighborhoods. Two of the three OJJDP/SAMHSA model programs selected for implementation under the MINUTE Program include **Let Each One Teach One** (intergenerational therapeutic mentoring delinquency prevention model) and **Creating Lasting Family Connections** (parent training model). All of the models selected address risk factors for high risk youth and their parents.

3. Description of the strategy for providing gender-responsive programming for females. The third OJJDP model program selected is designed for high-risk females. **Girls' Circle** has been piloted and proven effective with females of color. The model integrates relational-cultural theory, resiliency practices, and skills training into a specific format designed to create positive connections, personal and collective strengths, and competence in girls.

4. Goals for the year.

A. Impact on the community: Goal 1 – Continue to provide delinquency prevention education, activities, and peer counseling to Hooterville/Browning County youth identified by the Area Juvenile Court system as being at high risk for becoming delinquent. **Goal 2** – Continue to encourage and guide parents and caregivers of high-risk youth in obtaining and using the skills, goals, strategies, and knowledge needed to reconnect families and assist in delinquency prevention approaches with their child(ren). **B. Strategies for achieving goals:** – Continue to strengthen existing partnerships with the Area Juvenile Court system and with a local church that will provide the site for the MINUTE Program. – Meet with and involve referees' families/caregivers within 48 hours of referral, in their home or at another safe, less restrictive environment, to conduct a family assessment and develop Individual Family Plans for delinquency prevention. – Use proven and outcome-based programs to intervene early and quickly for the benefit of youth who are at risk of developing emotional or behavioral problems because of physical, peer, family, or mental stress. **Rationale:** Each OJJDP and/or SAMHSA model selected for MINUTE has been tested in urban areas with similar populations. Evaluation outcomes show significantly high post-test results for youth and parents. The models are endorsed by OJJDP and/or SAMHSA. Dreaming For Youth has been designing and implementing therapeutic mentoring programs statewide since 2001 with demonstrated success. These models address both national and state outcomes for delinquency prevention.

5. SMART objectives for each goal.

Objective 1a – 60 percent or more of youth in the MINUTE Program will exhibit desired changes in incidences of peer and family relationships, antisocial behavior, ATOD abuse, views about teen sexual relationships, and self-criticism by the end of the fourth quarter. **Objective 1b** – 80 percent or more of youth enrolling in the MINUTE Program will demonstrate resiliency skills by completing their mentoring experience and peer counseling requirements, and by achieving other protective-factor-building goals by the end of the fourth quarter. **Objective 1c** – 80 percent or more of youth enrolled in the MINUTE Program will complete a post-participation survey and convey satisfaction with their own preset outcomes and with their family's outcomes by the end of the fourth quarter.

Objective 2a – 50 percent or more of parents with youth enrolled in the MINUTE Program will demonstrate improved knowledge of ATOD abuse, family management skills, communication skills, family role-modeling of alcohol use, the need for youth involvement in community activities, and available community prevention/intervention services by the end of the fourth quarter.

6. How the project will be implemented. Dreaming for Youth, Inc. has already met with the county's Juvenile Justice Court judge to discuss the target population for SCCY and has developed a Memorandum of Understanding for high-risk, non-adjudicated school-age youth referrals to the MINUTE Program. In addition, over a dozen meetings have been held with our local church partner that resulted in setting days and times for MINUTE Program meetings. The new group of mentors/mentees will meet in single-gender groups once each week on different evenings. The local church's 15-passenger van will continue to transport (if needed) mentors and mentees to the church from school/home and return them home. Supervised gender-specific mentoring and counseling will continue to take place on Tuesday and Thursday evenings. Parent training and youth/parent teams will continue to be held on Saturday mornings for 90 minutes. Once notified of funding, the following program components will be implemented:

• **Let Each One Teach One (peer therapeutic mentoring):** Qualified social work staff will assist in recruiting, screening, and training older youth mentors from Hooterville Public Schools and local universities for this intensive peer role-modeling component. The youth selected for peer mentoring models will be academically and socially successful. This curriculum model is designed to train a specific number of older youth, who in turn, instill the philosophy of *each one teaching one*. These one-on-one mentoring matches (gender specific) will support self-efficacy and academic tutoring, and will minimize individual and school risk factors (for example, truancy and academic failure). Mentoring teams will meet for 60 minutes weekly over 48 weeks (two 24-week cycles) in a supervised setting (Dreaming for Youth, Inc. counselors will be present). The teams will have weekly discussion/activity goals. **Target:** All youth enrolled in the MINUTE Program.

• **Girls' Circle (structured support group):** During this ten-week curriculum (two ten-week cycles will be repeated), a group of girls of similar age and development will meet weekly with a Dreaming for Youth, Inc. counselor for 120-minute sessions. The girls will take turns talking and listening to one another respectfully about their concerns and interests. Staff will direct activities, including role-playing, drama, journaling, poetry, dance, drawing, collages, and clay figures. Gender-specific themes and topics will be introduced weekly, such as body image, goals, sexuality, drugs, competition, decision making, friendships, and trusting oneself. **Target:** All girls enrolled in the MINUTE Program.

• **Creating Lasting Family Connections (family-strengthening curriculum and peer counseling):** The six-week curriculum (four six-week cycles will be repeated) trains parents and youth. Parent trainings are designed to increase parent resiliency by improving their knowledge of ATOD abuse, family management and communication skills, family role-modeling of alcohol use, importance of youth involvement in community activities, and community services. In separate youth-oriented sessions, youth will learn to increase their resiliency through communications and refusal skills. Both the parent and the youth training encourage bonding within the family. Dreaming for Youth, Inc. counseling staff will introduce early intervention strategies and provide case management services. Case management services will continue for six months following the parent and youth trainings. When the family is having a crisis, in-home counseling will be provided by the Dreaming for Youth, Inc. case management staff. **Target:** All youth and parents enrolled in the MINUTE Program.

7. Annual work plan with quarterly format.
Table 1 – MINUTE Program Work Plan

Implementation Activities	1st Qtr.	2nd Qtr.	3rd Qtr.	4th Qtr.	Responsible Personnel
Orient/train any new staff on prevention models.	⊙				Executive Director
Develop procedures and logistics for court referrals and community program site.	⊙				Executive Director
Recruit, screen, train, and match mentors.	⊙	⊙			Program Director

4

Perform referral intakes, youth/family assessments, Individual and Family Service Plan development.	⊙	⊙			Program Director
Implement weekly components (3) – continuous session cycles.	⊙	⊙	⊙	⊙	MINUTE counseling staff
Hold monthly partnership and SCCY Regional Council interface meetings.					
Supervise, monitor, and make continuous improvement to program.	⊙	⊙	⊙	⊙	MINUTE counseling staff
Evaluate output and outcome indicators.		⊙	⊙	⊙	Third-party evaluators
Report data findings to SCCY staff.	⊙	⊙	⊙	⊙	Program Director
Conduct ongoing case management and follow-up for youth and families.	⊙	⊙	⊙	⊙	MINUTE counseling staff

8. Research-based methods and techniques to meet objectives and identification of evidenced-based programs used. *Let Each One Teach One,* which was rated as promising by OJJDP/SAMHSA, was piloted in Colorado with males, ages 11 to 13, with delinquency and academic problems. Pre-program, the treatment group had six school and individual risk factors. Post-program, youth emerged with six protective factors. *Girls' Circle,* which also was rated as promising by OJJDP, was piloted in California with girls, ages 9 to 18, with aggression/violence, sexual activity, ATOD abuse, and family functioning problems. Pre-program, the treatment group had 16 community, school, family, peer, and individual risk factors. Post-program, youth emerged with 14 protective factors. *Creating Lasting Family Connections,* which was rated as effective by OJJDP, was piloted in New York State with girls and boys, ages 9 to 17, with family functioning problems, delinquency, and ATOD abuse. Pre-program, the treatment group had 10 community, school, family, and individual risk factors. Post-program, youth emerged with 12 protective factors.

9. How the project demonstrates a collaborative effort and SCCY Regional Council interfacing. The MINUTE Program partnership includes Dreaming for Youth, Inc., Area Juvenile Court, a local church, Hooterville Public Schools, and local universities. The Dreaming for Youth, Inc. Program Director will be the point of contact for the SCCY Regional Council and will include the council in the independent evaluation process and share reports for program quality improvements. The Program Director will meet with the two partners weekly during the first two quarters and monthly thereafter.

10. Physical address, e-mail address, and telephone number for each site where activities will occur. All program components will be implemented during group and one-on-one sessions held at a local church.

5

C. **Performance Measures** (See attached Delinquency Prevention Performance Measures table.)

D. **Evaluation**

The MINUTE Program is designed to address multiple JJDP mandates leading to delinquency prevention and improvement of the juvenile justice system (planning, referral, and system-wide coordination) in Hooterville/Browning County. The MINUTE Program will adopt and implement three OJJDP and/or SAMHSA approved model curriculums for youth and their parents: *Let Each One Teach One, Creating Lasting Family Connections,* and *Girls' Circle.* All three address gender, cultural, and ethnicity learning model needs. Each model has been rigorously evaluated nationally and in Canada with treatment and experimental groups. All evaluators for the piloted programs used multivariate analysis methods to uncover direct and conditional relationships between the programs and outcomes and included treatment and experimental group comparisons. **Evaluation measures and data collection information for the proposed program are on the attached Delinquency Prevention Performance Measures table.**

Linear Logic Model Rationale for the MINUTE Program

Goals: Goal 1 – Provide delinquency prevention education, activities, and peer counseling to Hooterville/Browning County youth identified by the Area Juvenile Court system as being at high risk for becoming delinquent. **Goal 2** – Continue to encourage and guide parents and caregivers of high-risk youth in obtaining and using the skills, goals, strategies, and knowledge needed to reconnect families and assist in delinquency prevention approaches with their child(ren).

Objectives: Objective 1a – 60 percent or more of youth in the MINUTE Program will exhibit desired changes in incidences of peer and family relationships, antisocial behavior, ATOD abuse, views about teen sexual relationships, and self-criticism by the end of the fourth quarter.
Objective 1b – 80 percent or more of youth enrolling in the MINUTE Program will demonstrate resiliency skills by completing their mentoring experience and peer counseling requirements, and by achieving other protective-factor-building goals by the end of the fourth quarter.
Objective 1c – 80 percent or more of youth enrolled in the MINUTE Program will complete a post-participation survey and convey satisfaction with their own preset outcomes and with their family's outcomes by the end of the fourth quarter.
Objective 2a – 50 percent or more of parents with youth enrolled in the MINUTE Program will demonstrate improved knowledge of ATOD abuse, family management skills, communication skills, family role-modeling of alcohol use, the need for youth involvement in community activities, and available community prevention/intervention services by the end of the fourth quarter.

Activities: Objectives 1a and 1b – Staff model curriculum orientation and applications training. Development of procedures for court referrals and community program site recruitment, screening, training, and matching of mentors.
Objectives 1b and 2a – Referral intakes, youth/family assessments, individual and family service plan development. Weekly intervention components/activities.

Activities: Objective 1c – Monthly partnership meetings and SCCY Regional Council interface. Ongoing quality improvement and evaluation of outcome indicators. Evaluation reports to staff, board, and SCCY Regional Council. **Objective 2a** – Ongoing and follow-up case management for youth and families.

Outputs: Number of full-time equivalents funded by Federal Formula grant funds. Number of planning activities conducted. Number of program slots available. Number of youth served.

Outcomes: <u>Short-term</u> – Number and percent of program youth exhibiting desired change in targeted behaviors. Number and percent of program youth completing program requirements. Number and percent of program youth satisfied with program. Number and percent of program staff with increased knowledge of program area. <u>Long-term</u> – Number and percent of program youth exhibiting desired change in targeted behaviors.

Dreaming for Youth, Inc. will seek technical assistance in the MINUTE Program's implementation and evaluation process from a leading Psychologist and Consultant. <u>Data findings will be used to assess the program's effectiveness and take appropriate corrective actions that eliminate program weaknesses.</u>

E.   Project Personnel
1. Program Director (10 percent or 0.1 FTE): Planning, management, oversight, reporting, dissemination, collaboration, recruitment, screening, and training of mentors. The Program Director has 12 years of experience assessing and counseling at-risk youth and families.
Program Coordinator (50 percent or 0.5 FTE): Implementation, supervision, collaboration, information and referral director, assessment, lead case management counselor/supervisor, home visit specialist, and Juvenile Court liaison. The Program Coordinator has 10 years of experience providing individual and family therapy.
Clinical Social Worker (25 percent Contracted as Needed): Youth and family counseling, curriculum implementation, case management, and small group counseling facilitation. This individual has been a social worker for 11 years.
Social Worker (25 percent Contracted as Needed): Mentor recruitment, training, matching, and monitoring, and therapeutic mentoring responsibilities. This Social Worker has 10 years of case management experience.
Social Worker (25 percent Contracted as Needed): Youth and family counseling, curriculum implementation, case management, and Multisystemic Therapy. This Social Worker has more than 8 years of experience in providing counseling services to children, youth, and families under the Multisystemic Therapy model as a clinical therapist.
2. Other Personnel. The MINUTE Program will utilize up to 40 older, screened and trained, youth as volunteer mentors. Same gender peer mentor/mentee teams will meet weekly for one hour.

F.   Past Accomplishments
1. Outcomes and Outputs Achieved.
OUTPUTS:
-Federal Formula grant monies awarded for services: Requested $59,984; **Received 100 percent.**
-Number of FTEs funded by Federal Formula grant funds: **0.6 FTE.**

7

-Number of planning activities conducted: **30 single activities over the first three quarters.**
-Number of program slots available: Proposed 40; **Year-to-date: 29 slots filled.**
-Number of youth served: Proposed 40: **Achieved 29. 11 additional teens will be added beginning in May.**

OUTCOMES:
Short-Term:
-100 percent (29) of youth enrolled have exhibited desired change in targeted behaviors (e.g., substance use, school attendance, antisocial behavior, family relationships, and pregnancies).
-100 percent (29) of youth have completed program requirements.
-100 percent (29) of youth were satisfied with the program.
Short- and Long-Term:
-100 percent (2 staff and 3 independent contractors/social workers) increased their knowledge of program area.

2. Goals and Objectives Not Met and Explanation. All Year 1 Goals and Objectives **have been met** with the 29 youth already enrolled.

G.   Future Funding Strategies
1. After SCCY Ends. The grant applicant is aggressively seeking funding through the local school district and from the State Department of Education to provide delinquency prevention services. In addition, the grant applicant has secured the services of a national grant writing consultant to help pursue federal funding that incorporates mentoring programs for high-risk youth. The grant applicant will apply for funds from the U.S. Department of Health and Human Services, Administration for Children and Families – Mentoring Children of Prisoners.
2. Maintaining First Year SCCY Service Levels. The grant applicant will supplement the cost of the MINUTE Program with other grants and contracts in order to meet the funding reduction formula mandated by SCCY of 75 percent in Year 2 and 50 percent in Year 3.

8

Index

BUSINESS, CAREERS & PERSONAL FINANCE

Accounting For Dummies, 4th Edition*
978-0-470-24600-9

Bookkeeping Workbook For Dummies†
978-0-470-16983-4

Commodities For Dummies
978-0-470-04928-0

Doing Business in China For Dummies
978-0-470-04929-7

E-Mail Marketing For Dummies
978-0-470-19087-6

Job Interviews For Dummies, 3rd Edition*†
978-0-470-17748-8

Personal Finance Workbook For Dummies*†
978-0-470-09933-9

Real Estate License Exams For Dummies
978-0-7645-7623-2

Six Sigma For Dummies
978-0-7645-6798-8

Small Business Kit For Dummies, 2nd Edition*†
978-0-7645-5984-6

Telephone Sales For Dummies
978-0-470-16836-3

BUSINESS PRODUCTIVITY & MICROSOFT OFFICE

Access 2007 For Dummies
978-0-470-03649-5

Excel 2007 For Dummies
978-0-470-03737-9

Office 2007 For Dummies
978-0-470-00923-9

Outlook 2007 For Dummies
978-0-470-03830-7

PowerPoint 2007 For Dummies
978-0-470-04059-1

Project 2007 For Dummies
978-0-470-03651-8

QuickBooks 2008 For Dummies
978-0-470-18470-7

Quicken 2008 For Dummies
978-0-470-17473-9

Salesforce.com For Dummies, 2nd Edition
978-0-470-04893-1

Word 2007 For Dummies
978-0-470-03658-7

EDUCATION, HISTORY, REFERENCE & TEST PREPARATION

African American History For Dummies
978-0-7645-5469-8

Algebra For Dummies
978-0-7645-5325-7

Algebra Workbook For Dummies
978-0-7645-8467-1

Art History For Dummies
978-0-470-09910-0

ASVAB For Dummies, 2nd Edition
978-0-470-10671-6

British Military History For Dummies
978-0-470-03213-8

Calculus For Dummies
978-0-7645-2498-1

Canadian History For Dummies, 2nd Edition
978-0-470-83656-9

Geometry Workbook For Dummies
978-0-471-79940-5

The SAT I For Dummies, 6th Edition
978-0-7645-7193-0

Series 7 Exam For Dummies
978-0-470-09932-2

World History For Dummies
978-0-7645-5242-7

FOOD, GARDEN, HOBBIES & HOME

Bridge For Dummies, 2nd Edition
978-0-471-92426-5

Coin Collecting For Dummies, 2nd Edition
978-0-470-22275-1

Cooking Basics For Dummies, 3rd Edition
978-0-7645-7206-7

Drawing For Dummies
978-0-7645-5476-6

Etiquette For Dummies, 2nd Edition
978-0-470-10672-3

Gardening Basics For Dummies*†
978-0-470-03749-2

Knitting Patterns For Dummies
978-0-470-04556-5

Living Gluten-Free For Dummies†
978-0-471-77383-2

Painting Do-It-Yourself For Dummies
978-0-470-17533-0

HEALTH, SELF HELP, PARENTING & PETS

Anger Management For Dummies
978-0-470-03715-7

Anxiety & Depression Workbook For Dummies
978-0-7645-9793-0

Dieting For Dummies, 2nd Edition
978-0-7645-4149-0

Dog Training For Dummies, 2nd Edition
978-0-7645-8418-3

Horseback Riding For Dummies
978-0-470-09719-9

Infertility For Dummies†
978-0-470-11518-3

Meditation For Dummies with CD-ROM, 2nd Edition
978-0-471-77774-8

Post-Traumatic Stress Disorder For Dummies
978-0-470-04922-8

Puppies For Dummies, 2nd Edition
978-0-470-03717-1

Thyroid For Dummies, 2nd Edition†
978-0-471-78755-6

Type 1 Diabetes For Dummies*†
978-0-470-17811-9

---

* Separate Canadian edition also available
† Separate U.K. edition also available

Available wherever books are sold. For more information or to order direct: U.S. customers visit www.dummies.com or call 1-877-762-2974.
U.K. customers visit www.wileyeurope.com or call (0)1243 843291. Canadian customers visit www.wiley.ca or call 1-800-567-4797.

INTERNET & DIGITAL MEDIA

AdWords For Dummies
978-0-470-15252-2

Blogging For Dummies, 2nd Edition
978-0-470-23017-6

**Digital Photography All-in-One
Desk Reference For Dummies, 3rd Edition**
978-0-470-03743-0

Digital Photography For Dummies, 5th Edition
978-0-7645-9802-9

**Digital SLR Cameras & Photography
For Dummies, 2nd Edition**
978-0-470-14927-0

**eBay Business All-in-One Desk Reference
For Dummies**
978-0-7645-8438-1

eBay For Dummies, 5th Edition*
978-0-470-04529-9

eBay Listings That Sell For Dummies
978-0-471-78912-3

Facebook For Dummies
978-0-470-26273-3

The Internet For Dummies, 11th Edition
978-0-470-12174-0

Investing Online For Dummies, 5th Edition
978-0-7645-8456-5

iPod & iTunes For Dummies, 5th Edition
978-0-470-17474-6

MySpace For Dummies
978-0-470-09529-4

Podcasting For Dummies
978-0-471-74898-4

**Search Engine Optimization
For Dummies, 2nd Edition**
978-0-471-97998-2

Second Life For Dummies
978-0-470-18025-9

**Starting an eBay Business For Dummies,
3rd Edition†**
978-0-470-14924-9

GRAPHICS, DESIGN & WEB DEVELOPMENT

**Adobe Creative Suite 3 Design Premium
All-in-One Desk Reference For Dummies**
978-0-470-11724-8

**Adobe Web Suite CS3 All-in-One Desk
Reference For Dummies**
978-0-470-12099-6

AutoCAD 2008 For Dummies
978-0-470-11650-0

**Building a Web Site For Dummies,
3rd Edition**
978-0-470-14928-7

**Creating Web Pages All-in-One Desk
Reference For Dummies, 3rd Edition**
978-0-470-09629-1

**Creating Web Pages For Dummies,
8th Edition**
978-0-470-08030-6

Dreamweaver CS3 For Dummies
978-0-470-11490-2

Flash CS3 For Dummies
978-0-470-12100-9

Google SketchUp For Dummies
978-0-470-13744-4

InDesign CS3 For Dummies
978-0-470-11865-8

**Photoshop CS3 All-in-One
Desk Reference For Dummies**
978-0-470-11195-6

Photoshop CS3 For Dummies
978-0-470-11193-2

Photoshop Elements 5 For Dummies
978-0-470-09810-3

SolidWorks For Dummies
978-0-7645-9555-4

Visio 2007 For Dummies
978-0-470-08983-5

Web Design For Dummies, 2nd Edition
978-0-471-78117-2

Web Sites Do-It-Yourself For Dummies
978-0-470-16903-2

Web Stores Do-It-Yourself For Dummies
978-0-470-17443-2

LANGUAGES, RELIGION & SPIRITUALITY

Arabic For Dummies
978-0-471-77270-5

Chinese For Dummies, Audio Set
978-0-470-12766-7

French For Dummies
978-0-7645-5193-2

German For Dummies
978-0-7645-5195-6

Hebrew For Dummies
978-0-7645-5489-6

Ingles Para Dummies
978-0-7645-5427-8

Italian For Dummies, Audio Set
978-0-470-09586-7

Italian Verbs For Dummies
978-0-471-77389-4

Japanese For Dummies
978-0-7645-5429-2

Latin For Dummies
978-0-7645-5431-5

Portuguese For Dummies
978-0-471-78738-9

Russian For Dummies
978-0-471-78001-4

Spanish Phrases For Dummies
978-0-7645-7204-3

Spanish For Dummies
978-0-7645-5194-9

Spanish For Dummies, Audio Set
978-0-470-09585-0

The Bible For Dummies
978-0-7645-5296-0

Catholicism For Dummies
978-0-7645-5391-2

The Historical Jesus For Dummies
978-0-470-16785-4

Islam For Dummies
978-0-7645-5503-9

**Spirituality For Dummies,
2nd Edition**
978-0-470-19142-2

NETWORKING AND PROGRAMMING

ASP.NET 3.5 For Dummies
978-0-470-19592-5

C# 2008 For Dummies
978-0-470-19109-5

Hacking For Dummies, 2nd Edition
978-0-470-05235-8

Home Networking For Dummies, 4th Edition
978-0-470-11806-1

Java For Dummies, 4th Edition
978-0-470-08716-9

**Microsoft® SQL Server™ 2008 All-in-One
Desk Reference For Dummies**
978-0-470-17954-3

**Networking All-in-One Desk Reference
For Dummies, 2nd Edition**
978-0-7645-9939-2

**Networking For Dummies,
8th Edition**
978-0-470-05620-2

SharePoint 2007 For Dummies
978-0-470-09941-4

**Wireless Home Networking
For Dummies, 2nd Edition**
978-0-471-74940-0

OPERATING SYSTEMS & COMPUTER BASICS

iMac For Dummies, 5th Edition
978-0-7645-8458-9

Laptops For Dummies, 2nd Edition
978-0-470-05432-1

Linux For Dummies, 8th Edition
978-0-470-11649-4

MacBook For Dummies
978-0-470-04859-7

Mac OS X Leopard All-in-One Desk Reference For Dummies
978-0-470-05434-5

Mac OS X Leopard For Dummies
978-0-470-05433-8

Macs For Dummies, 9th Edition
978-0-470-04849-8

PCs For Dummies, 11th Edition
978-0-470-13728-4

Windows® Home Server For Dummies
978-0-470-18592-6

Windows Server 2008 For Dummies
978-0-470-18043-3

Windows Vista All-in-One Desk Reference For Dummies
978-0-471-74941-7

Windows Vista For Dummies
978-0-471-75421-3

Windows Vista Security For Dummies
978-0-470-11805-4

SPORTS, FITNESS & MUSIC

Coaching Hockey For Dummies
978-0-470-83685-9

Coaching Soccer For Dummies
978-0-471-77381-8

Fitness For Dummies, 3rd Edition
978-0-7645-7851-9

Football For Dummies, 3rd Edition
978-0-470-12536-6

GarageBand For Dummies
978-0-7645-7323-1

Golf For Dummies, 3rd Edition
978-0-471-76871-5

Guitar For Dummies, 2nd Edition
978-0-7645-9904-0

Home Recording For Musicians For Dummies, 2nd Edition
978-0-7645-8884-6

iPod & iTunes For Dummies, 5th Edition
978-0-470-17474-6

Music Theory For Dummies
978-0-7645-7838-0

Stretching For Dummies
978-0-470-06741-3

Get smart @ dummies.com®

- **Find a full list of Dummies titles**
- **Look into loads of FREE on-site articles**
- **Sign up for FREE eTips e-mailed to you weekly**
- **See what other products carry the Dummies name**
- **Shop directly from the Dummies bookstore**
- **Enter to win new prizes every month!**

* Separate Canadian edition also available
† Separate U.K. edition also available

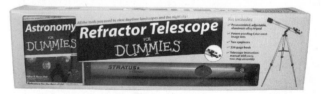